TELLING
GOD'S STORIES
WITH POWER

BIBLICAL STORYTELLING

IN ORAL CULTURES

"In this pioneering study, Paul Koehler describes the extraordinary energy that has been unleashed by the careful process of teaching oral culture people to tell the stories of the Bible by heart to their family and friends in their villages. Paul outlines in detail the actual story processes that were used in teaching this and records the impact that it had for specific persons in their communities. The implication of this study is that the whole enterprise of Christian missionary outreach needs to be reconceived in relation to the congruence betweeen oral cultures now and the oral cultures of biblical times."

Thomas E. Boomershine, Ph.D.
Prof. of NT and Founder, Network of Biblical Storytellers

"Paul Koehler in over a decade of experience has captured the essence of power in telling and teaching God's stories to pastors leading churches among low literacy congregations. This book is a needed resource for any one equipping pastors and evangelists to work effectively among people where low literacy and orality are factors. I highly recommend Telling God's Stories With Power."

J.O. Terry, Bible Storying Pioneer and Consultant

"Dr. Koehler's storytelling ministry is impressive and inspirational! Telling God's Stories with Power sums up his beautiful way of communicating the message of Jesus Christ to the pre-literate two-third worlds and the post-literate Western world in the original oral form. This book raises Jesus from death to tell his glad tidings to all of us again."

Andrew Sung Park, Professor of Theology
United Theological Seminary, Dayton, OH

"The participants in this program absorb a reproducible method of turning the written word into a spoken word, to be recalled and used at will. Having once learned the process of story-telling, they are equipped to use their written Bibles to learn more stories, and so the use of Scripture in oral form will expand."

Bible translator (unnamed for security reasons)

Telling God's Stories with Power: Biblical Storytelling in Oral Cultures
Copyright ©2010 by Paul F. Koehler

Published by William Carey Library
1605 East Elizabeth Street
Pasadena, CA 91104 | www.missionbooks.org

Johanna Deming, copy editor
Jonathan Pon, graphic design

William Carey Library is a ministry of the
U.S. Center for World Mission
Pasadena, CA | www.uscwm.org

Printed in the United States of America

14 13 12 11 10   5 4 3 2 1

20101000BP

Library of Congress Cataloging-in-Publication Data

Koehler, Paul F.
Telling God's stories with power : biblical storytelling in oral cultures / by Paul F. Koehler.
    p. cm.
Includes bibliographical references and indexes.
ISBN 978-0-87808-465-4
1. Intercultural communication--Religious aspects--Christianity. 2. Storytelling--Religious aspects--Christianity. 3. Bible stories. 4. Missions. 5. Intercultural communication--Study and teaching. 6. Bible stories--Study and teaching. 7. Storytelling--Study and teaching. 8. Missionaries--Training of. I. Title.
  BV2082.I57K64 2010
  266--dc22
                    2009053170

TELLING
GOD'S STORIES
WITH POWER

BIBLICAL STORYTELLING

IN ORAL CULTURES

WILLIAM CAREY
LIBRARY

CONTENTS

ILLUSTRATIONS

TABLES

OVERVIEW

The learning style of oral communicators differs in many ways from that of print learners. Yet most Christian workers still use literate methods when working among oral learners even though conventional teaching and communication methods often prove inadequate in such contexts. Among the more serious drawbacks are incongruence with local learning styles, ineffectiveness, and lack of reproducibility. In addition, because of their foreignness, conventional methods of evangelization often tend to engender resistance.

As awareness of this problem began to surface over the past two decades, biblical storytelling, or storying, was proposed as a solution. Since then, significant fieldwork has been done by missionaries who have used storytelling to evangelize and plant churches. But relatively few have yet tried to establish formal training programs designed to equip indigenous people as effective biblical storytellers.

In this project in South Asia, the primary research strategy was the multiplication of storytellers through intentional training and the collection of verbatim reports of their field experiences. Each storyteller was required to train at least one other person, emphasizing the relayed transfer of stories to subsequent generations of learners.

The training consisted of six modules over 15 months. After each module the workers returned to their fields where they practiced telling the stories until the next training event. During the program the storytellers mastered 100 biblical stories in chronological order from the Creation through the Ascension. As they told these stories in the villages, the stories became a powerful witness to God's love. Consequently many people came to faith in Christ and more than 200 new congregations were planted. Additionally, a large number of people who had not attended the central training also learned to tell many of the stories. Relayed story transfer extended as far as the fourth and even the fifth generation of learners.

In this study, storytelling was found to be superior for knowledge transfer and for bypassing resistance to the gospel in oral contexts thus presenting clear evidence of the effectiveness of biblical narrative among oral learners.

FOREWORD

In the last couple of decades there have been major paradigm shifts in the way we do missions. One of the challenges has been discovering how to equip church planters who were ministering to primarily illiterate and semi-literate cultures. We have learned that using traditional, literate methods of preparing Christian workers was not proving to be effective. Along with this challenge was the question of how to produce discipleship material that was culturally relevant but easily reproducible.

What seemed like a major training obstacle was just an opportunity for the Lord to bring us back to the basics of simply teaching the Word of God through Storying. As you will learn in this book, Chronological Bible Storying is a method of presenting Bible stories in a chronological sequence from the story of creation through the story of the resurrection.

But does it work? Does telling simple Bible stories really penetrate the heart with conviction and prepare the heart for the gospel message? The answer is a resounding yes.

Our experience with storying in N.E. India has proven to be much more effective than we ever imagined. When Paul and Teresa Koehler came to lead our first storying workshop, our hope was that by the end of the year, three training modules later, we might realize 10 or 15 new churches planted. But we soon realized that God had other plans.

About 100 workers representing multiple people groups and several languages attended that first week-long training. They committed to memory 14 Bible stories beginning with Adam and ending with Jacob. As the week progressed we noticed the excitement building as they began to realize that they were being equipped with more than just a few stories. They realized they now had a strategy. They began to visualize how they would use the stories to evangelize their villages.

One of the people groups represented at the training was the Patuas. For many centuries the Patuas have been the oral newspapers for their society. They traveled from village to village singing their own compositions while unrolling hand-painted scrolls featuring current events and stories of Hindu gods and goddesses. After the training module these three men returned to their village and led 40 families to Christ using the Bible stories and story scrolls they had prepared during the training module. Now there are 18 churches among the Patuas.

One Bengali lady was so excited about storying that she returned to her village and immediately taught 200 others to tell the stories. Many came to Christ and were baptized and several new village churches were planted.

In another town a long standing Hindu temple was flooded after an unusually heavy rain. Because the flood waters defiled the temple it was permanently closed. Six of the temple workers were suddenly out of a job. Their official caste work had been to carry water into the temple to fill the basins of the idols. One of our church planters saw their despair. He approached these men and told them the 14 Bible stories he learned in the training. All six accepted Christ and were baptized and now they are church planters reaching their own people group with the gospel of Christ through Bible storying.

Why do I believe in Bible storying? Because it works! Chronological Bible Storying is a back to the basics approach that enables the gospel to supernaturally penetrate the culture and then develop disciples of Jesus Christ. It removes barriers, helps make cultural connections and allows the Holy Spirit to make the Scripture alive and relevant.

This book is a culmination of observation and field experience. Paul Koehler's passion for the lost, his love for the world and his commitment to accurately telling the stories of the Bible make this book a must read for every missions-oriented believer. The book you hold in your hand is not just an academic look at Storying but represents years of field application in multiple language groups and cultures.

Larry Bennett
President
New Dimensions International

PREFACE

Recently when my wife and I were telling biblical stories, a friend became inspired as she listened. For years this woman had struggled to witness to others. She said that she always felt like David trying to fight in Saul's armor. But as she listened to us, she immediately said, "I can do that!" This is a common response of believers who hear biblical storytelling for the first time. They immediately grasp its potential and feel it is something they themselves could do.

This book is a product of my own journey as I confronted the challenges of teaching the Bible in parts of the world where people are unaccustomed to a Western style of learning. When I started developing an oral Bible program I had no idea of becoming a biblical storyteller myself. I simply wanted to train others to share the Word of God in ways that would fit their context better. It wasn't until later that I realized how unprepared I was to do this. Strangely, I don't think I had ever told a Bible story, not even to a children's class. And far from being a natural storyteller, my friends say I can't even tell a joke.

But a couple of years later, I made a crucial decision to stop preaching. Laying aside more than 30 years of sermon notes to try to become a biblical storyteller was not an easy choice. But I knew from experience that incarnational ministry often requires us to give up things we rely on (and which make us comfortable!) to share in the life world of those to whom God has called us. In this case, it was the learning style of my target group that I had to embrace. I soon discovered that moving from literacy to orality demanded a significant shift in my approach to ministry because oral communicators have a radically different way of processing information.

WHO IS THIS BOOK WRITTEN FOR?

This book was conceived as a response to a field problem, but it grew to maturity in the context of an action research doctoral project. The standards of reliability and validity common to doctoral programs helped to ground the project theoretically as well as practically. Thus it is a combination of the academic and the practical.

If you are new to biblical storytelling, this book presents a complete but simple introduction to the subject. It will be especially helpful for people who want to learn about using biblical storytelling in cross-cultural contexts and who want to train others as storytellers.

It was written primarily for missionaries who are engaged in evangelism, discipling and church-planting in cross-cultural contexts where orality is a significant factor. While it may be of interest to biblical theologians or to storytellers in other contexts, it is not primarily intended to address their concerns. Instead I have focused specifically on those who would attempt to train biblical storytellers in a missionary context. Field practitioners are often closest to oral peoples, so they are perhaps most aware of the limits of academic learning.

HOW TO READ THIS BOOK

I've found that many practitioners are interested in the "bottom line." They want to know, "What can I do with this?" This book is organized in a way that lets you begin reading where you are most comfortable. You may prefer to jump right in and start reading our account of how we trained the storytellers (Section Two). Others will want to take time to understand the theory first (Section One). You can even start with Section Three and read what the participants in the project have to say about it. My hope, of course, is that you will read the entire book, regardless of the order in which you choose to do so.

Knowing about orality and understanding why narrative works will make you more effective in communicating the Gospel among oral people. So in Section One, I lay a foundation for understanding the all-important differences between orality and literacy. I examine these from their biblical, historical, pedagogical and cultural perspectives to understand the place of narrative in knowledge transmission. Section Two describes the field project. It provides details on the various parts of the training model, the procedures I followed, and the reasons behind each. Tracing the movement of the biblical stories across four generations of tellers and listeners, it gives extensive examples from the storytellers' own experiences.

Finally, Section Three explores the findings from the research derived from three instruments: a database of verbatim reports by the storytellers; a follow-up questionnaire administered to 54 field leaders in areas where the program was applied; and the results of a comprehensive examination given to the storytellers at the end of the two-year program.

Perhaps the best way of gauging the effectiveness of a training program is to listen to the stories of those who have been affected by it. In Chapter 11, five storytellers relate how their lives were transformed through the oral Bible project.

The appendixes have additional information of interest to those who are storying or training storytellers. For example, Appendix H, "Comparing Storytelling with Other Methods," and Appendix J, "Case Instance Examples," contain many fascinating verbatim reports by the storytellers themselves.

OUR CHALLENGE

Throughout history storytelling was the chief way of learning and passing information along to others. It was eclipsed for a time by print media, but today it seems God is restoring storytelling to the church. The challenges we face in communicating the gospel have never been greater, while many of our past practices are no longer effective. Whether we consider the large number of unreached, nonliterate people groups or the postmodern generation that is often postliterate as well, storytelling can have an important part to play in the mix of strategies for reaching people today.

ACKNOWLEDGMENTS

Special appreciation is offered to my dear wife, Teresa Hineman Koehler, who is to be credited with sharing much of the labor of this project. Through many long discussions, she helped develop ideas that went into this book and served as a sounding board, a critic, an encourager and companion. Working with translators, she transcribed hundreds of pages of recorded field reports. Her leadership with the learning groups as coach and mentor was equal to my own work. This was a cooperative endeavor in every way—it would have been impossible to carry out alone.

I am also grateful to the Indian Evangelical Team, its leaders and workers, for their willingness to enter into a partnership and provide opportunity for the development and growth of this program. I have special appreciation for P. G. Vargis who has been my mentor and friend throughout this process, and for IET president Joy Thomas who had the vision to extend the program throughout the organization.

This work has been built on the labors of many who have gone before me. I have endeavored to give credit to each where possible. However, recognizing that it is the product of a lifetime of study and experience, I realize there may be instances where this was not done. If so, I beg forgiveness of those who contributed and express my deep appreciation to all who had a part in its development.

Finally, my deepest appreciation is for the storytellers themselves. It was through their collaboration that this project developed. They taught me most of what I know about storytelling in oral cultures.

Chapter One

INTRODUCTION

*The shortest distance between a human
being and truth is a story.*

—ANTHONY DE MELLO

After finishing high school, Bhibuti attended Bible college for two years to prepare for ministry. Now he was eager to preach the gospel to people in the villages of the interior of his country. But when he finally arrived at his station and began preaching, the unschooled villagers seemed baffled by his sermons. They puzzled over the theological terms he used; after awhile they gave up trying to understand him. Some would come to the church for the singing and then slip out as soon as the sermon started.

However, their response changed dramatically when Bhibuti started learning biblical storytelling. The same villagers who had been bored with his sermons listened delightedly to the stories he told them from the Bible. They found they could understand the spiritual themes and soon began growing in their Christian faith. Church members told him, "Because you are telling us the stories, now we can understand everything. Before you were not telling the story, and we were not understanding anything."

Just as exciting to Bhibuti was the realization that the believers had started telling the stories to their friends and neighbors. He appointed some of them to go tell the Bible stories in other villages. As their listeners heard the stories of how God had blessed people just like them, faith was birthed in their hearts and many believed in Jesus. New congregations of believers began to spring up and now Bhibuti is pastoring a dynamic, growing church.

BACKGROUND

In 1994 the Indian founder of a large indigenous church-planting agency asked my help in training the midlevel leaders of his rapidly growing organization.[1] Concurrent with this, my wife and I began an extended study program that culminated in earning masters degrees in Intercultural Studies at Fuller Theological Seminary School of World Mission.[2]

Although I had served as a missionary in Latin America for many years, I was still unprepared for the complexity of India's worldview and its social mosaic. I found that working in this context presented vigorous new challenges to communicating and teaching the Bible. Given my prior missionary experience and recent study at Fuller, I somewhat naively assumed that I had mastered the communication skills that would be needed. I worked hard to prepare lessons that were simple and comprehensible, seeking to offer the Christian workers practical training that would help them improve their field practice. In spite of their limited formal schooling and consequent unfamiliarity with western modes of learning, most seemed to enjoy the workshops and welcomed the instruction.

However, hints soon began to emerge that all was not well. It seemed that little of what I taught was being put into practice by the workers. When I asked them simple questions requiring minimal deductive reasoning they were unable to respond. Slowly I began to sense the huge barrier that exists between people with a preference for oral communication and print-oriented communicators like me.

At first it was tempting to blame the learners or even spiritual forces for this failure to communicate. But eventually I became convinced that I needed to find a better way of communicating with them. This began my quest for a more effective teaching method.

I tried alternative learning techniques like active training and role play; I added goal setting and accountability procedures, and sought other ways to make the training sessions more effective. These changes helped the seminars become better at transferring content that could be remembered by the learners and which they could put to use in their fields. But the equipping structure was still a western model that depended mainly on lecture.

This led to a bigger concern: if I taught the workers with techniques that were foreign to their context, how would they themselves learn to teach in ways that fit their context? In other words, to be reproducible the pedagogical model itself had to complement the learning styles found in the culture. If the pastors were unable to transfer the knowledge they had gained, how would the churches they served ever become strong and self-reliant?

This need for a more compatible equipping model eventually led me to begin developing the oral Bible training program. My studies at Fuller had laid a foundation in the disciplines of missiology, cultural anthropology and Christian communication which informed this project. Research in Fuller Seminary's McAlester Library in Pasadena, California and at the University of South Alabama in Mobile helped advance the search for a more user-friendly approach for oral cultures. I was looking for Bible teaching methods that were compatible with oral learning styles, and which would allow biblical knowledge to flow all the way to the fringes of each people group regardless of their level of schooling.

To my surprise, storytelling began to emerge as the strongest contender. Shortly afterward, I started testing biblical storytelling among some of the same oral communicators I had worked with previously. In what turned out to be a four-year pilot project, 56 men and women of all ages learned to tell significant portions of the Scriptures in story. Each storyteller was also required to train another person to tell the stories.

Building on the experience gained through the pilot project, in 2006 I started a second generation oral Bible program in a different region of the country. Sixty full-time Christian workers from half a dozen states enrolled in a structured two-year program to be trained as biblical storytellers. This book describes their experiences and tells what I learned among them during 20 months of field research.

In this second phase I also completed a D.Min. program at United Theological Seminary in Dayton, Ohio. My mentor was Tom Boomershine, the author of *Story Journey: An Invitation to the Gospel as Storytelling* (1988) and founder of the Network of Biblical Storytellers. *Telling God's Stories with Power* grew from the doctoral thesis I completed in November 2007.

PURPOSE

The intent of this project was to develop a storytelling equipping model that would promote relayed transmission of the Scriptures among peoples of oral cultures.

In literate cultures theological learning typically focuses on transforming knowledge and meaning by restructuring it in new ways. Oral communicators do not understand this because it relies on a cognitive style that is only possible for those who have well-developed literate skills. Grant Lovejoy explains, "Without the technology of reading and writing, primary oral communicators dare not break what they know into hard-to-remember abstract lists or categories. They resist literate-style analysis because they cannot be sure to get all the pieces back into proper place through the use of memory alone. Hence they communicate in holistic rather than analytic ways."[3]

An oral communicator's way of using what he or she learns is not to manipulate it mentally but to apply it to life in concrete ways. Oral communicators typically ground their cognitive styles and learning patterns in concrete experiences related closely to the lifeworld in which they live. This is known as concrete-relational thinking. Walter Ong explains, "In the absence of elaborate analytic categories that depend on writing to structure knowledge at a distance from lived experience, oral cultures must conceptualize and verbalize all their knowledge with more or less close reference to the human lifeworld, assimilating the alien, objective world to the more immediate, familiar interaction of human beings."[4]

The contrast between concrete and analytical communication can be illustrated by considering the meaning of statistics. What does it mean to talk about a 90 mph wind? Only after having spent ten hours in a hurricane and then walking outside to see the destruction the next day can it be properly understood. What does 40 degrees below zero mean? How about 12 inches of rain in four hours? Concrete descriptions of these events stand out in contrast to analytical ways of stating them.

Concrete-relational thinking may use metaphors of familiar objects to express thoughts, feelings, or quantities that are not easy for oral learners to grasp otherwise. Furthermore, while an analytical thinker generally deconstructs and analyzes the component parts, a concrete-relational thinker tends to view and talk about things holistically.[5] As far back as 1923, Lucien Levy-Bruhl described the wide divergence between the thinking styles of westerners and concrete-relational thinkers:

> The two mentalities which encounter each other here are so foreign to one another, their customs so widely divergent, their methods of expressing themselves so different! Almost unconsciously, the European makes use of abstract thought, and his language has made simple logical processes so easy for him that they entail no effort. With primitives, both thought and language are almost exclusively concrete by nature.[6]

Surprisingly, the Bible is uniquely suited for communicating with such oral peoples. Tom Steffen points out, "The concrete mode of communication dominates both Testaments and is conspicuously evident in all three basic literary styles [narration, poetry, thought-organized]."[7]

When the church was not as far removed from its oral roots as it is today, this concrete way of thinking and expressing ideas was valued. In 1785 a young

William Carey was seeking ordination from the Baptist Church in Olney, England, but he was turned down after the members heard him preach. They decided he needed a period of probation. Mr. Hall of Arnsby, criticizing the attempt, said, "Brother Carey, you have no *likes* in your sermons. Christ taught that the Kingdom of Heaven was *like* to leaven hid in meal, *like* to a grain of mustard, and etc. You tell us what things are, but never what they are like." [8] Whereas Carey was speaking in ideas, Mr. Hall was describing the learning preference of oral communicators who understand best when things are taught in concrete ways related to that which is already familiar to them.

Louis Luzbetak tells of an Indian religious man who was complaining to a group of missionaries about the methods they were employing: "You say that you bring Jesus and new humanity to us. But what is this 'new humanity' you are proclaiming? We would like to see it, touch it, taste it, feel it. Jesus must not be just a name, but a reality. Jesus must be illustrated humanly." [9]

The thesis of this research is that storytelling is a more effective way of relaying Bible knowledge in oral contexts than methods that grew from print technology. From the time of its post-Reformation renaissance, Christian missionary work was carried out according to a literate model. It has largely continued to base its strategies on literacy right up to the present time. Figure 1 shows the complexity of using such a literate transfer model to reach oral communicators with the gospel.

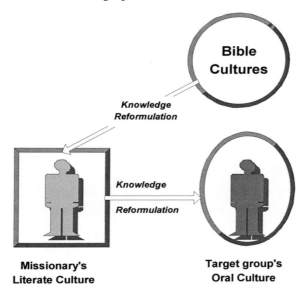

Figure 1. Literate Transfer Model

Because the knowledge of God was originally revealed in Bible cultures that were predominantly oral, it was necessary to reformulate the message twice: once into our literate culture and again into present-day oral cultures. This placed a great handicap on the missionary and also a heavy burden on the oral receptor to try to grasp ideas presented in an alien cognitive style. It greatly restricted the transmission of the biblical message throughout the missionary era.

In an effort to reach Hindus by providing the Scriptures in their own vernacular, William Carey and his associates, Marshman and Ward, translated and printed the Bible in Bengali, Oriya, Marathi, Hindi, Assamese, and Sanskrit and also translated parts of it into 29 other Indian languages. In the biographical film, "A Candle in the Dark" William Carey holds his first newly printed page of Scripture in the Bengali language. Referring to the printed words on the page, he proclaims, "These are my missionaries."[10] If printed words were indeed his missionaries, they failed to reach most of the people of Bengal or any other part of north India in the following 200 years. Statistics show that even today less than 1% of the people of North India are Christians. Carey's choice of literacy as the principal vehicle for Gospel communication was typical of most missionaries who came after him.

In contrast, the oral Bible model (Figure 2) lets both missionary and oral receptor focus directly on the Bible by using storytelling. Since in this model the transmission of Bible knowledge never passes through the missionary's literate culture, the cultural distance from the Bible to the oral target is far shorter.

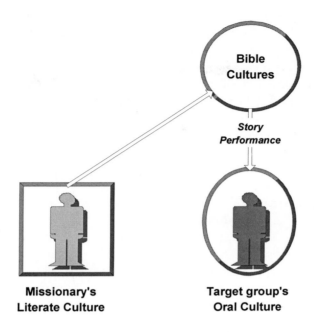

Figure 2. Oral Bible Transfer Model

Because many present-day oral cultures resemble cultures that are found in the Bible, this approach greatly simplifies the task of communicating the gospel message.

METHODS

This book is a descriptive case study grounded in personal observations and in data Teresa and I gathered while training the storytellers. Their unique experiences while applying biblical storytelling in diverse field contexts, and replicating the training strategy to equip more than 400 other storytellers, provided many opportunities for interviews, field reports, questionnaires and informal surveys. From the hundreds of oral accounts of their storytelling experiences that we recorded and transcribed, I was able to identify and code more than 50 significant themes.

A case study can be defined as a method for learning about a complex instance, based on a comprehensive understanding of that instance obtained by extensive description and analysis taken as a whole and in its context.[11] But since this was an action research (AR) project, description and analysis alone were insufficient. The purpose of AR is to develop practical solutions to real-life problems. The resulting knowledge is deemed credible only when it has been generated and tested in practice, and participants must also be able to use the knowledge that emerges.[12] AR refers to the conjunction of three elements: research, action, and participation.[13] Kurt Lewin (echoing the earlier work of John Dewey) said, "The best way to understand something is to try to change it."[14] This understanding is gained through repeated attempts to produce change in particular directions, in a partnership between the researcher and local stakeholders. The repe..ted action-reflection-action cycles bring about the development of better concepts and practices. The changes are the proof that a particular hypothesis is, or is not, correct.

Davydd Greenwood aptly describes the role of an action researcher as a coach, instead of a director or boss.

> The coach counts on local people to be the talented players and helps them improve their skills and strategies. A boss takes over the direction, management, and control of subordinate local groups and acts for them, further disempowering them … and usually guaranteeing that whatever changes are produced will not continue to produce locally initiated changes over the long run.[15]

Partnership is demonstrated through respect for local knowledge, careful consideration of context, empowerment as a goal, long-term relationship between insiders and outsiders, cogeneration of knowledge, local ownership, and respect for cultural insiders as peers.

Another important point, according to Greenwood, is that AR is a form of research that "… aims to increase the ability of the involved community or organization members to control their own destinies more effectively…"[16] In the oral Bible project, the participants were empowered by enabling them to learn and share the Bible with others through storytelling. Thus they are no longer entirely dependent on a trained specialist such as a pastor to learn, understand and proclaim the Word of God. This also empowers the local church because multiple voices are proclaiming God's Word instead of only the paid professional worker.

OUTLINE AND SCOPE

This book consists of an Introduction, three Sections and a Conclusion. The Introduction (Chapters 1 and 2) sets out the purpose and methodology of the study, identifying the areas of need, problem and concern. Section 1 (Chapters 3, 4, 5, and 6) deals with four theoretical foundations for the study: biblical, historical, pedagogical and theological. Section 2 (Chapters 7, 8, and 9) describes the field project, while Section 3 (Chapter 10 and 11) contains the findings from the research. The final chapter (Chapter 12) is the conclusion and summary, with recommendations for further development.

Although the project described in this book was limited to one region of the world, it extended to a wide variety of communities. The storytellers represented more than a dozen different language groups with highly diverse cultures. Beyond this, they applied the storytelling among still other cultures ranging from modern to extremely primitive. Their hearers were from tribal, Hindu, Buddhist and Muslim backgrounds, and various castes both high and low. Men and women of all ages as well as children were involved. This broad application of biblical storytelling offered insights that can be useful in other regions and countries.

Still, it is important to remember that no training model is universally applicable. Like all training programs, this one will have to be adapted to fit each new context. My hope is that principles and insights gained here will enable the reader to craft a similarly effective biblical storytelling program in his or her own sphere of ministry so it becomes a strategy tailored specifically for those people.

Chapter Two

A WORLD OF ORALITY

*There have been great societies that did
not use the wheel, but there have been no
societies that did not tell stories.*

–URSULA LE GUIN

Effective communication is at the heart of teaching and learning. However not everyone learns in the same way. Mismatched cognitive styles can result in poor communication, hindering the transfer of knowledge from teacher to student.

Learning preferences vary from person to person but they also follow patterns determined by one's educational experiences and the particular culture in which an individual lives. When the disjuncture between learning styles is minimal, transfer of knowledge is only impeded. In cross-cultural communication, however, the differences in learning styles can be so vast as to completely block the communication process.

Charles Kraft defines the purpose of communication as that of bringing a listener to understand a message in a way that substantially corresponds with the intent of the communicator.[17] When there is dissonance between the distinctive cognitive style of a communicator on one hand and the learning preference of a listener on the other, the message that is heard and interpreted by the listener may not accurately reflect the intent of the communicator. It may be distorted or even misunderstood entirely. This is because knowledge cannot be transferred from one human being to another simply through words and sentences that contain particular meanings. Rather, the message must be reconstructed by the listener.* When the listener uses lenses that differ greatly from those of the communicator, it is reasonable to assume the reconstructed message will have little resemblance to the original.

Kraft's theory of receptor-oriented communication indicates that to be effective communicators of the gospel, we must abandon the notion that it is normative for God to meet everyone within the same framework of concepts and customs by which he became known to us.[18] In practical terms, this means that a Christian communicator must make every effort to enter the audience's frame of reference using language, cultural concepts and symbols that are understandable to them. This, of course, includes employing culturally suitable teaching and learning styles.

ORAL VS. LITERATE LEARNING STYLES

Perhaps the greatest disparity in learning styles is between print-oriented learners and oral learners. Walter Ong, in his definitive work on orality and literacy, proposed that when a culture moves from orality to literacy a restructuring of consciousness takes place.

> Without writing, the literate mind would not and could not think as it does, not only when engaged in writing but normally even when it is composing its thoughts in oral form. More than any other single invention, writing has transformed human consciousness.[19]

In other words, because literate people can read and write, they are able to think differently. Richard Jensen compares it to putting new "software" into the human brain.[20] This affects all aspects of a literate society including radically altering the way the church communicates with people. Jensen writes,

> When preaching came under the tutelage of the literate world it changed immensely. Preaching began to be characterized by linearity (three points), propositional content, an analytical nature, left-brain communication, and metaphors of illustration. Christian proclamation moved from "thinking in story" to "thinking in ideas." The goal of preaching moved from participation to understanding. Homiletical textbooks from the time of Gutenberg until very recently have taught us to preach by "thinking in ideas." [21]

---

* This follows the constructivist theory of education propounded by Bruner, Piaget and others.

Michael Cole, in extensive research with the Kpelle people of Liberia, found significant differences between the functional cognition of nonliterate and literate people.[22] For instance, when nonliterates were presented with a logical deductive problem where conclusions should follow from the premises presented in the problem statement, they often tried to handle the problem by relying on what they knew/did not know independently for solving the problem. In other words, the "if … therefore" of logic was ignored. In further experiments Cole found that some of the experiences involved in formal education changed this approach to problem solving.[23]

In their manual on the Chronological Bible Storying model, James Slack and J. O. Terry state that while different learning preferences exist among people in every culture, there are two dominant, or primary, learning preferences. These are oral culture communication and literate, word-culture communication.[24] Harry Box goes further and includes orality as an important element of worldview that is common to all oral peoples:

> In considering the worldview characteristics of oral, event-oriented people, we are not simply considering the worldview of a particular culture, but rather an aspect of worldview that has strong features of commonality in many cultures.…
>
> There is a marked contrast between the worldview characteristics of oral communicators and literacy-oriented people. This is not simply at a superficial, surface level, but rather at a deep worldview level and is particularly significant in the whole area of communication. To move from an oral worldview position to a literacy-oriented worldview position, or vice versa, requires a major worldview shift.[25]

Box believes that "… regular principles of communication can be applied to a group of people as broad in scope as the oral societies of the world, and successful results can be predicted with reasonable confidence."[26] This recognition has major implications for missionary practice among oral peoples.

It follows that the most significant factor influencing selection of teaching techniques in this project was the functional orality of the people involved. Because their cognitive style and learning preference is radically different from that of print-culture people, it was essential to discover ways to communicate using their frame of reference. Box points to this issue when he says, "This has been a problem with many Christian communicators from western countries in that they have used conceptual thinking as the basis of their communication strategy, and also taught it to their oral-oriented receptors as a superior system to use in communicating the Christian message to others."[27] This not only impedes learning, but also limits the further transmission of the message to other oral communicators.

Borrowing from Walter Ong's work, Richard Brown created a comparison between the contrasting ways that oral communicators and print communicators think and learn (Table 1):[*]

* Richard D. Brown, "Designing Programs for Oral Cultures," *Notes on Literature in Use and Language Programs* 46 (December 1995): 34 (page numbers are from Ong, *Orality and Literacy*).

Table 1. Comparison of Oral and Literate Learning Styles

Oral communicators ...	Print communicators ...	Ong
... learn by hearing (hearing-dominance).	... learn by seeing (sight-dominance).	121
... learn by observing and imitating, by listening and repeating, by memorizing proverbs, traditional sayings, stories, songs, and expressions.	... learn by reading nonfiction, by studying, examining, classifying, comparing, [and] analyzing.	8–9, 41, 43
... think and talk about events, not words.	... think and talk about words, concepts, [and] principles.	12, 61
... "use stories of human action to store, organize, and communicate much of what they know"; information is "embedded in the flow of time" usually on a "story line."	... manage knowledge "in elaborate, more or less scientifically abstract categories," and store it in print rather than in stories.	140, 141
... memorize information handed down from the past.	... seek to discover new information.	41
... value tradition.	... value novelty.	41
... reason from experience and association.	... reason logically, with analysis and explanation.	172
... organize nonnarrative speeches, such as exhortations and sermons, largely by mentioning events associated with the point being made or the words used.	... organize nonnarrative speeches, such as exhortations and sermons, by laying out a logical progression of thoughts.	165
... tend to communicate in groups.	... tend to communicate one-to-one.	69, 74
... learn mostly in interaction with others.	... learn mostly alone.	69
... cannot think about something very long without dialogue.	... can think about something for a long time while making notes about it.	34
... communicate by joining sentences with conjunctions such as "and," "then."	... communicate by joining sentences with subjunctions like "while," "after."	37
... frequently use words in set phrases, such as sayings, proverbs, riddles, formulas, or just descriptions such as "brave soldier."	... generally use words independently, with few set phrases.	38
... appreciate repetition, in case something was missed the first time.	... do not like repetition, since material missed can be read again.	39
... like verbosity (many words to say little), because speaking is fast.	... like brevity (few words to say much), because writing is slow.	40

LITERACY AND ILLITERACY

Some widely held assumptions about the function and spread of literacy have little basis in fact. They stem from a literate worldview that cannot imagine people living and functioning effectively without knowing how to read and write. From this viewpoint, "illiterate" is a derogative word that suggests someone is backward and impoverished. Box writes,

> It is important for people of Western cultural origin to realize that this oral system of communication is not just something superficial, barely able to do the job of passing simple messages, and which is waiting for the Western literacy oriented system to come along. Rather, it is a complex system requiring numerous skills, and is perfectly adequate to communicate at all levels of the society and to all situations.[28]

Another misconception is that the world's population is now mostly literate with only pockets of illiteracy remaining. This could not be farther from the truth. Estimates are that as many as two-thirds of people worldwide have a strong preference for oral communication.[29] For them, reading takes a minor role, if any at all, in the ways they gather and share the information needed to live their daily lives. Even in developed countries like the United States, competence in reading is far from universal. A 1992 study by the U.S. Department of Education showed that only 18–21% of adults in the U.S. showed sufficient reading skills to be rated either literate or highly literate.[30] A follow-up survey in 2003 found that among adults who had taken graduate courses or had graduate degrees, only 41% scored as proficient, compared with 51% a decade earlier which points to a further distancing from literacy and literate methods.*

This leads us to a third myth, which is that illiteracy is decreasing and will conceivably become insignificant in our lifetime. After all, we might ask, with the push for literacy from so many directions, surely illiteracy will be "eradicated" before long? Contrary to this belief, in many countries the percentage of nonliterate people is actually increasing because literacy efforts are not keeping pace with population growth, and because most oral communicators see no reason for learning to read.

Each country has its own definition of literacy. In some countries everyone who has attended school for a year or two is counted as literate. Nations also

---

* In this study, proficiency was measured by ability to read lengthy, complex abstract texts and analyze information in the documents. Interestingly, this description seems to accurately describe the biblical text, at least as it is commonly presented in churches in the West.

tend to inflate their literacy rate to appear more advanced than they are. Major international lenders such as the World Bank include national literacy rates in their lending criteria, so it makes sense for a country to claim as high a percentage of literacy as possible. Grant Lovejoy believes that in most cases it would be more realistic to reduce the claimed literacy levels by at least half.[31]

ORALITY IN INDIA

According to official statistics, India has made great strides toward literacy. In 1961, only 28% of Indians could read (40% of males, 15% of females). The total number of nonliterates then was 167 million. By 1991, government figures claimed that the literacy rate had improved to 52% (64% males, 39% females). Nevertheless, because of the population explosion, during this same time the number of nonliterates *doubled* to 330 million. Even now, among tribal and low caste people the official literacy rate is still only 30–35%, with literacy for women being as low as 9–10% in some states.

India has a long history of oral competency. Orally transmitted religious epics such as the Ramayana, the Mahabharata, the Vedas and the Puranas date to around 500 B.C. or even earlier, a time comparable to the Greek epics. C. J. Daswani writes, "All early literatures in India were composed, transmitted and preserved orally and were reduced to writing much later."[32] Even then, reading them was strictly limited to the privileged Brahmin caste. A person of a lower caste—or a woman of any caste—who dared to learn to read the Sanskrit language risked harsh penalties like having molten lead poured into their ears and having their tongue cut out.[*] The Brahmins were so obsessed with the idea of safeguarding their knowledge that for eons they did not commit any of the sacred chanted Vedas to writing, instead preserving their secrecy through oral tradition out of fear that written scripts could be easily stolen.

Later, during the ascendancy of the Muslim culture in the Moghul period, the system of oral literacy continued. Although the founder of the Moghul empire, Babur (1504–1525), is remembered for keeping a detailed personal journal, his grandson, Akbar (1556–1605), the greatest Moghul ruler of all, found no personal use for literacy. Instead he preferred to hear oral arguments before making his decisions. As is still common today, the Muslim Quran was passed on orally, its written form serving mostly as an aid to oral recitation and memorization.[33]

A preference for oral communication persists even in 21st century India. As J. P. Losty phrases it, "The belief in the superiority of the spoken word

---

[*]   An oft-quoted statement from the Manu Smiriti.

over the written word has always been very strong in India, and survives to this day."[34] It is still considered unscholarly, for example, to depend on books when chanting Vedic hymns or singing.

A news item on BBC radio pointed to the likelihood that even many middle class Indians may not feel entirely comfortable with printed instructions. In 2002, Electrolux Appliances announced that they were bringing out a new talking washing machine just for India. This "washy talky" would help people through the various spin-wash cycles by speaking 90 phrases in fluent Hindi, English or Tamil.[35] This is an indicator that there is still a preference for oral communication even in homes where people may have extensive formal education.

Other examples are seen in the hundreds of political parties in India that are represented at the polling places not by their written name but by a unique graphic symbol, and by India's prolific film industry (known as Bollywood because it is in Bombay) that produces more movies every year than any other film industry in the world. India's smallest rupee coins bear the symbol of a hand with one or two fingers extended to distinguish one coin from the other. Recently the Indian government began recommending pictorial warnings on cigarette packs when it was discovered that most of the people dying from cancer cannot read written warnings because they are illiterate.

Throughout India, religious festivals often transform marketplaces and other public spaces in cities and towns into impromptu outdoor theaters featuring live dramatization of the Hindu epics. A large stage is erected where a drama troupe or a *pandit* (storyteller) presents episodes of the Ramayana, the Mahabharata or the Puranas before large crowds of listeners. These well attended *katha* performances often last for three or four nights in succession.[36]

To demonstrate the high-orality/low-literacy context of India one must look no further than the publishing industry. A published body of literature in a particular language suggests there are enough readers of that language to make publishing and selling books viable. About 300 languages are still spoken in India. Recent statistics show that Indian publishers annually print 70,000 different titles in 24 of these languages. Half of the publications are in Hindi or English with the rest divided among 22 other languages—and none at all for the remaining 275 Indian languages, which, by definition, are languages that belong to groups of primary oral communicators.[37]

The Indian educational system also points to a strong residual orality. Walter Ong cites Jack Goody when he says, "The residual orality of a given chirographic culture can be calculated from ... the amount of memorization the culture's educational procedures require."[38] In India schools from kindergarten to university depend heavily on rote memorization. A student's ability to memorize facts and repeat them on exams largely defines India's educational system.

A villager named Ismail Hembrom had studied through high school using borrowed schoolbooks. I asked him, "Did you have any books at home?" As though the question were slightly ridiculous, he answered that there were no books and no time to read them anyway. So even people like Ismail who manage to get through ten years of formal education may still not use reading as part of their normal environment. Despite their ability to read and write, functionally they are still oral communicators.

ORAL STORIES IN PEASANT CULTURES

Connections between ancient and present-day oral cultures give Bible narratives unique appeal to people from tribal and peasant contexts. They often understand instinctively that which must be explained to a Christian from a literate culture. Familiarity with idolatry, the spirit world, blood sacrifice, cleansing rituals, religious food laws, village life, poverty, illness, death, agriculture, social hierarchy, power differential, kinship obligations, sacred groves, rights of primogeniture and so forth give Bible stories great credibility.

In 1978 it was estimated that two billion people, or half of earth's population, could be categorized as peasants.[39] Today it is likely that this number is significantly larger. It includes not only rural cultivators but also multitudes of "urban peasants" who have migrated to the city without seeing their status in life changed appreciably. The vast majority are oral communicators.

David Filbeck defines peasant society as, "... a part-society dependent upon and subordinate to an elite segment that stands in control of all society." Peasants are mainly rural, living in relation to market towns. Although traditionally agricultural, significant numbers earn a living from nonagricultural occupations. Robert Redfield (1956) characterized peasant society as "intermediate between the tribe and the modern city...." In fact, many tribal groups that were formerly autonomous and self-sufficient now more closely resemble peasant cultures. The most accurate definitions of peasant society are based on economics and power: "The peasant must contend with a dominant elite who hold the power to demand a part, if not all, of the peasant's surplus...."[40]

The striking similarities between many aspects of biblical cultures and that of present-day peasant cultures provide important avenues for communication of the gospel. By taking advantage of these natural connections, stories from biblical cultures can relate the Bible message directly to today's peasant societies. Filbeck writes,

> If there is any one social type that more closely resembles biblical times, especially the social context of the first century Palestine, it is peasant society.... If the social context wherein Jesus of Nazareth preached was peasant in character, then how he encoded the Good News of the Kingdom ... should serve as the model for communicating the gospel cross-culturally in peasant society today.[41]

Parallels are numerous. For example, agriculture is central to most peasant societies. The great Israelite festivals were important because, in addition to having religious and historical significance, they marked the rhythm of the agricultural year.[*] Many of the storytellers in the Oral Bible pilot project were from the Santal tribe which traditionally celebrated seven annual festivals connected with agriculture.[†] Researcher Joseph Troisi, who lived among the Santals for a year and a half in the 1970s, writes, "Since Santal religion is so intimately related to agriculture—their chief source of livelihood—special emphasis is given to those rituals and festivals that mark every important stage of the Santal agricultural cycle."

Another aspect is economic necessity. The peasant's most basic concern is to produce enough food to feed his family plus a surplus that can be sold or traded for other necessities of life. Impoverishment has more than one cause, but a principle reason can be misfortune of one kind or another. S. Estborn writes,

> The monsoon and the crop may fail, other losses or sickness may come, money had to be borrowed at high-interest [from the money-lender] and the poor villager may have to mortgage his property

---

[*] Pentecost at the beginning of June marked the wheat harvest and was known as the Feast of the Harvest. The Festival of Tabernacles at the end of September came at the end of the grape harvest and was known as the Feast of Ingathering (Exo. 23:14-16).

[†] No Santal would dare to begin planting rice before the festival of *Erok Sim* because they believe it would bring ruin not only upon the individual, but upon the whole village. The festival of first fruits known as *Janthar* is also regarded as sacred. It is strictly taboo for anyone to eat of the first fruits until ceremonial rituals have been performed to the spirits on behalf of the whole village. The spirits are honored by being offered the first fruits of the land. The Santal harvest festival called *Sohrae* is held after the rice paddy has been reaped, threshed and stored. *Sohrae* lasts for six days and six nights during which the Santal code of sexual conduct is relaxed. When the festival is over, offerings are made to atone for the misconduct that has taken place. Joseph Troisi, *Tribal Religion: Religious Beliefs and Practices Among the Santals* (New Delhi: Manohar, 1979, 2000), 21, 137, 138, 126-127.

and soon it is lost and he is reduced to a miserable slave of the large landowners. For a large number of village Christians the problem is how to get food from day to day. They are very much the same kind of people as those poor and hungry people who surrounded our Lord (Luke 6:20ff) and to whom he preached the good news.[42]

The misfortunes mentioned by Estborn correspond to many Old Testament narratives such as those that were told about the prophets Elijah and Elisha. Stories about abusive political leaders, famines and moneylenders, illnesses and the deaths of children parallel the daily lives of peasants everywhere.

A third significant area of correspondence with biblical cultures is belief in the power of magic and of evil spirits. In the stories of the Old Testament, magicians are found in royal courts from the Pharaohs to the kings of Babylon. Robert Alter refers to this when he describes Balaam's actions in Numbers 23 as "... paganism, with its notion that divine powers can be manipulated by a caste of professionals through a set of carefully prescribed procedures."[43] Incidents referring to evil (unclean) spirits are evident in stories throughout the Gospels and in Acts. These often appear in confrontation with the power of God.

The Santals' belief in spirits and in magic is typical of many present-day tribal and peasant groups. Troisi writes:

Santals are aware that ... the course of nature is at times affected by agencies outside their sphere of control. To cope with the mysterious supernatural world, the Santals, like other tribes at the same level of culture, have evolved a system of beliefs and practices. According to them, the supernatural world is populated with a large number of supernatural spirits called bongas and with a large number of impersonal supernatural powers. They are believed to shape the course of nature and of human events....

Guasdal (1960) records the names of 178 different spirits who are said to be prevalent among the Santals. ...The Santals regard themselves as living, moving, and having their being in this world of supernatural entities.... Mountains, rocks, rivers, trees, etc., are believed to be inhabited by various powers.... [Their] relation towards these supernatural spirits is one of reverential fear, dependence, submission, and propitiation (Troisi, 21, 71, 73, 77, 240).

When anthropologist and Bible translator Jacob Loewen read an early draft of Mark's Gospel to Choco tribal Christians in South America for the first time, he noted the power that biblical narratives have in contexts where there is a belief in spirits:

> Bible reading in an area where witchcraft is being practiced can be a revealing experience.... I began to realize that they were appreciating something about the gospel narrative that I could not, or at least did not, [appreciate] to the same degree as they.... I have had to conclude that since they had been so very conscious of the evil spirit forces as non-Christians, these new converts were now equally conscious of the presence of the Spirit of God.[44]

In these cultures, belief in evil spirits and the power of magic often makes people anxious and fearful. Even the shamans and priests who are appointed to control the spirits fear them. Hearing a biblical story about God's power over spirits can bring hope and release from this fear and bondage.*

People in other cultures sometimes interpret Bible stories in ways that to us seem unexpected and even surprising. Because of the subordinate position they occupy in society, peasants experience much insecurity in their lives. Since poverty equates to powerlessness, the poor have always sought ways to equal the scales. Susan Niditch, in her book, *Underdogs and Tricksters*, shows how Bible stories about such characters can become heroic stories for the poor and dispossessed.

> The underdog is the poor relative, the youngest son, the exile, the ex-prince, the soldier of a defeated army—the person, in short, who is least likely to succeed and yet does. The underdog evokes our sympathies ... and when they succeed we succeed.[45]

Characters like Joseph, Moses, Gideon, and David are examples of underdogs who through God's help and their own wisdom or physical ability overcame difficult situations. Ruth is an example of an underdog who was able to exchange her marginal existence as a foreigner and a widow for a higher, more secure status. Another wonderful underdog story is that of Esther. Overcoming her low status as an adopted orphan and a member of a despised ethnic group, she was chosen to be queen of the foremost nation of that time. She retained her position in spite of

---

* See Chapter 11 for case studies that show the Santals' sense of powerlessness and desperate fear of the spirit world.

deadly threats from a powerful enemy and turned the tables to save her own people from destruction.

Underdog characters have universal appeal to people who are marginalized and oppressed. However they find special glee in trickster stories. Niditch describes the trickster as a subtype of the underdog:

> A fascinating and universal hero, the trickster brings about change in a situation via trickery. Underdogs who are also tricksters ... survive because they have the nerve to use their wits.[46]

Trickster stories have special attractiveness for those who are not part of the establishment. In such contexts a trickster is seen as admirable because of the injustice that is imposed by the dominant culture.

Niditch points out that Genesis includes many trickster stories. Leah, the unloved wife, trades mandrakes for sexual intimacy with her husband (30:14–18). Jacob makes striped sticks to overcome the unfair contract enforced by his uncle Laban (30:37–43). The twice-widowed Tamar tricks her father-in-law, Judah, by posing as a prostitute. Turning the tables on him, she achieves elevated status as the mother of twin sons (Gen. 38). Even Joseph's story includes the trickster motif at key points, although Joseph's use of it is presented as wisdom and not as tricksterism.[47] Abraham (12:10–20; 20:1–18), Isaac (26:1–17), Jacob (25:29–34), Rebekah (chapter 27), Laban (chapter 29) and Dinah's brothers (chapter 34) are other characters who through trickery succeeded in achieving their aims.

Biblical stories about such unlikely heroes enable listeners who may be paralyzed by their own powerlessness, to believe that despite the uncontrollable forces and chaos in their lives, God will help them overcome their difficult circumstances and limitations.

In conclusion, the parallels between biblical cultures and present-day peasant cultures contribute powerfully to the attraction that Bible stories have for village people everywhere. The connections are both broad and instinctive, in most cases requiring little explanation. A biblical story is a form of the message that so closely parallels their own culture, it is simple for them to understand and easy to pass along to others.

Stories for Ministry

My name is Dasrath. Some months ago I visited a family that was worshipping idols. I shared the story of the Prophet Elijah's encounter with King Ahab and Jezebel and the idol priests (1 Kings 18). After telling them that story, I also told them about Jesus, how he was born, how he died on a cross and how he rose again. I told them, "These are true stories," and they believed all those stories.

After hearing those stories, that entire family believed in Jesus. Shortly afterward at the time of the Dussehra festival, when all the Hindu people in their village worship their god and decorate their idols, they chose not to participate. On December 30th we baptized four members of that family.

Then the people around them started to criticize them. They began to scold them and caused much fear in that family. So I went to their house and shared the story about Saul. I told how Saul used to persecute the Christians. But God chose Saul for ministry, and Saul became Paul and started his ministry. I told them, "I believe these people will also be changed like Saul was. Don't fear—Jesus is with you." I also told them a story about Peter (Acts 12:1–24). "Because of his ministry, Peter was imprisoned. But God sent his angel and the angel delivered Peter from that jail. In the same way, God will help you to overcome whatever problem you are experiencing in your life." So I encouraged them in this way to stand with God.

I visited another Hindu family in that same village. A woman named Toojhima was sick, so I told the story of the woman who had the issue of blood (Mark 5:25–34). I said, "If you believe in Jesus, then God will heal you completely." After hearing this story, she came to faith. She said, "I believe in Jesus. Please pray for me." A week later when I visited that home again, Toojhima was so happy to see me. She said, "Pastor, you prayed for me and Jesus healed me completely!" She got salvation. She accepted Jesus Christ, and last month she also took baptism.

Section One

THEORETICAL FOUNDATIONS

Chapter 3

ORALITY IN THE BIBLE

Jesus was not a theologian;
He was God who told stories.

—MADELEINE L'ENGLE

The noted behavioral psychologist, B. F. Skinner, observed, "A culture is no stronger than its capacity to transmit itself. It must impart an accumulation of skills, knowledge, and social and ethical practices to its members."[48] This is equally true for a community of believers. Biblical leaders from Moses to Paul were all deeply concerned with the vital importance of transmission of revealed truth within the communities they served.

Much like present-day India, most of Israel's people in biblical times led agrarian lives. They worked the land, lived in villages led by elders, and throughout biblical history they continued to tell stories, preserve custom and law, and cite proverbs orally. Some individuals were probably regarded by their communities as especially good storytellers, but all would have shared in the oral culture.[49] Few people knew written works by having seen and read them themselves; instead they received the messages and content verbally. Even the rare individuals who had read the works would normally quote them from memory, not by referencing a written text.[50]

TRANSMISSION OF BIBLICAL KNOWLEDGE THROUGH STORYTELLING

From our modern perspective, it is difficult to imagine a world without literacy. Nevertheless, writing—as we know it—is a relatively recent innovation. Eric Havelock explains,

Up until about 700 years before Christ the Greek peoples were non-literate. About that time they invented a writing system conveniently described as an "alphabet," the Greek word for it. The use of this invention in the course of 300 to 400 years after 700 B.C. had a transformational effect upon the behavior of the Greek language, upon the kind of things that could be said in the language and the things that could be thought as it was used.[51]

Earliest human "writing" was by pictographic symbols; logograms (written symbols representing a spoken word) came later and began to allow a wider range of expression. Systems such as cuneiform in Sumeria and hieroglyphics in Egypt developed as early as 3000 B.C. However, these were quite limited and required a skilled class of specialists to interpret them. The Semitic systems that arose between 1500–1000 B.C. consisted entirely of consonants, and thus were useful largely as an aid to memory since they were difficult to decipher apart from oral interpretation. The genius of the Greeks was to take certain of the Semitic consonant signs and use them for vowels, thus creating the first phonetic system for transcribing human speech.[52]

Biblical texts indicate the existence of at least some literate people in Israelite society from as early as the tenth century B.C. A dramatic narrative in 2 Samuel 11 tells of David sending a letter to his general, Joab, at the hands of Uriah, whom he intended to kill.

During the eons before writing developed, God's progressive revelation was preserved solely by passing it orally from one generation to the next. The prophet Joel shows this oral process of knowledge transfer: "Tell your children about it, let your children tell their children, and their children another generation." (Joel 1:3). This pattern for transferring knowledge consisted of parents "teaching" it to children, literally by repeating the words again and again as though sharpening a sword:

And these words which I command you today shall be in your heart. You shall teach them diligently to your children, and shall talk of them when you sit in your house, when you walk by the way, when you lie down, and when you rise up. You shall bind them as a sign on your hand, and they shall be as frontlets between your eyes. You shall write them on the doorposts of your house and on your gates.* (Deut. 6:6–9).†

---

* Niditch theorizes that this "writing" was more iconic or symbolic than for the purpose of providing a record of the words in case they were forgotten. It was meant to invest the individual and the home with the power of the Torah. (Niditch, *Oral World,* 87).

† Unless otherwise noted, Scripture passages in this document are from the New King James Version (NKJV).

But how was it possible to recall such an accumulated body of information? The answer is simple—as the canon developed, much of it was specifically structured for remembrance and oral transmission; genre such as proverbs, poetry, songs and genealogies made it easy to recall and repeat to others. In fact, most of the Bible was originally given to be heard rather than read.

Louis L'Amour was one of America's foremost authors of cowboy novels. Up to the time he began writing at the age of thirty, L'Amour traveled widely and had many and varied experiences. After his death, his wife wrote:

> During his travels he would occasionally compose poems, and it always seemed remarkable to me that he could both create and remember them without writing them down; it seemed as if he could not forget a line or even a word. Louis explained that before the development of writing, poetry was one of the tricks ancient people used to remember stories. The rhyme and meter of each line would help you to remember the next. Because of this, poems that told a story ... were very popular with the hobos and sailors of his day. They were men with few possessions, some even illiterate, and so they were, in a way, like those prehistoric people who carried their literature in their heads.[53]

The preponderance of narrative in the Scriptures suggests that the most common way of recalling and passing knowledge along was simply through hearing and telling stories. As a father walked along the road with his son or a mother worked at home with her daughter, they were to be telling and retelling God's stories. At bedtime and when they got up they were to recount again and again the mighty acts of God. In these stories of God's interactions with specific historical characters who were central to the development of the Jewish faith, children would learn of God's attributes, his demands and his power.

It was, in fact, nothing less than the Jewish worldview which was to be formed and sustained through rehearsing these stories. N. T. Wright observes, "Stories are actually peculiarly good at modifying or subverting other stories and their world views."[54] As long as the Jewish people knew and told their own stories, the stories of other nations and other gods were of little effect.

These stories were often connected to specific events or objects. For instance, a rainbow in the sky would be a reminder of the story of God's salvation from the great flood. Similarly the annual festivals like Passover were intended to memorialize important events in Israel's history. Each part of the Passover ritual was structured as a memory aid. God said, "When you do this each year your children will ask, 'Why are you doing this? What does it mean?' " (Exo.12:26–27). That was a reminder to tell them the story of the historical and symbolic event.

Another example is found in Joshua 4:1–9. After miraculously crossing the Jordan River into Canaan, Joshua was told to take 12 stones from the dry riverbed as a reminder of what God had done: "That this may be a sign among you when your children ask in time to come, saying, 'What do these stones mean to you?' " In this way stories were linked to specific places, events and objects, and were told informally as well as on formal occasions. The core of knowledge transmission was storytelling.

JESUS' EXAMPLE

Jesus followed this same communicational pattern, often linking his stories and sayings to impromptu questions by his hearers. Other opportunities arose from everyday happenings and even current news events.

Since literacy was still relatively rare, an oral methodology was essential. Catherine Hezser, in *Jewish Literacy in Roman Palestine*, maintains that the Jewish literacy rate was lower than that of the Greco-Roman society of which it was a part.[55] Since even in classical Greece literacy rarely exceeded 10%,[56] Palestinian literacy would have been quite low. In fact, Meir Bar-Ilan believes that in some rural towns and settlements the literacy rate was below 1%, and some villages may not even have had one single individual who could read. He asserts, "It is no exaggeration to say that the total literacy rate in the land of Israel at that time (of Jews only, of course) was probably less than 3%".[57] William Barclay writes, "Jews were not 'the people of the book' in the sense that every Jew possessed the book, and read and studied it…. [They] were 'people of the book' … because the book was the container of the law which was inserted into their minds, and graven upon their hearts by oral teaching."[58]

Hezser describes Jewish literacy using the image of concentric circles:

> At the center one has to imagine a very small number of highly literate people who could read literary texts in both Hebrew/Aramaic and Greek. Then there was another, slightly broader circle of those who could read literary texts in either Hebrew/Aramaic, or Greek only. They were surrounded by people who could not read literary texts but only short letters, lists, and accounts. A broader proportion of the population may have been able merely to identify individual letters, names, and labels. They as well as the vast majority of their entirely illiterate contemporaries had access to texts through intermediaries only.[59]

It seems clear that estimates of anything approaching universal literacy are the projections of a literate culture upon what in reality were overwhelmingly oral contexts of the biblical eras. Hezser points out that many of the conditions necessary for the development of literacy were lacking. This included the availability of schools, the cost and distribution of texts, low status for teachers and few inducements to seek education. James Crenshaw writes,

> Economic conditions, the demands of daily chores—tending sheep and goats, preparing land for cultivation, attending to olive groves and vineyards—discouraged formal schooling. The modest economic rewards available to trained scribes and the limited prospects of advancement did little to offset this situation. Few families could afford the luxury of sending boys away to school, especially during the labor intensive seasons of planting and harvesting crops.[60]

In the absence of paper (which had not yet been invented) even common writing materials were prohibitive. Broken pot shards (*ostraca*), and wood, stone, leather or wax tablets were commonly available but were hardly suitable for anything other than short letters, receipts or lists. A roll of papyrus to copy one of Paul's longer letters could have cost four day's wages while a high quality copy of the book of Mark might have required as much as ten day's wages.[61] Obviously only the wealthy could afford to own books. Because of this, even schools depended to a large degree on memory and not on print; scholastic learning consisted largely of oral memorization of the texts.

It is also important to recognize that for an oral communicator, reading a written document does not carry the same weight as living speech. In the first half of the second century, Papias of Hierapolis alluded to this viewpoint when he explained that his five volume work was written on the basis of what he had learned from personally hearing those "who had accompanied the 'elders' and that for him the 'living and abiding voice' was a much more profitable source than written books."[62]

For the transmission of knowledge to be effective in such a context, it had to match the learning preferences of a predominantly oral population. In agreement with this supposition, it appears that Jesus followed an almost purely oral strategy. Using the oral communication system of his day, he chose to address his teaching to a mostly nonliterate target group instead of to the educated elite.* In fact, Jesus was so committed to oral communication forms

---

* Although there are many stories about Jesus arguing over Scripture with the scribes and Pharisees, the educated classes were not his target group. Rather he tailored his appeals toward small businessmen, artisans, farmers and fishermen. The 12 he chose as his disciples (most of whom were unschooled) are representative of this class.

that it has caused some scholars to doubt that he was literate.[63] His use of chiasmus, rhyme and meter, as well as metaphors, repetition and alliteration made his sayings easy to learn and recall. He created parables as fascinating stories, using plot, characterization and dialogue. His spoken words were full of memorable sounds that delighted the ear. He took well-known proverbs and outdid them with new proverbs of his own making, linking his new sayings with the old ones so they would be easy to remember.

In this way, even without writing his teachings would easily transfer from person to person. Jesus' use of oral methods not only enabled everyone to learn—it also ensured that everyone could teach, thus facilitating the transmission of his words across a much broader area than he was able to reach personally.

The results of his oral training methods are obvious in the amazed reaction of the Jewish leaders to Peter and John's speech to the Sanhedrin. "Now when they saw the boldness of Peter and John, and perceived that they were uneducated and untrained [unschooled] men, they marveled. And they realized that they had been with Jesus." (Acts 4:13).

PAUL

Against this idea that oral communication was the primary means of knowledge transmission displayed in the Bible, some point to Paul's epistles. They use these as justification for seeing thought-ordered prose as a higher form of communication than story or other oral forms. It is true that at first glance Paul's Greek rhetoric and logical discourse seem foreign to oral storytelling. However, this overlooks important evidence that suggests storytelling was a more integral part of Paul's communication than just reading his epistles would indicate.

Because writing is fundamentally different from oral communication, a present-day reading of Paul's epistles cannot fully reflect the style and content of his spoken messages. Even so, significant evidence of oral patterns can be discerned. According to John Harvey, recognizable oral techniques like chiasmus, inversion, alternation, inclusion, ring-composition, word-chains, refrains, and concentric symmetry abound, especially in Paul's longer letters.[64] In the first century it was common for letters to be intentionally composed for public recitation using oral forms such as these.

Whitney Shiner, Tom Boomershine and others have pointed out that writing (and reading) in Paul's day contrasted sharply to modern usage. Instead of a solitary occupation in which one person writes in solitude to another who then reads in solitude, the message was dictated orally to a copyist who would later read it aloud to the intended audience, perhaps even incorporating much of the nonwritten communication of the author, such as body language, tone of voice, facial expression, gestures, and so forth.

It can also be shown that storytelling was not uncommon to Paul's experience. From the beginning, the power of storytelling proved to be a significant factor in his conversion to Christ.[65] It is likely that the image of Stephen telling the Old Testament stories at his trial burned in Paul's conscience and eventually helped bring him to his knees before Jesus. Second, clearly Paul told the story of his own conversion over and over and this became an important method for his presentation of the Gospel.[66] Third, although we have little record of Paul's sermons or teachings, in at least one instance where his sermon is recorded, it consisted of a series of selected Old Testament stories and the story of Jesus.[67]

Paul saturated his letters with references to the Old Testament. In just four of his epistles—Romans, 1 and 2 Corinthians, and Galatians—he includes 88 quotations from the Old Testament and 58 Old Testament allusions. Another 17 Old Testament allusions are found in Philippians and 1 Thessalonians.[68] In the letters he wrote, well-known stories would not have been repeated in full for the sake of brevity. But Paul's repeated allusions to these stories suggest that they were familiar to his converts. Incidents from the lives of Adam, Abraham, Lot, Sarah and Hagar, Jacob and Esau, Moses, Elijah and others formed the basis for some of Paul's strongest lessons.[69] It is likely that for the Gentile converts at least, this familiarity with the Jewish narratives was because Paul regularly told these stories as he preached and taught. N. T. Wright goes so far as to assert that Paul's teachings are extensions of Old Testament stories he had in mind as he wrote his letters. In other words, Paul was rescripting well-known Jewish stories, placing Jesus as the culmination.[70]

In addition to story, Paul's extensive use of metaphor shows sensitivity to the oral cognitive styles prevalent among his listeners. In 1 Corinthians 2, he describes a communication style that included a reliance on metaphor: "These things we also speak, not in words which man's wisdom teaches but which the Holy Spirit teaches, comparing spiritual things with spiritual..." (1 Cor. 2:13). Notice the concrete metaphors he employs in 1 Corinthians chapter three: planting, watering, and harvest, building a house, the refiner's fire, the body as temple of God, and food for babes. Other metaphors are found in chapter 9:7–13 (soldier, agriculture, priesthood); 9:24–27 (athletes); chapter 12 (a body); 14:7–13 (musical instruments, languages); 15:36–38 (seeds); 15:39–41 (comparison with nature: earthly and heavenly bodies); and 16:13 (a soldier's virtues). These word pictures would stick in a hearer's mind long after Paul had finished speaking.

Some may object to my portrayal, instead pointing to Paul as preacher exemplar. Perhaps part of the reason for this confusion lies in a misunderstanding of what the Bible means by the word "preach." Paul's preaching, which was from the world of the ear, differed in many ways from sermons that are developed in a world of print.

Hans Weber cites discussions in response to the Heidelberg Catechism (1953). He writes:

> The New Testament knows a *much more varied proclamation* of the Gospel than may be presumed from our word "preaching". …a sign that we have lost much of what in early Christianity was a living reality. Proclamation, in the Bible, always has a *dialogic* and *dramatic* character…. [Through] the communication of God's speaking, those thus addressed are taken into the great drama of redemptive history. This dialogic and dramatic character of divine speaking not only justifies but demands the dialogic and dramatic way of proclamation.[71]

This differs from present-day preaching in which the sermon is commonly understood to be a lecture or speech prepared in linear style that presents a series of propositional statements, sometimes illustrated by examples. Such sermons typically endeavor to extract a deeper meaning hidden behind the biblical text; the points to be made are then abstracted from the text and the listeners are left with the abstract principles in place of the text. This concept of preaching bears more resemblance to the European university system of an earlier age than to the biblical era. Mark Ellingsen writes,

> The classic three-point sermon, a didactic type of preaching often heard from many of these pulpits, which had its origins in the nineteenth century, abandons the biblical world and its literary forms. Instead of an actual presentation of that world, one receives from this model sermons about biblical topics. [72]

There are about a dozen Greek words in the New Testament that are at times translated into English as some form of the word "preach." Charles Kraft believes each of them could be translated simply "communicate." [73] An example of how these words are used is found in Luke's description of Paul's communication in the Jewish synagogue in Thessalonica:

> And Paul, as his manner was, went in unto them, and three sabbath days reasoned (*dialegomai*) with them out of the scriptures, opening (*dianoigo*) and alleging (*paratithemi*), that Christ must needs have suffered, and risen again from the dead;

and that this Jesus, whom I preach (*kataggello*) unto you, is Christ (Acts 17:2–3; KJV).

From this verse and others it appears that Paul took advantage of an array of communication forms in his preaching.

In conclusion, both Jesus and Paul were concerned with the vital importance of the transmission of knowledge leading to obedience. Jesus' final words to his disciples in Matthew 28:18 reflect this: "Go therefore and make disciples of all the nations, baptizing them in the name of the Father and of the Son and of the Holy Spirit, teaching them to observe all things that I have commanded you." Jesus had modeled for them how to do this. All they would have to do is repeat what they had learned from him following his same oral teaching techniques.

Likewise Paul urged Timothy, "And the things that you have heard from me among many witnesses, commit these to faithful men who will be able to teach others also." (2 Tim. 2:2). Paul was aware of the critical importance of passing the baton from one generation to the next. He was not content just to equip his Timothys and Tituses—he knew his work could not be considered successful unless they in turn passed it along to others. It was essential for Timothy to be part of a chain that would transmit the teaching of God's Word from person to person and generation to generation.

Learning and repeating stories of the events of Jesus' life became the everyday activity of the average believer in the early church; those who were scattered by persecution preached the word wherever they went.[74] Except for this the dispersion of the church would have been a disaster. Obviously it was not the written word that these believers carried and proclaimed—they had been given the Word in a communication medium they themselves could use. Through stories, the Word of God multiplied and became known across a wide area.[75]

How Storytelling Changed My Ministry

My name is Sunil Kumar Sadhu. When I first came to the storytelling training, I had already completed one year of training in the local Bible School and my two years of field experience, and then I went to the central Bible School for further studies. I thought, "This storytelling program is nothing. I've already learned all this." But when I started learning to tell the stories, and as I entered into the depth of this program, only then could I really understand its value.

In the Bible School, I had learned different things such as authorship, canonization, and different theological views and so on. But here I began to learn the reality and the depth of the Bible. I was able to gain more through this storytelling program than anything I had learned throughout my studies in Bible School.

The way I used to preach, I would need a long time to prepare my message. That was the only way I could preach. But now without any preparation, I can preach at least fifty messages or fifty sermons. Without a Bible, without any preparation, without any observation, I can preach now. This is my confidence and it is my faith even.

In my church some of the people have been to school but others are illiterate. When I used to preach, I was preaching about theological views and ideas. But it was not touching my congregants and it was not very effective. If we preach and give the theological views, then the educated ones may understand. But after I began using storytelling, everyone could understand, both the literate and the nonliterate.

Everyone told me, "Brother Sunil, you are preaching so differently now. Your messages are so beautiful. Whatever you were speaking before we could not understand it. But now we are able to understand you very well." (January 2008)

Chapter 4

THE DEVELOPMENT
OF BIBLICAL STORYTELLING

The important thing is the tale,
the well-told tale, not he who tells it.

–DEAN KOONTZ

Many missionary efforts in the past seemed to be as much about the superiority of the missionary's culture as they were about bringing the Good News of eternal salvation to the lost.* Gary McGee, professor of church history, writes, "Late nineteenth- and early twentieth-century Protestant mission leaders and missionaries, among them John R. Mott and James S. Dennis, shared the prevailing optimism that progress and Christian civilization would march forward together until the kingdom of God had been established on earth."[76] Schooling and literacy were central to this philosophy aimed at uplifting the "natives."

Nevertheless, there were always some missionaries who used biblical storytelling to teach the Scriptures to their converts. Tom Steffen and J. O. Terry list a number of these in their article, "The Sweeping Story of Scripture Taught Through Time."[77] As early as 1620, Paul Hsu's daughter trained

---

* "Around the 1950's an important change in viewing culture occurred, a shift from a classical understanding of culture to an empirical one. The myth, for that was what it really was, that there was only one culture for all peoples, namely, the Euro-American civilization, was debunked with the discovery and recognition of cultures, different and varied. Belied too was the West's claim to cultural superiority." Jose M. de Mesa, "Making Salvation Concrete and Jesus Real: Trends in Asian Christology," *SEDOS* (Jan. 1999).

professional storytellers to take the gospel to the villages of China and supported them from her father's money.[78] Another was noted Presbyterian missionary John L. Nevius (1829–1893) who found that telling the stories of the Bible was an effective way of developing churches in China and Korea. He described how this was done:

> We have the Scripture story exercise. Someone previously appointed tells the story; the leader of the meeting then calls on different persons one after another to reproduce it in consecutive parts; and afterwards all present take part in drawing practical lessons and duties from it. There is never time for more than one story, and often that one has to be divided, and has two Sundays given to it....
>
> I give great prominence to learning and reciting Scripture Stories and Parables, and nothing has been found to produce more satisfactory results. It excites interest, develops thought, and furnishes in a simple form a compendium of Bible History and Christian Duty; while a careful training in relating Bible Stories and drawing practical lessons from them is one of the best ways of developing preaching talent wherever it is found.[79]

V. S. Azariah became the first Indian bishop of the Anglican church in 1912. Stephen Neill relates how Azariah presided over the churches in his area during a large movement to Christ. Around 3,000 people were being baptized every year, and his flock grew from 50,000 to 150,000. Neill says, "When Azariah baptized very simple people in the villages, he would make them put their hands on their heads in Indian fashion and say with St. Paul, 'Woe is me if I preach not the gospel of Christ.' People said to him, 'How can such very simple people bear witness to Jesus Christ? They are from the depressed classes and the majority of them are illiterate.' Azariah smiled and said, 'Well, if a man knows only one Bible story, he can go and teach that story among them and then come back and learn another Bible story.'"[80]

Another missionary known for using biblical storytelling was Gladys Aylward (1902–1970) who taught Bible stories to freight-hauling muleteers in China. The movie, "The Inn of the Sixth Happiness" (1958), is based roughly on her life.

Chronological Bible Storying

In the second half of the twentieth century, a dramatic rethinking of the missionary task and its accompanying methodologies began to take place.

Among the many changes that developed was the gradual reemergence of biblical storytelling as a primary and systematic methodology, with a view toward bypassing the prerequisite of adapting to literate thinking which had so long been a barrier to the spread of the gospel in oral cultures.

One early instance is that of Dutch Reformed missionary Hans Ruedi Weber. As a young man, Weber was sent to disciple some 30,000 nominal Christians in Luwuk-Banggai, Indonesia in 1952. There he discovered the power of stories for communicating the Scriptures to oral people. Weber wrote,

> We spoke the same language, yet we did not understand each other. Our methods of thought and communication were entirely different. When we asked the meaning of a word unknown to us, the illiterate would not give a synonym, or a more or less abstract transcription, but he would 'paint' in words, quickly and unfailingly, a picture that illustrated the exact meaning. In describing a person the illiterate would not talk about his character but rather tell significant stories about him.[81]

This insight led Weber to begin developing biblical storytelling. He concluded, "If you tell a story well, illiterates will listen attentively a whole night long."[82] Weber also developed a system of drawing simple pictures or mnemonic symbols to help nonliterates remember the stories. Even though Weber served as a missionary for just four years (only 12 months of that among the oral people of Luwuk-Banggai), his ideas later proved foundational for many of the Chronological Bible Storying (CBS) methods that were developed in the following decades.

The next major milestone in the development of CBS came in the 1970s. In his work among the Palawaño people in the Philippines, missionary Trevor McIlwain began using what came to be known as Chronological Bible Teaching.[83] McIlwain felt that the professing Christians among the Palawaños lacked much of the basic foundational teaching, including the gospel of grace, on which true Christianity rests. So he developed a series of Old Testament and Gospel lessons based on Bible stories which he presented in chronological order. As McIlwain's ideas spread, they were adapted by other Philippine missionaries including Tom Steffen.[84]

Indisputably McIlwain's was a literate approach, not one based on storytelling *per se,* nor with the unique learning preferences of oral communicators in mind. He simply wanted a way to teach the Palawaños certain doctrines that he considered important. His primary contribution— and it was a huge one—was to recognize that the New Testament could only be properly understood when it was seen against the backdrop of the

Old Testament, that is, a chronological approach. As Chronological Bible Teaching led to Chronological Bible Storying, the heritage of McIlwain's literate philosophy continued to leave its imprint on the CBS movement, which in practice was slow to fully appreciate the deep-level differences between the cognitive styles and learning preferences of oral and literate people, and the power of story as story.

McIlwain's approach was next adopted by a handful of Baptist missionaries, among them J. O. Terry, who was introduced to Chronological Bible Teaching in 1988. His first attempts at teaching expositionally from a chronological series of Bible references were ineffective, but through these experiences he came to recognize the primacy of the stories themselves. As Terry began to witness the results of telling the Bible stories and their appeal to oral communicators, he concluded that simply telling the stories was far more effective than teaching expositionally. So in 1990 a decision was made to begin emphasizing the role and value of the intact Bible story. To distinguish this from McIlwain's model, the term *Chronological Bible Storying* was chosen.[85] This model also borrowed strongly from work done by Jacob Loewen in Latin America during the 1950s and 1960s.[86]

In the following years, CBS was further developed and popularized by leading Southern Baptists such as James Slack, Avery Willis, and Grant Lovejoy, among others. In 2001, a number of major mission agencies banded together to form the International Orality Network (ION) to promote the use of biblical storytelling in the mission force worldwide.[87]

WHERE NEXT?

Some of the key distinctives of the CBS model to this point have been a chronological approach, the telling of intact biblical stories (as contrasted to exposition), and the use of worldview studies for selecting appropriate stories to interface with particular cultural and religious issues in a given people group.

Chronological Bible Storying was developed for the most part by missionaries who were strongly influenced by their seminary backgrounds. This western theological approach was formative in how CBS proponents originally perceived and organized the task of biblical storytelling. The starting point was a list of essential doctrines that, like rungs on a ladder, would enable a person to gain enough theological knowledge to come to salvation.[88] After the missionary had compiled this list of essential doctrines, in conjunction with worldview studies, he or she then selected Bible narratives that would teach these doctrines.

I chose a different approach, one that sought to have the hearers identify with how Bible characters *experienced* God in the narratives, so that through those experiences the hearers might come to know God in the same manner. Instead of doctrines, the structure for the story track was biographical; that is, it was based on the lives of key Bible characters presented in chronological order. Starting in Genesis, the storytellers became intimately acquainted with Adam, Noah, Abraham, Isaac, Jacob and Joseph by learning a cluster of three to five stories about each one in chronological order. They soon began to identify with the characters and draw life-lessons from how God had dealt with them. By presenting the Scriptures as biographical portions, it was made more attractive and more memorable.

While theological understanding is a part of the process, the primary emphasis is on identification, felt needs, application, and experiential knowing. This seemed to me to be more compatible with the learning style of oral communicators, and to approximate more closely the way the Bible stories were originally told.

Caution is always in order to ensure that we do not impose our own theological categories on people who are of different cultures than ours. Peter Chang notes,

> Theological education evolves in the larger context of culture and is closely related to people's thinking style. In the western academic scene, linear thinking has been the dominant mode. It is largely analytical, objective, logical and systematic.[89]

From Chang's description, it becomes clear that western theological categories are largely incompatible with the cognitive styles of oral learners.* It is safe to assume that any theology that grows authentically from an oral culture will look and sound different from ours. This does not mean that context has equal weight with the Bible in development of doctrine. Rather, it respects the fact that Christian believers in many cultures have grappled with the same biblical truths and discovered how to best express them in their own context. It is important to grant this freedom to our hearers instead of imposing our own preconceived outcomes. Tom Boomershine writes,

> The most critical element in sharing these stories is to protect the freedom of the listener. Biblical stories are not designed to persuade or to manipulate a listener into agreement. To be sure, there are appeals, and the stories are structured to invite response. But the

---

* For more about the cognitive styles of oral learners, see the following chapter.

freedom of the listener to respond in a variety of ways is built into the stories. They do not have only one meaning but open out onto a broad playground of meaning. There the listeners are invited to play…. It is an invitation to enter into an event.[90]

Jesus never hesitated to give people freedom to ponder for themselves what his stories and teachings might mean. Apparently he did not feel he had to convince them of the rightness of his doctrine or position.

TWO KINDS OF THINKING

This issue goes much deeper than just a difference in style. Jerome Bruner is widely known for his research and defining theories in the areas of cognition, language, and education. Bruner believes there are two modes—and only two—of cognitive functioning or ways of knowing and constructing reality. The first is reasoning which Bruner refers to as paradigmatic thinking. This is the kind of thinking that is employed in propositional theology. The second way of knowing is the narrative mode. He writes,

A good story and a well-formed argument are different natural kinds. Both can be used as a means for convincing another. Yet what they convince *of* is fundamentally different: arguments convince one of their truth, stories of their lifelikeness. The one verifies by eventual appeal to procedures for establishing formal and empirical proof. The other establishes not truth but verisimilitude.[91]

Being inconclusive is antithetical to logical thinking. However, in Bruner's concept it is the very "subjunctivity" of a good story that recruits the listener's own imagination and allows for the recreation of the story using his or her own life experiences and cultural tool kit. "[It is] the creation of implicit rather than explicit meanings. For with explicitness the reader's degrees of interpretive freedom are annulled."[92] Bruner adds, "To be in the subjunctive mode is to be trafficking in human possibilities rather than in settled certainties."[93] The object is to enlist the listener in the "performance of meaning under the guidance of the text."[94] In other words, subjunctivity enhances the possibility of participation by the listener in the story event.

The author's act of creating a narrative of a particular kind and in a particular form is not to evoke a standard reaction but to recruit whatever is most appropriate and emotionally lively in the reader's repertoire. So, "great" storytelling is about compelling human plights that are "accessible" to readers. But at the same time, the plights must be set forth with sufficient subjunctivity to allow them to be *rewritten* by the reader, so as to allow play for the reader's imagination.[95]

Bruner goes on to describe this process:

As our readers read, as they begin to construct a virtual text of their own, it is as if they were embarking on a journey without maps— and yet, they possess a stock of maps that *might* give hints. And besides, they know a lot about journeys and about mapmaking. First impressions of the new terrain are, of course, based on older journeys already taken. In time, the new journey becomes a thing in itself, however much its initial shape was borrowed from the past.[96]

This process is crucial because it promotes internalization and ownership of the new stories. The important role of discovery in the learning process will be discussed more fully in the next chapter. For now we can conclude that making truth explicit, which is a strength of propositional theology, is quite different from a storytelling approach.

Each of these two modes of thinking provides a distinct way of constructing reality. The paradigmatic mode seeks to transcend the particular by higher and higher reaching for abstraction;[97] it looks for universal principles that can be shown to be true regardless of context. It strives for explicit definition of truth. In contrast, narrative thinking is a way of knowing that places knowledge in human experiences located in a particular time and place. It calls on the listener's own emotions and imagination to reconstruct reality through clues, riddles, whispers and descriptions instead of formulas and appeals to logic. Because it models life, it is content with inconclusiveness and mystery. It invites the listener to an exploration of possibilities.

The evangelical appeal to reason derides such an approach to decision-making. It scoffs at emotionally charged discourse and emotional responses, arguing that the only authentic decision is a logical one based on a cool consideration of facts. One proponent of this position expressed it like this, "Persuasion involves disclosure of the facts to create thoughtful decision-making on the part of the participants. Awakening people's ability to intellectually make decisions rather than react to emotionalized manipulations is fundamental to positive long-lasting change agendas."[98]

Even though there are many instances of opinion leaders using emotionalism to foster their own ends, it does not follow that appeals involving emotional responses are fundamentally wrong. Whitney Shiner describes the Greek rhetoric of the first-century as one which "stressed the importance of emotions and recognized that emotion was superior to rational argument in convincing an audience."[99] In one of his writings, Cicero has Antonius point out, "Men decide far more problems by hate, or love, or lust, or rage, or sorrow, or joy, or hope, or fear, or illusion, or some other inward emotion, than by reality, or authority, or any legal standard, or judicial precedent, or statute."[100] Quintilian criticized those who crowded their speeches with logical proofs:

> That is suitable for dialectical controversies among learned men but not for the lawcourts, where the judges are frequently ill educated. In order to vindicate truth in that circumstance, we must rely on the charm and force of our discourse and appeals to emotion.... Proofs, it is true, may induce the judges to regard our case as superior to that of our opponent, but the appeal to the emotions will do more, for it will make them wish our case to be the better. And what they wish, they will also believe.[101]

In contrast, the Stoics believed that emotions were mere fancies and frivolous opinions and the wise man should be free from emotion. Cicero criticized them for this, saying, "Their meagre little syllogisms are mere pinpricks; they may convince the intellect, but they cannot convert the heart..." [102]

American evangelicalism has strong precedents for emotional appeals and emotional responses. Jonathan Edwards' best known sermon was entitled, "Sinners in the Hands of an Angry God." In it he vividly depicted the agonies of those who do not plead for God's forgiveness. Edwards preached this sermon all over New England and through it helped usher in the Great Awakening. Even though he simply read the sermon from the pulpit, its words so affected the listeners that it often brought terrified responses. Despite reservations about the excesses that sometimes occurred, in his 1746 *Treatise on Religious Affections*, Edwards argued that true religion resides in the heart, the seat of affections, emotions, and inclinations.[103]

Even the great evangelist Charles Finney, a lawyer by training, admitted using acting skills in his preaching. He wrote in his own defense against those who criticized him for it:

> If ministers are too stiff to learn even from an actor the best method of diffusing the warmth of burning thought over a congregation, let them remember that while they are turning away and decrying the art of the actor, and attempting to support

what they call the dignity of the pulpit, the theatres can be thronged every night.[104]

James Stephens beautifully expressed this distinction between the two kinds of thinking when he wrote, "I have learned that the head does not hear anything until the heart has listened, and what the heart knows today the head will understand tomorrow."[105]

In his paper, "Narrative Theology and the Dogmatic Use of the Bible," Maarten Wisse addresses the question of whether a narrative approach to theology necessarily results in weaker claims than a more propositional approach. He argues that, in many respects, a narrative approach can be said to make equally strong or perhaps even stronger claims than a propositional approach:

> Abstract dogmatic claims are sometimes strong in a theoretical sense—i.e., they claim universal validity and truth, but they may well be weak in a practical sense ... because of a loose connection to our real life world....
>
> A narrative's claims are many times intimately connected with our real life situation. That which is the weakness of a propositional formulation of the faith, is the strength of a narrative presentation of it.... In addition, a narrative does not argue for its picture of the world. It only tells the story as if so that what is told is seemingly obvious. If we take these two arguments together, a narrative's claims may well be equally strong or even stronger than those of an abstract dogmatic formula. A narrative may combine the strength of a real life picture with the tricks of rhetoric, so that the reader is moved by the story almost without having the ability to decide whether he agrees with the message or not.[106]

A perceived advantage of the abstract propositional approach in scientific thought is that resulting principles can have a more universal application. However, Wisse believes that narratives can also have universal appeal: "... we sometimes speak about 'universal stories' which appeal to universal experiences in human lives. In that sense, the message which the story tells may well have universal significance."[107]

Paradigmatic thinking is the product of millenniums of literate culture; it is a specialized skill that is only acquired through years of formal schooling. Lacking this specialized training, people who are oral communicators typically construct reality through narrative. For a missionary from the West, the challenge of an oral culture is no less than learning how to communicate all over again.

It is not easy to embrace the demand to relinquish our areas of strength. Jonathan Wilson describes an experience he had as a new missionary in Japan:

> When I first came to Japan I tried my hand at "kendo", the Japanese way of the sword. A very kind man agreed to coach me and for a summer I worked at learning this martial art. Perhaps the most frustrating thing was that I had already studied western sword fighting, or "fencing" in college. What I thought would be a help, was really the biggest hindrance—because everything I knew already was actually wrong and now had to be unlearned![108]

Because most westerners tend to default to paradigmatic thinking, any program that purports to teach oral communicators must confront this issue. Otherwise the assumption can be maintained that literacy-based, propositional, expositional teaching is "real" teaching and that storytelling is only a starting point toward this goal. If, indeed, storytelling is seen simply as a veneer that can be overlaid on top of paradigmatic ways of thinking, it is an indication that there has not yet been a deep-level comprehension of the huge differences between literate and oral communicators. This is perhaps the biggest single barrier to application of an effective biblical storytelling strategy in an oral culture.

In a sense, laying down our own cognitive style and choosing to communicate according to the learning preferences of those we serve is incarnational ministry, much as Christ did when he came from heaven to earth. Incarnational ministry means letting go of some of the things we have learned to rely on and which make us comfortable in order to share in the life style of our target group. In this case, it is their learning style that we must embrace. We have grown accustomed to preaching messages that were mainly about ideas—now we must learn to think in narrative and tell the biblical stories in such a way that the biblical characters come to life in the hearts and minds of our listeners.

In conclusion, the rewards for making this cognitive shift are great. Beyond the all-important aspect of being able to communicate the gospel to oral communicators in their own terms, we may even find that some of our own richest learning experiences come from narrative. Through the power of imagination, the Bible can grant understandings that it does not communicate through the faculty of reason.

The Pujari

My name is Nitual Dhanful. Once I went to a new village where I was telling the Bible stories. There was a village idol priest there, a pujari, who thought there were no Christians in his village. To reach the house where I was telling the stories we had to walk right past the house of the Hindu priest and through his patio.

So over some days he began to notice me going there and started to look me over, to monitor my movements, wondering where I was going. One day he followed me to the place where we worship. While I told the stories, he stood around the corner listening.

A Hindu mother who was there told me, "There was a pujari here, and he was asking about you. They are strongly opposed to Christianity in this village, so he may be planning to get the others in the village to destroy you or have some charges brought. He is the main man here. So you be careful when you are coming here to do these things."

But from then on I started to share the stories even more boldly and the pujari was always standing outside listening. One day I asked someone what his name was, and from then on I kept his name on my prayer list. I prayed saying, "Lord, please help me to have an introduction to him." After some days we met each other and I was able to speak with him. This pujari told me, "I listened to all the stories you are teaching here. Are you coming to this village to convert people?" And we had some arguments.

But after some time he also gave me some prayer requests to pray for. He confessed, "As I heard your stories I was not able to sleep. Some evil forces were coming to wake me up while I was sleeping. So please pray for me." And we prayed for him.

Now he is coming to our church regularly. I told him, "If you believe, you will receive salvation. He said, "I believe. But

I'm the main Hindu priest here. If I accept Jesus or become a Christian, what will people think? They will throw me out of the village. So I will come to the church secretly and pray."

Then I told him the story of Noah. I said, "Just like Noah was in that village, the Lord chose him and told him to prepare a ship. He was a good man, a very strong man. There were other people there who were able to do all kinds of things. But the Lord selected him only. And the people were laughing at him while he was preparing the ship. In the same way, you have to prepare a ship or an ark here in your village. If you accept the Lord, you will receive salvation like Noah."

I told him many such things and he believed. Just before coming to training this time I saw him, and now he is pressing me to baptize him! I told all this to my coordinator, so a baptismal program might even have taken place while I was here this week.

So that's how we won this temple priest. Now please pray for his followers to also come to Christ and also pray for all the other villagers of that place.

Chapter 5

STORIES AND LEARNING

Amusement does not go with learning,
for learning is a painful process.

—ARISTOTLE

The process of teaching-learning is meant to facilitate the transmission of knowledge or skills. It is of crucial importance to every society for without it the society's accumulated store of wisdom and knowledge would be lost with each generation that passes. Researchers and educators have studied the field of education extensively for the last century and a half to better understand how transfer works and to improve its effectiveness.

In the 1960s, there was a popular theory that learning and remembering depend on changes in the molecular structure of certain chemicals that are incorporated in body cells. Experiments were published offering evidence that skills had been transferred by taking materials from the brains of trained animals and injecting them into the bodies of untrained organisms.[109] Efforts to repeat such experiments more often than not failed to demonstrate transmission of skills. While it would be wonderful if one could take a language injection and wake up the next morning speaking fluent French, it will probably never be that simple.

How does knowledge transmission occur? In this section we will look at different aspects of this process, with special regard to oral cultures.

THE EDUCATIONAL ROLE OF STORIES

Storytelling is as old as history and yet as modern as the latest Hollywood film. Whether gathered around a village campfire listening to a traveling storyteller recount enchanting tales or sitting in a theater watching a hit movie with spectacular computerized effects, people everywhere are fascinated by stories.

From the beginning of human history, knowledge passed from person to person and generation to generation in the form of stories. People everywhere relied on the oral wisdom embodied in the proverbs, poems, stories and songs of their culture. This was a time when storytellers were warmly welcomed wherever people congregated and socialized - beneath a shady tree, at a busy market place, walking along a dusty road or sitting around a cooking fire at night. Listeners followed their stories with rapt attention, often participating in the storytelling ritual by asking questions, interjecting comments, laughing or even shedding a tear. But most importantly, they repeated the stories to others; and so each person became part of the media fabric of his or her culture.

Stories entertain, but they also have a more serious role to play by teaching people about a society's norms. Cultural values are preserved in stories that are passed from one generation to the next.

A society's stories serve as interpreters giving the meaning of life events. For example, in a tribal culture sickness may be attributed to having displeased a dead ancestor. In another culture happiness may be linked to romantic love. In each case there will be many stories that embody and thus reinforce these beliefs. This is true for important concepts in every society.

It is reasonable to assume that if we want to change a society, we may start by teaching it new and different stories. When people start believing different stories it is only a matter of time until they throw off the restraints the old stories imposed on them. In this sense, stories are revolutionary.

Ballads are stories that are told in song—Andrew Fletcher, a seventeenth century Scottish patriot observed, "If a man were permitted to make all the ballads, he need not care who should make the laws of a nation."[110] Nigerian author Ben Okri stated it inversely, "Stories can be either bacteria or light; they can infect a system, or illuminate a world.... To poison a nation, poison its stories. A demoralized nation tells demoralized stories to itself."[111] A biblical storyteller in India commented,

> I have come to understand how powerful stories are. Many people
> in my tribe live according to the religious myths that they believe.
> They are animists who worship spirits, rivers and trees. They do not

even understand the stories well; nevertheless they worship just like the story. In the same way, as they begin to believe the Bible stories their lives will change.[112]

A story becomes a doorway to a possible world because it offers the listener a glimpse of a future that is not simply a repetition of the past. Michael Goldberg describes it like this: "Narratives offer us a relatively safe way to explore our 'options' without first having to experiment with our own lives. They help us imagine what might follow from taking up and acting on one set of convictions rather than another."[113] N. T. Wright concurs, stating that the stories Jesus told "… invited his hearers into a new world, making the implicit suggestion that the new worldview be tried on for size with a view to permanent purchase."[114]

In the long-running Star Trek television series, the story line often revolved around a visit to an unexplored world. No matter which episode we watched, we knew that when Captain Kirk sent a team down from the spaceship Enterprise, anything was possible. In fact it was highly likely that the scientific laws and cultural norms that governed the Enterprise's world would not correspond at all with those on the new storyworld. On the other hand, from the perspective of the new world, the world of the space travelers would also seem illogical.

The dissimilarity between a story-listener's world and the biblical universe can be as profound as any fictional Star Trek episode. When people enter the biblical storyworld, the barriers that permanently fixed the boundaries of their life no longer define those limits. The impossible suddenly becomes possible, the illogical becomes logical, and hope can replace hopelessness.

Kevin Bradt describes his experience with those who came to him for counseling:

I noticed how lives, relationships, problems, all were structured as stories, some that stretched back across time and culture and seemed to repeat themselves in every generation, often with the same disastrous consequences. Sadly I learned that some people could not even imagine changing the stories they were born into, no matter how much they suffered as a result.[115]

"The babe in the cradle," G. K. Chesterton says, "knows about the dragon. He needs the stories to know about St. George."* Chesterton was talking about the need for hope. One of the greatest tragedies a human being can experience is to live without hope. For peasants in a country like India, hopelessness is often a part of life. Even the gods offer no hope—the best they can expect is that their gods will leave them alone. All the old stories go over and over in their minds, saying, "No hope, no hope, no hope." Until one day, a storyteller comes by with a new story, a story that says loudly, "There is hope!" There is hope because there is a God who loves you! This is the change that can occur when a biblical storyteller begins to recount a biblical story.

A beautiful Shadri tribal girl named Anita lived in a village in India. As a teenager she became mentally disturbed and would often run away to live in the forest with the wild animals. Time after time Anita's family brought her back home, but she was never at peace. Sometimes they even had to tie her with ropes to keep her from leaving. Her family members were not Christians, but finally in desperation they sent for a Christian pastor from a nearby village. Pritichan Das told them the story of the Gadarene demoniac from Mark 5:1–20, and other Bible stories. After he prayed for Anita to be healed, the evil spirit left her and soon she enrolled in the biblical storytelling training program. Even though Anita is completely unschooled, she learned to tell many of the Bible stories. When she sings the song about the Prodigal Son, the personal loss she experienced comes through in the hauntingly beautiful melody and words. She is still the only believer in her family, but she continues to serve God faithfully.

LITERACY AND ORALITY

It can be difficult for a person from a highly literate society to grasp the barriers to Christian communication that exist in places like India where literacy is the exception and not the rule. Because reading is synonymous with western education it can seem strange to conceive of systems of learning that do not depend on it. Yet in many cultures, schooling is not a significant part of the education process even today. The commonly held assumption that it is only a matter of time until nearly everyone will be able to read is clearly a myth. As has been pointed out, over half the world's population are oral communicators and in many places the percentage of

---

* "Exactly what the fairy tale does is this: it accustoms him for a series of clear pictures to the idea that these limitless terrors had a limit, that these shapeless enemies have enemies in the knights of God, that there is something in the universe more mystical than darkness, and stronger than strong fear." G. K. Chesterton, *Tremendous Trifles* (New York: Dodd, Mead and Company, 1909), 130.

nonliterate people is increasing because literacy programs are not keeping pace with population growth.

India's educational system was inherited from 200 years of British rule; it owes much to the sacrificial work of western missionaries. S. Y. Shah writes,

> During the nineteenth and early twentieth centuries the Christian missionaries of British India were actively involved in literacy programs as they wanted the members of their church to read the Bible. Since the bulk of the converts to Christianity were illiterates, literacy had become an important concern among Indian missionaries. Though most of them were teaching illiterates with great missionary zeal, they had observed that it took almost three years to make an illiterate adult literate. They realized that an illiterate church meant "without Bible, weak and in danger" and hence were keen to develop a quick method of teaching.[116]

This concern for education continues today. India's educated upper-class is largely the reason India has progressed as far as it has in the modern world. Many Hindus now consider an English-medium education in a Catholic or Protestant school to be essential for their children's future.

Nevertheless most of India's more than one billion people still have little or no formal education. A third of the adults in India have never attended school at all. Another third may have gone to school for a short while but then reverted to nonliteracy again afterward.

One should not conclude, however, that this means such nonreaders are ignorant. Rather, they have found literacy to be superfluous because they are taught in an oral system that fits them thoroughly to live life within their own context.

Despite this predominantly oral environment, countless Indian Bible training institutes are wedded to a western pedagogical model. This is problematic because graduates are typically sent to villages where people are not equipped to think in the propositional and abstract ways that are part of western education. Approaches that depend on unfamiliar communication forms borrowed from a literate society not only present cognitive barriers, they also cause feelings of inferiority when nonreaders are required to use literacy-based methods to be able to take part in the life of the church. Furthermore, non-Christians can be alienated by the foreignness of communication forms that are often used for evangelism, producing antagonism and resistance that have nothing to do with Christianity's beliefs.

The leader of a large church-planting organization in India confided to me,

We discussed giving extra support to the workers who studied more. It sounded good. But I faced some practical problems: those who have a degree many times did not baptize anyone, whereas the village preachers were baptizing 30 or more every year. It is a fact that the results of Bible college graduates in winning people and baptizing them is not as good as those who have little or no training.[117]

J. O. Terry wrote in similar fashion regarding his training of storytellers: "I have found that it is often the less-theologically trained members of our teams who do the best job of storying and who seem to have both the vision and the discipline to develop story sets, teach them and train storyers."[118]

Those who inhabit a print world forget that it is not easy to become literate. Reading is a complex system, akin to learning a new language but even more difficult because it also demands a different way of thinking. It is estimated that for a person from an oral community to become truly literate requires eight years or more of formal education, and afterward that the person continue applying their reading skills. In fact, it is not uncommon to find even highly educated people who still retain an oral cognitive style. Grant Lovejoy relates how Lynne Abney, M.D., worked alongside an Arab cardiologist trained in Cairo:

He could quote long passages from the same massive cardiology textbook that she had used in medical school. Yet if the patient displayed symptoms of multiple problems, the cardiologist could not reason deductively to diagnose which was the patient's actual ailment. His rote-memory education enabled him to retain massive amounts of information but did not teach him the logical, analytical thinking processes that are considered essential to western education. In actual practice, this physician is a residual oral communicator even though he has completed many years of schooling.[119]

There are two distinct ways of conceptualizing literacy. The first is as an ability to interpret marks on paper which we call reading. This skill varies greatly among oral communicators. Even rudimentary reading skills are helpful to an oral Bible project because storytellers can use their Bibles to refresh their memories and as a plumb line to keep the told stories accurate. However this should not be confused with true literacy. Jakob Neilsen, an expert on website usability, points out that "… lower-literacy users exhibit very different reading behaviors than higher-literacy users: they plow text rather than scan it…. The most notable difference between lower- and higher-literacy users is that lower-literacy users can't understand a text by glancing at it. They must read word for word and often spend considerable time trying to understand multi-syllabic words."[120] Basic readers commonly use their finger to point out individual words as they struggle through the text. Although this level of literacy would be useful for buying something at a shop or perhaps reading a train schedule at a railway station, it is inadequate for understanding complex documents such as the Scriptures or religious pamphlets.

The second way of conceptualizing literacy is as a literate style of thinking. A literate cognitive style is a learned skill that is unavailable to oral communicators and thus must be avoided in our transmission of the gospel. To depend on this thinking style for any part of learning, teaching or interpreting the Word of God is to limit the Bible, relatively speaking, to a select few, that is, to those whose minds have been trained through long years of formal education and much practice to handle information in a literate manner. This is not a difference of degree but rather a difference in kind. As has been pointed out, a literate style of thinking is, in effect, part of a radically different worldview.

A CHURCH-COMPATIBLE TRAINING MODEL

An important consideration in designing ministerial training programs is that the structure of the educational program itself often becomes a model for the students. Dayton and Fraser write: "Nor must we forget the power of imitation. The resulting church often models itself after the community from which it heard the good news. Frequently the structures developed by the evangelizing agency become an essential heritage...."[121]

In most theological training institutions, students learn in a system that is highly dissimilar from the one where they will be serving in their ministries. If the goal of a training program is to multiply new churches, it is better for the training model to correspond as closely as possible to the desired church model in the particular culture toward which the training is being projected. Since India is still primarily a nation of villages, any innovation must be thought of in terms of villages and village life. Dayton and Fraser conclude,

> The ideal organizational structure would be one that is similar to structures already present in the culture. Or alternatively it may be a structure that members of the culture are already adopting because *they* see it as workable and effective.[122]

Figure 3 describes the typical way that training occurs in most missions agencies. Novices (usually young men) are extracted from their village context and sent to a formal Bible school where over several years they are trained to become ministers of the gospel. They learn to read, preach, sing, witness and exercise leadership in ways that are pleasing to the school administrators. Then they graduate and are sent back to a village.

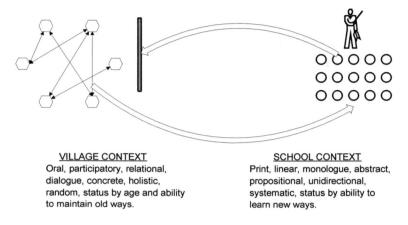

VILLAGE CONTEXT
Oral, participatory, relational,
dialogue, concrete, holistic,
random, status by age and ability
to maintain old ways.

SCHOOL CONTEXT
Print, linear, monologue, abstract,
propositional, unidirectional,
systematic, status by ability to
learn new ways.

Figure 3. Literate Equipping Model

However, the very process of going through this training has largely unfitted them for communication with their own people. Now a strong barrier exists that keeps them from being effective in an oral context. This resistance is often blamed on the people they are trying to reach instead of being identified as a consequence of the type of training the worker received. Paul Hiebert points out that many aspects of western education are alien or even offensive to communal people groups:

> This emphasis on competition and personal achievement is foreign to many societies.... [Children] are taught at an early age not to compete or to take issue with others, especially those of their own age or older. Consequently, in school they help each other complete their homework and do not try to be the first to complete their lessons.... And in sports they do not like to keep score because they do not want to win over others in their group.[123]

In the oral Bible project, I chose to employ a training structure of cooperative learning groups because it resembles the interpersonal communications that are typical of a village context. In fact, group orientation is a primary characteristic of oral communicators—learning in such cultures occurs in communication with others, not inside the mind of the individual student. Clark Bouton writes, "Dialogue is essential to learning in groups."[124] Bouton gives the rationale behind the use of learning groups: "The goal … is to develop a teaching method that actively engages students in a learning process that enables them both to acquire a knowledge of the material and to develop their skills in the process of acquiring that knowledge."[125] Instead of being passive listeners, the participants in cooperative groups learn by doing and in dialogue with other members of the group.

In addition to story-learning, elements such as worship, *koinonia*, the sharing of personal faith stories, times of prayer and the celebration of the Eucharist helped provide a spiritual learning environment. As much as possible the story learners were active participants in all aspects of the learning process. They also contributed leadership roles. In short, they were made to feel that they were members of a body, not students in a class. Thus the training program not only taught content but also modeled ways of learning and relating that would fit the new churches the participants would be expected to plant in the future. If the learners simply reproduced the various elements of the biblical storytelling training program in their own mission context, a viable church could be the result.

THE AFFECTIVE ASPECT OF LEARNING

Learning takes place not only in the cognitive dimension; it can also involve the realm of human emotions. In fact, enduring learning is more likely to occur when the emotions are engaged.

That which engages the emotions is often far more transformational than a simple statement of facts or even a logical, well-presented argument. This dynamic is basic to effective storytelling. For example, when the prophet Nathan wished to reprove King David, he chose a story to tell that, through the king's love for justice, tapped into David's feelings (2 Sam. 12).

Max McLean, a professional biblical storyteller, describes his philosophy about telling the stories of the Bible:

> The Bible is meant to touch us in the deep, deep recesses of our turbulent souls. We may not comprehend all that it is saying to us. But it clings to our innermost being and won't easily let go. At the end of a [storytelling] presentation many of the comments are not about what was learned, but rather what was felt. The Bible is not just a book that you read. It is also a book that you experience. That is what gives me confidence to speak its words and to convey its thoughts.[126]

The Jewish people have long used stories to convey truth. When a rabbi was asked: "Why does a parable possess such great power?" he, of course, answered with a parable:

> Once upon a time, Truth went about the streets as naked as the day he was born. As a result, no one would let him into their homes. Whenever people caught sight of him, they turned away and fled. One day when Truth was sadly wandering about, he came upon Parable. Now, Parable was dressed in splendid clothes of beautiful colors. And Parable, seeing Truth, said, "Tell me, neighbor, what makes you look so sad?" Truth replied bitterly, "Ah, brother, things are bad. Very bad. I'm old, very old, and no one wants to acknowledge me. No one wants anything to do with me."
>
> Hearing that, Parable said, "People don't run away from you because you're old. I too am old. Very old. But the older I get, the better people like me. I'll tell you a secret: Everyone likes things disguised and prettied up a bit. Let me lend you some splendid clothes like mine, and you'll see that the very people who pushed you aside will invite you into their homes and be glad of your company."
>
> Truth took Parable's advice and put on the borrowed clothes. And from that time on, Truth and Parable have gone hand in hand together and everyone loves them. They make a happy pair.[127]

It has been demonstrated that engaging the affective part of a listener's nature will intensify learning and aid in long-term memory retention. LaNette Thompson describes an experiment that measured people's emotional involvement in learning. Positron emission tomography (PET) is used to study neural activity in the brain. In 1995 a group of experimenters led by P. C. Fletcher used PET to locate areas of the brain that were activated when subjects silently read three different kinds of stories. The results showed that with simple stories that did not require the reader to empathize with the characters, only three regions of the brain were activated, whereas with stories where the reader identified with the characters, four areas of the brain were activated (this modeled an earlier French experiment where the subjects merely listened to the stories). The stories contained intrigue, competition, and deception. Hence, the subjects became involved with the characters by thinking of their motives and mental states.[128]

Author and consultant David Straker offers this advice for attempting to influence others: "Do not try to convince someone of something outside their belief system using logic."[129] This is even truer when dealing with those who are not educated in logic and argumentation, since such people tend to reason from their experience. Tom Steffen categorizes these two contrasting approaches as evidential apologetics and experiential apologetics.[130]

One activity that can greatly amplify this emotional understanding of the stories is group interactive storytelling (dramatization). As the storytellers get "inside the skins" of the various characters they portray, they gain unique perspectives of the story events. In the oral Bible training, evenings were routinely devoted to presenting the stories as drama. Each learning group would select one of the new stories they had learned that day to present to the larger group. The humor, pathos, dialogue, plot and action of the stories all contributed to making a deep and lasting impression. Typically the groups portrayed even the smallest details of each story in their dramatic presentations, and by the end of the evening both listeners and performers had understood and internalized the stories at a new level.

THE POWER OF DISCOVERY

A primary reason for avoiding exposition in the biblical storytelling approach is to allow the listeners to discover truth for themselves. N. T. Wright points to the power of story as an extended metaphor:

> Stories function as complex metaphors ... [which] consist of bringing two ideas close together, close enough for a spark to jump, but not too close, so that the spark in jumping illuminates for a moment the whole area around, changing perceptions as it does so.[131]

Wright's comment emphasizes the power of implicit over explicit truth. Making room for discovery engages the listener's own imagination. Henry Ward Beecher named imagination as the most important prerequisite for effective preaching, calling it "the God-power in the soul," that is, "the power of conceiving as definite the things which are invisible to the senses, of giving them distinct shape."[132] Secular storyteller Ben Haggarty recounts the experience of a colleague who was performing in a New York school. "One of the girls was hanging back at the end," he recalls, "and came up to the colleague quite aggressively, and said, 'What did you do to my head? You put something in my head, what did you do?' She realized this girl had never experienced imagination before." [133]

Historically, schools have been organized around the banking concept of education, a term first popularized by Paulo Freire, who wrote, "In the banking concept of education, knowledge is a gift bestowed by those who consider themselves knowledgeable upon those whom they consider to know nothing."[134] This approach reflects a view of people as containers or receptacles needing to be filled by a teacher. Education becomes the act of depositing material into the learner's mind; the learner's task is to receive, memorize, and repeat (withdraw) it. In such teacher-centered education the focus is on what is taught instead of on what is learned.

Many disagree with this view of knowledge as a commodity that can be poured from one mind to another. Lev Vygotsky (1896–1934) was a Russian educator who followed the constructivist theory of learning. Gordon Wells explains Vygostky's stance:

> Minds are not containers of knowledge propositions; nor can knowledge be directly transmitted through text or talk, because it must be constructed by each individual knower.... In treating knowledge as a thing that people possess, it loses sight of the relationship between knowing and acting.... Knowledge is created and re-created between people as they bring their personal experience and information derived from other sources to bear on solving some particular problem.... Neither the participants' understanding nor the knowledge representation can be appropriated by others unless they too engage in some comparable problem solving.[135]

This debate goes back at least as far as the dichotomy between the Hebrew and the Greek approaches to learning. The Greek view was that knowledge is a body of information, while the Hebrew concept of learning was equated to knowledge which is experienced, that is, it was intended to cause the learner to obey the divine message and integrate it into the person's life. Ted Ward writes, "In the Hellenistic exalting of intellect and rationality, the concern for acting on one's knowledge was assumed to be unimportant; it was seen as virtually automatic or even irrelevant. What one *knows* was the important matter."[136]

Our western educational system emphasizes the Greek approach which focused almost exclusively on cognitive excellence. A relevant quote from Michel Eyquem de Montaigne (1533–1592) seems to frame this discussion: "We can be knowledgeable with other men's knowledge but we cannot be wise with other men's wisdom." Until learners mix the information they are being taught with their own experiences and personal store of knowledge and apply it to a specific context, it remains someone else's knowledge.

When teaching adults, it is important to recognize that, unlike children, adults bring a large store of varied experiences to learning. Teaching which fails to value and draw on their experience devalues them as persons. In the storytelling model of learning, participants should be given opportunity to recall their own stories, to hold them alongside the biblical stories and to verbalize their significance to others. Tom Boomershine writes, "When our/my story is connected appropriately with the story of God, there is revelation. It is a sacramental moment when ordinary human reality discloses the presence of God."[137] For Boomershine, it is important to make "connections" between the story events and life events the teller has experienced.

> Somehow the telling of personal stories about how the stories have had meaning for others gives them a context.... Relating how others have experienced the stories provides a framework of experience that is broader and gives permission for people to listen to the stories in a variety of ways. When left free to listen, people often make connections with the story that are surprising as well as fully appropriate. No counselor could ever foresee the helpful connections that sometimes emerge.[138]

Like fish caught by a net, it is the intersection of one's own story with a particular Bible story that "captures" the person. Some, like the drunkard Somarsing, may be deeply touched by the story of the prodigal son because it intersects with the story of their own life.* A woman in the United States was paging through the various television channels one night when she happened to hear Daniel O'Donnell singing "By the Rivers of Babylon." The lyrics, "How can we sing the Lord's song in a strange land?" touched her deeply as this story intersected with her own experience of the world as an alien place where she had often felt like a stranger. Consequently spiritual renewal came into her life.

Discovery is one of the most important principles of learning. People inherently feel that, "Truth which you tell me is your truth—truth that I discover for myself is my truth." The very act of discovery seems to give ownership. Charles Kraft observes:

> It is in the process of discovery rather than in the simple hearing of someone else's discovery, presented in predigested form, that the deepest, most abiding kind of learning takes place. This is likely the main reason why God's written Word is presented to us in experience-

* Chapter 11

oriented casebook fashion rather than as a predigested theology textbook…. Note that what Peter perceived as discovery was labeled revelation by Jesus (Mat. 16:15–17). Apparently revelation and discovery are the divine and human aspects of the same process.[139]

In an expositional presentation there is little room left for discovery. The speaker usually only refers to a biblical text in passing, giving it at the most a quick reading. Most of the time is spent extracting truths it contains and adding explanations and illustrations in order to teach these truths to the listeners as clearly and efficiently as possible. In contrast, a story promotes discovery.

One cannot simply hold a story at arm's length and examine it mentally—a story gets down inside and makes itself at home. In an interesting comparison, biblical scholar William Barclay likened truth to a distasteful medicine:

Whenever a foreign object threatens to enter the eye, the eye automatically closes. That is an instinctive, reflex action. In like manner, whenever the human mind hears something that it does not want to hear, it automatically closes its door. There are times when truth can hurt; but sometimes a distasteful drug or an unpleasant treatment must be accepted if health is to be preserved.

To extend Barclay's analogy, we might think of storytelling as sugar-coating the bitter-tasting medicine of truth to get it inside where it can do its healing work.

Referring again to the biblical example in 2 Samuel 12:1, the prophet Nathan trusted the story he was telling to accomplish this in the king. If Nathan had explained the story (or what *he* thought it meant) it might have aborted what God was doing in David's heart. People often tend to resist others' efforts to manipulate them into a certain point of view or a particular interpretation. But when God speaks to a heart, it is a different thing altogether.

So how does one encourage discovery in storytelling? One of the best ways is to provide space after the story is told to ask open-ended questions and stimulate discussion aimed at helping the listeners grasp the truths the story presents. These may be questions such as, "What did you hear God saying to you in this story?", "What was there about this story that excited you?", or "Which character in this story would you like to be and why?"

When I asked this last question in regard to the story in Joshua chapter 1 and 2, a young man in India replied that he would like to be Rahab. Since Rahab is portrayed as a prostitute in the story, this of course got a laugh from the other students, so I asked him to explain. He replied, "Because she won her entire family to God." (Josh. 6:23). Often a time of sharing such as this helps the learners discover deep truths that will never be forgotten. LaNette Thompson tells how a story discovery was instrumental in breaking through the worldview of a young Muslim man:

> It wasn't until I was using the story of Jacob's dream with a young Muslim man that I realized the significance of this story to Muslims. When asked, "How can we approach God?" the young man said automatically, "By our good actions." I then said, "Name Jacob's good actions that encouraged God to come to Him." He thought and thought, then replied finally, "He hadn't done anything good." I saw on his face that first crack in a worldview that believes we have a relationship with God because of our actions.[140]

It is impossible to end this section without stressing again the importance of dialogic interaction in the discovery process. Vygostky described meaning as a function of the process of transforming inner speech into public speech, a constructive process that occurs *during*, rather than after, the process of articulation.[141] The opportunity for the listener to reformulate in his or her own words the truth that he or she is learning is essential to discovery. Knowledge is both reconstructed and co-constructed in the course of dialogic interaction with others.[142] In school settings, the western cultural values of efficiency and time management work against this; classroom dialogue typically is seen as a wasteful expenditure of time. The solution, of course, is to reduce the amount of content that must be covered to allow time for this kind of learning.

The Value of an Example

A central cord of Bible stories is that they provide us with human examples. People have a natural tendency to imitate that to which they are consistently exposed. This is such a strong part of human learning that it even happens unintentionally. For example, in our speech patterns we may find that we picked up a figure of speech from someone we were around or that our accent changed because we were living in a different region. In fact, much of what we are—in our mannerisms, our way of speaking and reacting to others— was not consciously learned; rather it was communicated to us by simple observation and subconscious imitation of another person.

Early theorists in the field of imitation suggested that imitation is an instinctual or constitutional tendency. We imitate, not because of a rational consideration of the consequences, but because we are evolutionarily hardwired to imitate.[143] Recent brain research tends to confirm this. Neuroscientists have discovered mirror neutrons that fire both when an action is observed and when it is performed. The implications are that when human beings observe an action, they generate a plan to do the same action, or an image of doing it themselves.[144]

The intentional imitation of human examples has great power to mold and change people. Examples influence by revealing a pattern that can be reproduced, thus offering a possible example of a future self. [145]

In the classical or historical tradition exemplified by the Homeric epics such as the Iliad, education was understood in terms of the imitation of heroes. This model of learning continued through the Middle Ages as Christian teachers drew on the classical emphasis on imitation, infusing it with relevant biblical teachings. The author of *Moralium Dogma Philosophorum* argued that we must "choose a good man and hold his image ever before our eyes." Another teacher poet asserted that a student should "choose in his mind an excellent man and arrange his behavior according to that pattern." John Locke (1632-1704) believed that the use of human examples to teach children had "more force to draw or deter their imitation, than any discourse which can be made to them." [146]

This classical tradition of education was set in preliterate, primary oral contexts. Therefore, what we learn from examining it can be extremely helpful in communicating with oral learners today. According to Bryan Warnick, the classical model contains three elements: 1) the description of an example's action, 2) the description of the results of the action, and 3) an exhortation to do what the example did. Warnick notes that this way of learning has a cognitive aspect, but just as importantly it includes an affective element that gives the learner a feeling of attraction toward the exemplar, providing a motivational impulse. [147] He describes how this learning process functions:

> The cognitive element of learning is supplied when attention is drawn to the exemplar's actions and to the results that flow from the actions, thus allowing the observer to construct a mental representation of the actions and their consequences…. If the results are attractive, they inspire the observer to replicate the action. The exhortational element involves telling the learner to pay attention to the action and its results, while the consequences supply the motivation to imitate the action…. The information is about how to live; the model's life is taken as an example of the possible life that the students can have through imitation. The information is valuable because the observer can, in at least some sense, use the information to do the same thing

the model did and thus produce the same achievements.[148]

Warnick hypothesizes that at least two elements are necessary for something to become an example. First, a thing becomes an example when it "exaggerates a trait beyond average levels, since accentuation may be achieved through exaggeration. An example of a generous person would be someone who is even more generous than the average person.... The more different someone is from the norm, the more of an example the person becomes." But in addition, the example must be set in a situation that brings out and highlights both similarities and differences.[149] This may occur by contrasting differences in extremes, such as in the story of Lazarus and the Rich Man (Luke 16:19-31).

It is easy to apply these observations about learning from exemplars to biblical characters. In fact, this was the model that Paul used in writing to the Corinthians when he held up negative examples from the stories of the Hebrews who came out of Egypt: "Now all these things happened to them as examples, and they were written for our admonition, upon whom the ends of the ages have come." (1 Cor.10:1-11). Paul was saying, "This is what they did and these were the consequences of their actions. Do not imitate them." The author of Hebrews uses this same approach in a positive way to inspire believers to imitate the "heroes of faith" and thus triumph as they did (Heb.11).

In contrast to theoretical, abstract or propositional ways of communicating, a role model exemplar is a concrete way of learning. This is particularly important among oral communicators. In doctoral research in Papua New Guinea on David Kolb's Learning Style Inventory, Arden Sanders discovered that even the relatively well-educated students in the Bible school where he carried out his research overwhelmingly preferred concrete learning situations (apprehension) rather than abstract ones (comprehension). [150]

In my own research, I found that the biblical storytellers in India often choose to tell stories that teach through example, either positive or negative. To an alcoholic they may tell the story of the Lost Son (Luke 15:11-32) or the story about Noah's drunkenness and its consequences (Gen. 9:20-29). To an idolater they might tell the story of Nebuchadnezzar's image (Dan. 3) or Elijah on Mt. Carmel (1 Kgs. 18). For a person who is sick they may choose to tell the story of the sick woman in Mark 5:25-34 or the story of the leprous Naaman in 2 Kings 5. Such stories become powerful examples to the listeners, teaching them about the consequences and/or rewards connected to particular actions displayed in concrete ways through human exemplars. In addition to cognitive learning, the listeners are often motivated to change their behavior in imitation of the Bible character, or inversely, to avoid behavior that brought the negative consequences.

PRAXIS

Praxis refers to the difference between thinking about an idea and putting it into action. A curious feature of western schooling is its lack of attention to praxis. As long as the student is able to imbibe the information that is being taught and then repeat it on an exam, it does not seem to matter whether he or she can actually do anything in particular with it. Despite repeated research showing the weakness of this approach, educators continue to assume that students will automatically convert what they have learned into useful realities. To rectify this it is essential that praxis be designed into the course of study—a student learns primarily through what he or she does and not through what the teacher does. We learn to swim, not by passively watching others swim, but by swimming.

Learning through imitation is fundamental to many species. For example, baby ducks learn to survive by imitating their mother. The duckling simply follows her and does what she does. This is true for many species of birds and animals and for humans as well. But when a child in a literate culture reaches school age, he or she is expected to begin learning a body of facts (from books or lectures) that are separate from any practical application. Oral communicators in particular are not capable of learning in this way or of retaining such knowledge. For them the accumulation of knowledge must be integrated with praxis; it is not possible to separate the two as is typically expected of a print learner.

In oral cultures, there is no gap between learning and doing because learning is a hands-on activity—oral communicators typically learn by doing a task or by watching someone else do it. As soon as a boy is old enough to go with his father, he begins his education in what is expected of a man in his culture. Little girls learn how to carry out the responsibilities of a wife and mother by watching and helping in the home. In formal apprenticeships in such cultures, ideally the initiate learns by observing the master craftsman and then practicing successively more difficult tasks, which, incidentally, appears to be how Jesus trained his disciples.

One of the more debilitating aspects of formal education is its postponed application. Students are expected to spend many years in school before beginning to use what they are learning. An important principle in modern manufacturing is known as "just-in-time" (JIT) inventory strategy. For example, in the manufacture of automobiles with JIT, the chain of supply is managed so each part arrives just when it is needed. This is much more efficient than the older method of having warehouses full of fenders, bumpers and other parts sitting around until they are required by the assembly line.

This earlier way resembles the formal education process in which students spend from 12 to 20 years warehousing knowledge with the notion that someday in the future it will be needed. Consequently, the student eventually comes to believe that dissociation between learning and action is normal. If praxis can be designed into a program, it will help change this assumption.

In the oral Bible project, this was addressed in several ways. First, the cooperative learning groups gave students a forum in which to immediately start telling the stories as they were learning them. They also told stories in conjunction with the celebration of the Lord's Supper, in worship and through drama. Second, training was noncontiguous so there were always at least three weeks between training events. This gave participants the opportunity to practice telling the stories in their home areas. This task was assigned to them as fieldwork, and accountability procedures were used to verify compliance.

Linking learning with praxis strengthens the educational experience. Through praxis students increase their mastery of the stories. As they experience what happens when the stories are told in their field, they become excited about learning more stories. Praxis also tends toward transformation which is the object of Christian education.

Finally, through praxis there was immediate transmission of the stories to a third generation of hearers. All the participants told the stories to their own families and to their congregants, as well as to friends, neighbors and casual acquaintances. Each participant was also required to select and mentor at least one other person as an apprentice, teaching him or her to tell the biblical stories to others.

THE IMPORTANCE OF TRANSFER

Educators almost universally rely upon exams to assess the degree to which a student is assumed to have mastered the content of a course of study. Strangely enough, the student's ability to transfer this information to a third person is rarely measured. It is assumed that a student's academic standing will have a direct correlation to his or her future effectiveness at teaching others, even though there is no evidence for this.

The subsequent knowledge transfer quotient of a training program is a factor of both the reproducibility of its content and the learning methods that were used. Since learners tend to teach others in the same way that they themselves were taught, it is important to consider the training model's potential for reproducibility in the particular culture toward which it is directed. Training methods that harmonize with the preferred learning style of the target group will be most effective in transferring knowledge. We may assume that where reproducibility of either content or learning methods is low, it will be reflected in a low rate of transfer to third generation learners.

In accord with this assumption, George Patterson recommends adopting the perspective of looking beyond our students to focus on their ministry in a church or group (figure 4).[151] If we do this when selecting training methods, it will increase the degree of transfer in subsequent generations of learners.

Figure 4. Teaching for Transfer

The graph in Figure 5 is a hypothetical comparison between a Bible school model of training and a biblical storytelling program. It describes my perception of the way that knowledge transfer occurs in the two models. GEN1 (Generation one) represents the training program or institution itself. GEN2 represents the student, and GEN3-GEN6 are the downline links in the chain of knowledge transfer.

The first thing that is evident in the graph is the relative amount of content that is taught. In a formal Bible school, students exit the program knowing more about a greater body of facts. Although typically they have not learned much of the actual Scriptures, they have taken many courses about the Bible. In contrast, in an oral Bible project the students learn only Scripture (in story), but the body of content they master is far from comprehensive, at least initially.

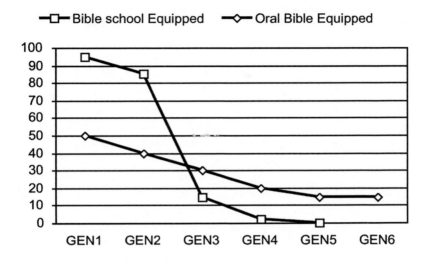

Figure 5. Comparison of two training models. Each generation (GEN) represents the hand-off of biblical knowledge from one person to another like links in a chain. GEN1 is the training program; GEN2 is the student; GEN3 is the person to whom the student passes on his or her knowledge.

In both training models the degree of transference from GEN1 to GEN2 is similar. The difficulty appears when the student (GEN2) tries to transfer what he or she has learned to a third person such as a congregant (GEN3). Even in print cultures the rate of transfer is far from remarkable. For example, how much of a typical Sunday morning sermon can a congregant remember on Tuesday or Wednesday? In predominantly oral cultures the transfer is even lower. The rate of 15% shown in the graph is charitable and would certainly only apply to exceptional individuals. In contrast, in the oral Bible model the transfer continues at more or less the same rate as in the training program itself and applies to most individuals regardless of literacy or age. In other words, most of what the student learned transfers to the congregants in a form that they can remember and reproduce.

By GEN4 in the Bible school model, transfer is negligible. For instance, when church members try to tell someone else what the pastor said, often the best they can do is invite them to come to the church, an unappealing option for most non-Christians. In contrast, in the oral Bible model, by GEN4 the transfer of Bible knowledge stabilizes and by

GEN5 a significant number of stories will have become part of the canon of the church.

If this is an accurate perception of the potential of this model, it means that in an oral Bible course such as this one, in which participants learned to tell 100 stories, at least 30 of these would become part of the canon of the local churches. Nearly every believer in these churches would be able to tell any of these stories at a moment's notice without depending on any written reference. Repeating those stories would become their standard strategy for evangelism and their instant response to every challenge to faith in Christ. Whether they are walking to market, working in the field, or traveling on a bus or train, it would be natural for them to repeat the stories to anyone they meet along the way. Of course, this repertoire of stories would include the key narratives of the gospel such as the Passion of Christ and would likely emphasize stories that are most suitable to the cultural worldview of that people.

There was inadequate time in this research project to fully test the accuracy of this hypothesis. However, the results discovered in the comprehensive exams were promising. In short, 45% of the apprentices scored as high as or higher than their GEN2 mentors, pointing to an exceptional rate of knowledge transfer. I will enlarge on this in Section 3 (Findings).

A final issue that needs to be addressed briefly is accuracy of transfer in an oral/aural context. Everyone is familiar with the "telephone" game in which a group of people sits next to each other in a circle. The first player whispers a phrase into the ear of the following person; that person then whispers the same phrase to the next person, and so on. The last person in the circle repeats the phrase out loud for everyone to hear. Of course, it always differs wildly from the original phrase. People have asked, "What is to keep that from happening to the told stories?"

There are two plumb lines that help keep an orally transmitted story accurate. First, thanks to the tireless efforts of Bible translators, many of the oral people of the world now have a Bible or Bible portion available in their own language or at least in an adjacent trade language. If even a few people can read, the written story will serve to keep the told story on track.

A more traditional oral safeguard is the fact that stories are never whispered. They are told aloud for the entire community to hear. Truth is held by the community as a whole, so a storyteller who changes a familiar story or tells it incorrectly loses face in the community. In the oral Bible project, the biblical storytellers were taught to correct one another as they were learning and telling the stories. It was common to see several in each learning group with their Bibles open, following along as the story was being told, ready to correct the teller.

In many ways stories are actually more capable vehicles for the transfer of truth than are literate methods. Rudyard Kipling once wrote, "If history were taught in the form of stories, it would never be forgotten." He could just as easily have added, "and the stories would always be passed along to others."

The Power of a Story

My name is Surash. One day in our village there was a village council meeting and they were all talking about us, saying, "They are low caste people. We should not allow them to take water from our well." As they were talking like that, I could not stop myself. I said to my sarpanch *(councilman), "Sir, please permit me to say something." I stood up and started telling the story of Creation. Then I said, "God has created Adam and you. From that first couple, Adam and Eve, all of us were born. We are all one; we are all brothers and sisters."*

They all agreed and said, "Yes, we are all one. Our father and our parents are one." Since that time they have showed me respect. Even the patwari *(revenue officer) respects us now. Whenever I go to his office he even invites me to drink tea. Before that, no matter what I said he would turn his back and walk away. But now whenever we meet in the market, or wherever he sees me, he greets me.*

Twenty to twenty-five people are attending my church. Before, in order to preach I would first take a pen and write out an outline. Then while I was preaching my message, some people would talk to one another and others would sleep! After attending this storytelling training program, I went back to my church and took my Bible and laid it on the lectern. Just as if I was telling a story I started speaking to them, and all the people were sitting quietly and listening very carefully.

After worship was over, some sisters came to me and asked, "Pastor, where did you learn these stories?"

I replied, "I went to a training program."

They said, "You did not know about this kind of Bible study before!"

It was because of my preaching that many people had stopped coming to church. But now I am preaching with the stories, and those same people who had stopped coming are attending again, and many new people are also coming.

Chapter 6

THEOLOGICAL FOUNDATIONS OF STORYTELLING

Storytelling reveals meaning without committing the error of defining it.

–HANNAH ARENDT

At its most basic, theology is simply organized thinking about God. Different ways of organizing those thoughts have resulted in different types of theology. Adherents of Chronological Bible Storying, which was mentioned in a previous chapter, follow the system known as biblical theology. Slack, Terry and Lovejoy write, "Prior to the advances of literacy in the West, the Gospel was shared primarily through narrative presentations. Biblical theology was the norm rather than systematic theology which presupposes literacy."[153]

An important aspect of biblical theology is progressive revelation, which means that God worked over time, with different people and through different means to reveal himself and his truth in the Bible. Biblical theology is historical in its orientation. It attempts to get into the minds of the authors of Scripture in order to arrive at the meanings they intended for their original readers. Because revelation is progressive, biblical theology fits well with the CBS rationale of telling the Bible stories in chronological order.

However, because biblical theology is a western construct, it naturally has been influenced by the Hellenistic reasoning and literate thinking common in the West which can make it seem foreign to oral communicators. Furthermore, in practice the emphasis on biblical authority can mean a corresponding lack of attention to the human realm. Wonsuk Ma writes,

> There is a strong emphasis on the biblical authority. And the goal is naturally to bring humans to terms with the reality of the divine realm. The theologizer takes the role of a proclaimer, as we often see from the Old Testament prophets. Hence, the primacy of the divine truth is clearly manifested. As a weakness, however, it tends to be detached from human needs and quests. As a result, theology exists for theology's sake, rather than making God's truth relevant for Christian recipients.[154]

In other words, the cross-cultural aspect of theologizing, that is, applying divine truth to a specific human setting and specific human needs, can be inadequate. CBS tries to address this by supplementary story selection based on ethnographic studies.

Yet another difficulty is that biblical theology normally focuses on the revelation of God and His people's understanding of His acts, and not on the religious experience of the people.[155] Other cultures tend to be much more interested in the experiential dimensions of religious life than in its cognitive and intellectual aspects.

A PENTECOSTAL THEOLOGY

From humble beginnings, in just one century Pentecostalism exploded worldwide to become the second largest community in Christendom after the Roman Catholic church with 400 to 500 million members. Together these two constituencies represent at least two-thirds of world Christianity.[156]

A Pentecostal theological framework fit the context of this project for two reasons: first, the agency where the project was carried out in India is Pentecostal/charismatic in belief and practice.* Second, Pentecostal theology itself is inherently oral. Swiss Pentecostal analyst Walter Hollenweger, in describing the orality of Pentecostal theology writes,

> In these preliterate, semiliterate, or postliterate cultures the medium of communication is—just as in biblical times—not the definition but the description, not the statement but the story, not the doctrine but the testimony, not the book but the parable, not a systematic theology but a song, not the treatise but the TV program, not the

---

* While there are differences in Pentecostal and charismatic theology, for the purpose of this book they will be treated as one.

articulation of concepts but the celebration of banquets. Desmond Tutu comments, "Why should we feel embarrassed if our theology is not systematic? Why should we feel that something is amiss if our theology is too dramatic for verbalization but can be expressed only adequately in the joyous song and the scintillating movement of Africa's dance in the liturgy?"[157]

Pentecostalism is far from monolithic in its beliefs; nevertheless certain theological distinctives common to all Pentecostals have been identified. Pentecostal missiologist L. Grant McClung lists some of these: literal biblicism, an experiential Christianity, the personality and power of the Holy Spirit, a strong Christology, and an urgent missiology.[158] Veli-Matti Karkkainen notes that Pentecostals have many theological doctrines in common with Evangelicals:

> Both Pentecostals and Evangelicals share conservative doctrinal views regarding the inspiration and authority of the Bible, the lostness of humankind without Christ, justification by faith, as well as priority of evangelism over social action. From Evangelical-Conservatives, Pentecostals inherited also the insistence on the necessity of conversion and emphasis on an individual's salvation experience. Pentecostals consequently came to stress the importance of "crisis"-experience rather than "growth"-experience in conversion.[159]

AN EXPERIENTIAL CHRISTIANITY

Instead of attempting to treat all of these, this section will focus on the practice of experiential Christianity which is at the heart of Pentecostal belief. I begin with this fundamental assumption: the Bible is a supernatural book, divinely inspired and preserved. Its stories are not mere human stories, but have within them God's power to transform human lives. When the stories of the Bible are told, we can expect that which happened originally to also happen today.

Wonsuk Ma writes, "Simply defined, theology is a process which takes the divine truth, the revelation of God, and applies it to a specific human setting."[160] He goes on to point out that historically God's revelation was contextualized into the western worldview which became identified with Christianity and vice versa. Charles Taber describes this:

> For reasons which are well known, as Christian thinkers reflected seriously on the Scriptures and began to construct creeds and

theological systems, they used the tools which they knew best and which best (in their context) offered them an approach for dialogue with non-Christians: the tools of philosophy and of law. That is, they opted for technical, abstract discourse.[161]

This is why in parts of the world such as Asia, Christianity is now viewed as a western religion despite its origins in the Mideast. Wonsuk Ma contends that what is needed is a "recontextualizing" into uniquely Asian worldviews and thought patterns. Taber goes on to quote Holth:

> There are certain features of traditional western theology which many Asians find objectionable. Generally speaking, Asians do not attach the same importance to formulated doctrines. Our keenness for analysis and system is something they find quite incomprehensible.[162]

In oral societies the church often develops biblical theologies that focus on the acts of God in history, particularly in the lives of Bible characters including, of course, Jesus Christ. In this vein, physician John Hercus compared the Bible to a medical doctor's reference source, describing it as God's casebook:

> God has recorded case after case to teach us how he encounters men [and] what he wants from this encounter. It is as though he has given us access to a lavish selection of case histories, so that every aspect of truth is demonstrated. Here is the greatest ward-round any student can undertake. All are cases needing treatment, and every aspect of their need, as of their treatment may be studied here in the official clinical records. They are all here, even a number of fatal cases with the full postmortem findings.[163]

As pre-Christians listen to these case stories from the Bible, they often identify strongly with characters in the accounts. Hearing of the concrete saving acts that the God of the Christians performed for other human beings, they can begin to know him themselves.* Initially oral people are attracted by God's love and power and his willingness to act on behalf of people like themselves. But as they continue listening, they also discover what pleases or displeases God, which leads them to the ultimate reality questions about judgment and eternal life.

---

* Orlando Costas argues that the gospel cannot be defined at all without reference to context, since the context is the stage where all comprehension takes place. Orlando Costas, *Christ Outside the Gate: Mission Beyond Christendom* (Maryknoll, NY: Orbis Books, 1982), 5.

Anthropologist Jacob Loewen observed that all too often the western-trained missionary approaches Christianity from the point of right belief. The missionary task is thus seen as replacing a wrong belief with the right belief. At one point Loewen asked a group of Lengua tribal people what mistakes missionaries had made. After hesitating, they answered, "They are scratching where it doesn't itch."[164] In other words, the missionaries were scratching where the missionaries itched, not where the Lengua people felt their own need to be.

The emphasis on right belief instead of on experiential Christianity tends toward surface change, leaving the core worldview issues relatively untouched. This has the potential to produce syncretism. Loewen writes,

> The right faith *is* the answer to man's problems.... [However] for many deeply evangelical people it essentially involves mental acceptance of a set of premises or doctrines as truth, and it frequently lacks the concomitant ingredients of commitment and obedience. This means that faith has largely been separated from life.[165]

Indian missionary statesman, E. Stanley Jones, agreed, saying,

> Christianity has followed Plato in his doctrine of ideas and in following him, emphasis has been thrown upon belief in religion. When this emphasis upon ideas was combined with the Roman tendency toward legal and exact phraseology, the stage was set for fierce clashes over doctrine and creed. A Christian was one who could repeat a correctly stated creed.*

Such an approach to religion as formulaic truth has never appealed to many people in the world. For oral people, life and religion are inextricably mixed together—there is no separation between the two. Hence theology that is not experiential has little power to transform their lives.

WHOSE THEOLOGY?

Each culture and people deserves the right to make their own theology, one that flows from their own experience of applying and understanding the Bible in their context. As Jose M. de Mesa states,

---

* E. Stanley Jones, *Christ at the Round Table* (New York: Abingdon, 1928), 127. Even though Augustine had great experiences in his life with Christ, he became instrumental in solidifying and legitimizing this system of hermeneutics.

Christology needs to be intimately linked with the culture, the particular way of feeling, thinking and behaving of a given people. This is important because a recognizable reference to lived experience is the first criterion for the meaningfulness of a given theological reflection. A Christology which is rooted in a culture ensures the intelligibility and relevance of Jesus in that culture.[166]

Wonsuk Ma suggests that the particular theology that is formed and how it is expressed depends largely on the issues that a nascent church faces in its formative stage. For example, after the devastating Korean War, Pentecostal missionaries brought a message of God's power and hope to meet the needs of people. During this period Pastor Yonggi Cho planted a church that eventually grew to be the largest in the world. His messages centered around two emphases; first, God's power to heal and solve human problems through the Holy Spirit; and second, human faith in God's miracle power. This combination resulted in a message of hope even for this world.[167]

The theologies of oral peoples will often reflect their experiences of God revealing himself by meeting their felt needs. The Psalms are full of examples recalling God's loving acts on behalf of His people as stimulation to adoration and faith. As these were rehearsed orally through song, they served as an experiential theology and statement of faith for God's people.

In missionary practice the indigenous Christian communities have often only been recipients of theologies formulated by others. Paul Hiebert writes,

Too often we have turned the task [of hermeneutics] over to religious "experts." Consequently, ordinary Christians are not encouraged to think theologically. They are expected to learn and obey the teaching of the experts. They are taught to be followers, not priests, in the church. The result is often a nominal Christianity in which people have little understanding of the doctrines they follow and of how these doctrines apply to their everyday lives. In such situations, church leaders become policemen who enforce their rules on the parishioners.[168]

Such communities could easily have their own theology that has been worked out from their experiences in conjunction with the Word of God by learning and telling the biblical stories and witnessing the present-day manifestation of similar events through their faith. Jose M. de Mesa writes, "A Christology articulated, however inchoately and imperfectly by a community is, to me, more meaningful to that community than anything done, as it were, for them by theologians or official church bodies."[169]

FELT NEEDS

Felt needs are the physical and other life needs of human beings for whom God elects to demonstrate His love and power by supernaturally intervening on their behalf. This is not synonymous with another missiological term, points of contact, which refers to the concept of theological common ground between Christianity and other religions. Sanders defines points of contact as "manifestations of general revelation that enhance communication of the gospel." They are "fragments of truth found in non-Christian cultures and worldviews that exhibit relationships to aspects of biblical truth."[170] As described by Sanders, the concept of points of contact deals with a system of belief. Hence it is abstract while felt needs are concrete.

When referring to felt needs, David Hesselgrave and others differentiate between spiritual and other needs almost as though spiritual needs alone have real significance.[171] Tom Steffen states this viewpoint clearly:

> For many heralds today, the gospel message is synonymous to felt needs. For example, if a person faces health problems, the good news becomes Jesus as Healer. If a person fears the spirit world, the good news becomes Jesus as the most powerful Spirit. If a person experiences financial woes the good news becomes Jesus as Provider. If a person experiences loneliness the good news becomes Jesus as Companion. While all of these are true in and of themselves, they are not the specific message of good news as defined by Paul, rather they are the results of that good news. ...For Paul, the good news meant God has accepted wholeheartedly and irreversibly Jesus Christ's sacrifice on the cross to restore our broken relationship with himself. The heralds of the gospel must focus their message on the redemptive efforts of Jesus Christ.[172]

As Steffen points out, the truth of redemption *is* the core of Christian belief. However, many would assert that physical healing, deliverance from evil spirits, and other kinds of provision are as much a part of the redemption as is the forgiveness of sins. Jack Hayford writes,

> The dynamic ministry of Jesus not only revealed God's heart of love for mankind's need of a Redeemer, but unveiled God's compassionate heart of mercy for mankind's need of a Healer. The will of God was

perfectly disclosed in His Son; we are to seek ways to fully convey that perfect revelation. Just as the Fall of man introduced sickness as a part of the curse, the Cross of Christ has opened a door to healing as part of salvation's provision. Healing encompasses God's power to restore broken hearts, broken homes, broken lives, and broken bodies.[173]

The Greek words *soteria* (salvation) and *sozo* (save) clearly seem to include more than just being forgiven and placed into the family of God, as central as these are. William Barclay points to Romans 1:16–17 as containing much of the quintessence of Paul's gospel. He then describes the meaning of the word *soteria* in verse 16: "Let us see just what this Christian *soteria*, this Christian salvation was. [First] it was salvation from physical illness (Mat. 9:21; Luke 8:36). It was not a completely other-worldly thing. It aimed at rescuing a man in body and in soul." [174] W. E. Vine describes *sozo/soteria* in a similar fashion: "*Sozo* 'to save,' is used (as with the noun *soteria*, 'salvation') of material and temporal deliverance from danger, suffering, and sickness as well as spiritual and eternal salvation granted immediately by God to those who believe on the Lord Jesus Christ." [175] Commenting on Luke chapter eight, Jack Hayford enlarges on this idea:

> The Greek word *sozo* offers Luke's unique perspective as a physician. A full range of encounters appears, manifesting Jesus' healing power: 1) The Gadarene, delivered from the demonic powers dominating him, is "healed," freed of evil powers that countermanded his own rational mind and physical actions. 2) The woman with the issue of blood (vv. 43–48) touches the hem of Jesus' garment, and Jesus says, "Your faith has made you well." 3) In v. 50, after being told the little girl is dead, Jesus declares: "Only believe, and she will be made well." 4) In v. 12, as Jesus explains the parable of the sower, the word "saved" is used of one's restored relationship with God through faith. Luke's precise account offers a complete picture of the Savior's concern to restore every part of man's life: (a) our relationship with God the Father; (b) our broken personalities and bondages; (c) our physical health; and (d) ultimately our rescue from death itself at the Resurrection. Jesus Christ is the Savior of the whole man.[176]

When the Gospels describe Jesus healing the sick and casting out demons, he is seen as showing what God the Father is like just as much as when he portrays love and forgiveness. It is entirely accurate to proclaim a God who cares deeply about the felt needs of women and men. Many Bible narratives clearly show God to be a powerful Savior meeting people's felt needs for material supply and physical protection, as well as for healing and deliverance.

Moreover, it is important to recognize that many times God graciously starts where we are, not where he is. Because spiritual needs are often unrecognized at first, he begins with a need that we do recognize—a felt need.* For example, when God heals someone who is ill, it can become an opportunity to draw that person to himself and begin dealing with spiritual issues in the person's life. This is evident many times in the accounts of Jesus' ministry in the Gospels. We might call these needs the "doors of God." To say that they are relatively insignificant next to spiritual needs is to overlook the many instances recorded in the Bible when God used felt human need to gain access to a person's heart and life. Like Mary Magdalene, "out of whom had come seven demons" (Luke 8:2), many people in the Gospels were known by the description of what Jesus had done for them. In fact, the names of *most* of those whom Jesus touched remain unknown—they are recorded only by the accounts of what he did to meet their felt needs.

Even though we have a message that is important for our hearers to know about, unless it deals with matters in which they are vitally interested it is not likely to have much of an impact. The message must relate directly to issues the listeners themselves feel are important. If we offer people a "Savior" who has no power—or who refuses to help with desperate felt needs here in the present—why would they want to trust Him for help in a future eternity?

As God demonstrates His love for individuals by caring for the needs they experience, they can begin to comprehend the good news of God's redemption in a personal way. Over and over in both Testaments God met people at their point of felt need. He fed them when they were hungry, healed them when they were sick, gave them victory over their enemies and comforted them in sorrow. Certainly God's love is a theological doctrine, often expressed as an abstract concept, but for oral communicators it will be best comprehended by experiencing a loving God acting on their behalf or on behalf of a family member who is in need—love that is demonstrated, felt and experienced, not just a doctrine to be learned.

R. Edward Miller writes about an incident that happened during evangelist Tommy Hick's nation-transforming crusade in Buenos Aires in the early 1950s:

> A little child of over three had been unable to walk without heavy steel braces; something was wrong in the bone structure of the leg. When the mass prayer was made, the mother took off the child's braces in faith; the child started walking. As he

---

* See Chapter 11 for stories that show how felt needs brought people to Christ.

ran up and down, the crowds began to cheer, to weep and to shout. Faith rose in many hearts and miracles began to happen spontaneously out in the crowds. A doctor who knew the child's case observed the miracle, then came over to where Hicks was standing. Grabbing him around the knees, he began to cry out, "I want this Christ; I want to be saved; I can serve a God who will do this for little children." [177]

Charles Kraft believes that a theology that is only cognitive and theoretical is inadequate—that Christian theology must also be experiential. Kraft proposed that for true Christian conversion people need to have three kinds of encounters with God. The first is an allegiance encounter; that is, a change from their old primary allegiance to an allegiance commitment to Christ leading to relationship. The second is a power encounter, which brings freedom from the bondages of sin and Satan through the spiritual power of the Holy Spirit. And finally, the individual must also have a truth encounter that is both cognitive and experiential as an antidote for ignorance and error. [178]

In power-oriented cultures people will more easily be convinced that their gods are inferior by witnessing the acts of a more powerful God than by force of logic alone. J. Herbert Kane wrote, "We in the West equate religion with truth, forgetting that in the Third World people equate religion with power. We ask, 'Is it true?' They ask, 'Does it work?' If it works, they want it; if it doesn't they don't." [179] A biblical example of this is found in the story of the prophet Elijah's victory on Mt. Carmel. It was the fire that fell from heaven that turned the people away from Baal and back toward the true God. Baal's impotence as well as God's omnipotence brought them to repentance (1 Kings 18:38-39). In a New Testament example, John the Baptist from prison asked Jesus, "Are You the Coming One, or do we look for another?" Jesus answered him not with logical arguments, but by pointing to the demonstrations of his power in curing the sick and casting out evil spirits (Luke 7:20-22).

This same dynamic was observed on many occasions during the oral Bible project. Storyteller Sanjaya's report is typical:

When our people were going to a certain place for outreach, the village people would beat them and send them away.... The village headman has one son. That boy was having fever and shaking in his hands. They told us, "If this boy will get healed then we will accept Christ." When we prayed for him, the boy became well, and they did believe and came to Christ. Now five people are going to take water baptism there.*

The appeal to logic developed during the time of the Reformation when Luther and others relied on the hermeneutical system associated with Augustine. Later the Protestant missionary movement attempted to use this same approach. However, the situation they faced was much different for they were now dealing with power-oriented peoples who worshiped other gods. Their reliance on logic in such cultures was inadequate and contributed to the slow advance of the church.

In the early 1980s, missiologist Paul Hiebert developed a concept that he called the "flaw of the excluded middle."[180] He noted that in the western view of reality typical of most missionaries there are just two worlds. The first is the observable natural world, while the second is the higher unseen sacred world that has to do with things beyond this life such as heaven and hell. However, according to Hiebert, many nonwesterners also recognize a middle world, a realm comprised of unseen powers like magic, witchcraft and spirits that affects every aspect of human life. Hiebert labeled this blind spot in the western worldview "the flaw of the excluded middle." When missionaries who did not understand this excluded middle world met people from cultures whose worldview strongly endorsed it, their theology was found to be inadequate. Pentecostal missionaries, whose theology was already highly experiential, had no difficulty dealing with third world beliefs in spirits and demons.

I found ample evidence of this in 1997 as I was carrying out research on the Indian context. I interviewed 28 Indian church-planters from 21 organizations varying in size from two of the largest church-planting organizations in India to several independent workers who were pretty much on their own. They were working with people from many different levels of society in both urban and rural areas. Nearly everyone I spoke with mentioned healings or other power encounters that had been significant both in contributing to their own conversion and to the conversions of others.

In a 1981 doctoral study designed to discover the primary reason people in India turn from Hinduism to Christianity, C. Zechariah documented that 61% do so because they, or someone close to them, were healed through the prayers of Christians. Another 20% became Christians through the exorcism of demons, either from themselves or from someone close to them. That is a total of 81% who became Christians because of experiencing or witnessing God's power.[181]

---

* See also Appendix J:3b.

In the oral Bible research, various types of felt needs emerged as important components of people's responses to hearing the Bible stories. These will be discussed in chapter ten.

In summary, to be an effective Christian witness in any culture it is essential to follow a system of theology that is suitable to the context. In oral cultures, biblical storytelling allows people to come to know God as they first hear of and then experience his power and loving acts on their behalf. They then categorize this theology by telling selected stories or singing songs that embody the truth or doctrine they wish to communicate. Most often these will have to do with concrete realities found in people's lives and will often relate to their felt needs.

Let Us Pray to the God of Him Who Told Us a Story

My name is Sanjeeb Kumar Digal. Usually I minister some distance from the town where I live, and we have to cross a river to reach our mission field. A wonderful incident happened there recently. A year ago I was on my way to my mission field which is called Bomboo. Some of the villagers farm small plots of ground when the river is low, and there are small huts nearby. One Sunday as I was going past, there was a young man about 18 years old who was in intense distress. He and his family are Hindus, so of course they did not speak to me. But I noticed him there.

I stopped and asked them, "What happened?" They told me, "It's stomach pain. From his birth onwards, he has been suffering with stomach pain."

So after getting their permission, I began telling them the story about Naaman from the Old Testament. Then I prayed and went on to my mission field. About six or seven months passed without knowing what had happened to the boy.

Two months ago they sent for me and said, "We are agreed that we want to accept Jesus now."

I asked them, "Why do you want that? When I came before you were not interested. What changed?"

They replied, "On that day we did not know you. And we did not know that your God is a great god. You told us a story and prayed for us and you went back, and still my son was not healed. Again we went to the doctor and again we went to another doctor, and we practiced several witchcrafts but he was not healed. So once again we remembered about you. And we remembered your God. So we took a decision in our family, "Let us once again call his God who told us a story. So we did that. And my son got completely healed on that day."

So after that healing took place they sent for me and gave me this testimony.

The words that we are telling will never come back without result. I had read this in the Bible, but now I understood it.

Section Two
Training Storytellers:

A DESCRIPTIVE CASE STUDY

Chapter 7

THE STORYTELLERS

*Tell me a fact and I'll learn. Tell me a truth
and I'll believe. But tell me a story and
it will live in my heart forever.*

–NATIVE AMERICAN PROVERB

In 1994 the founder of a large, rapidly growing indigenous missionary agency invited my help in training his organization's field leaders to increase their effectiveness. Over several years it became clear that despite their schooling most were still oral communicators, not prepared to think in the propositional and abstract ways that are considered essential to western education. To complicate things further, the training environment was highly multilingual. It was typical to have a workshop with 30 participants who spoke 15 different languages. The participants would endeavor to listen as the lessons were translated from English into one of the regional or national languages, but since these were second or even third languages, comprehension was difficult. Even the available interpreters were imprecise, not speaking either English or Hindi well. Trying to teach in such an environment was always a challenge and often frustrating as well.

I began wondering if there were teaching methods that would be more effective. After trying different techniques, I eventually settled on biblical storytelling and chose to develop a model that employed language-centric learning groups instead of lecture. By using oral stories and communal learning, this approach addressed the main communication issues with which I had struggled. In the following case study I describe how the storytellers were trained and include many personal accounts of their remarkable experiences while telling God's stories.

A PILOT PROJECT

In an initial oral Bible pilot project from 2001–2005, more than 50 men and women of all ages learned to tell significant portions of the Scriptures in story. The transferability of their new knowledge was equally important, so program participants were required to teach these stories to others, most of whom were even lower on the literacy continuum.

Over four years, five story tracks were taught: 1) a basic track covering 70 stories from Genesis to the Ascension; 2) thirty-five stories of the Life of Christ; 3) twenty-six stories from Acts; 4) a track of thirty-five women's stories; and 5) an extension track of fifteen stories taught by one of the program's graduates. The basic track and the life of Christ track were taught twice, while Acts, the women's track and the extension track were each taught once. The total number of Bible stories that each participant learned varied from 15 to 130 (Table 2):

Table 2. Number of Stories Learned in the Pilot Project

Number of stories learned	130	100	70	50	35	24	15	15
Number of storytellers	6	9	17	2	5	9	8	8

I found that it was possible to lead several tracks concurrently, much like the old one-room schoolhouse where children in several grades would study under one teacher. The synergy that resulted from having overlapping training groups was worthwhile. However, a trade-off was a loss of intimacy provided by a smaller group context.

The pilot project was carried out at the rather primitive facilities provided by an indigenous Bible school. Each month storytellers from four states came by train and bus, traveling between eight and ten hours to reach this central location. In two, three or four days of intensive training, they learned to tell between six and twelve new Bible stories, afterward returning to their homes. In the weeks between training intensives, they were required to practice the new stories, which they did by telling them over and over to family, friends and strangers in homes, marketplaces, schools, churches and other settings. The following month they would return to learn more new stories. Each training season lasted from four to six months, providing ten to 20 training days each year. The end of the training season was sometimes celebrated with an oral Bible festival to which the storytellers invited their family or friends.

I had hoped that if the pilot project proved effective it would be recognized by the agency leaders and implemented more widely throughout the organization. However, during the time the pilot project was being tested the organization went through a period of leadership change. The founder and president made a decision to seek someone else to take his place so he would be free to travel, speak and write. It took three years for this to be carried out, and meanwhile the agency was wary of launching any new programs.

THE ORAL BIBLE PROJECT

A breakthrough finally came in November 2005. The prior year, a new agency president had taken the reins of leadership. He was a man with a deep love for the Bible who was from a literate background himself. The agency had received a substantial financial gift designated for a social ministry project. The new president envisioned a large-scale literacy project to help villagers learn to read. Having heard about the oral Bible project, he decided to combine the two programs. Teresa and I would train biblical storytellers who in turn would teach the stories to literacy workers. They would then tell them in the remote villages where they were teaching literacy. The initial goal was to train 60 storytellers who would teach the stories to 500 literacy workers. As it turned out, the literacy component would prove to be highly useful in creating opportunities for the stories to gain entrance to hundreds of villages that were resistant to Christianity.

The first oral Bible training module was held in February 2006. I recruited three advanced storytellers who had graduated from the pilot project as my training assistants. Sixty-two full-time Christian workers with no previous experience as storytellers came from seven states. Many traveled more than 24 hours to reach the training location. To keep the groups from being too large, I scheduled the participants in two batches with identical four-day training events held back-to-back.

The training was held at the agency's brand-new central Bible college campus. As the biblical storytellers learned to perform the Bible dramatically in their own indigenous languages, students in the Bible college were busy studying in traditional academic classes in English. This made an interesting juxtaposition, to say the least.*

The workers who came for storytelling training were engaged in the

---

* See Appendix G for a comparison of the two training models.

intense challenges of ministry in pioneer areas where orality levels were high. Because they understood the limitations of a literate approach they were receptive to innovative practical methods that could help them in their ministries of gospel proclamation.

During the four days of this first module they learned to tell 12 stories:

Adam (3 stories)	Noah (+ Tower of Babel)
Genesis 1:1 to 2:4	Genesis 6:5 to 9:29
Genesis 2:5 to 3:24	Genesis 11:1–9
Genesis 4:1–12,16–17, 25–26	
Abraham (4 stories)	Jacob (3 stories)
Genesis 12:1–8; Gen. 13:2–18	Genesis 25:19–34
Genesis 15:1–14,17–18; 16:1–16	Genesis 27
Genesis 18:1 to 19:29	Genesis 28:10–22
Genesis 21:1–7; 22:1–19	

Table 3. List of Stories Learned in the First Training Module

After completing the training module the new storytellers returned to their home areas where they were told to practice telling each story no less than three times.*

Six weeks later when they came for their second training event, 94% had completed their field assignment resulting in 32,386 story encounters (a story encounter is one person hearing one story).† Despite being in areas with deeply entrenched resistance to Christianity, the participants reported that as a result of hearing one or more stories from God's Word, 87 people had become Christians. They had baptized two of the converts and 40 others were being prepared for baptism. Eighty-one individual Hindus, Muslims, and Buddhists had attended a Christian worship service for the first time, and five new worshipping groups were planted.

Over the next two years, the storytellers continued to learn new stories. Altogether they would receive 240 hours of training in six modules, learning to tell 100 stories from Creation to the Ascension. This is equivalent to knowing 65 Old Testament chapters and 800 verses from the New Testament by heart. After completing their comprehensive exams, half of the original 62 participants would

---

* See Appendix C for a sample field report form.

† This total is conservative since a third of the participants said they told stories to more people than they had room to include on their field report forms (there was room to list only three tellings for each story).

graduate from the course having become accomplished biblical storytellers.

A SYSTEMS MODEL OF TRAINING

The training structure was a systems model comprised of three elements: participants, process and product (Figure 6). Because the training was given in modules followed by intervals of field application, it allowed for feedback from the storytellers' field experiences to improve the training process.

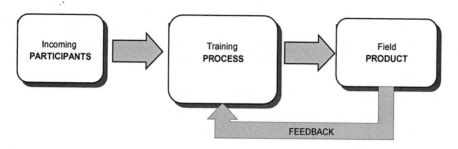

Figure 6. Systems Model of Training

In the remainder of this chapter and the next two chapters, I describe the three major elements of the system: participants, process and product.

DESCRIPTION OF THE PARTICIPANTS

The trainees (61 men and one woman) were all literate, having on average almost 12 years of secular education plus two years of Bible school. Despite their years of formal education, it was possible to glimpse an underlying orality shared by many. For example, 62% had mothers who could not read, and 38% had fathers who could not read. When asked how many books were in their childhood home, 11% had only their required schoolbooks. 33% had between one and five books, and 16% replied that they had no books at all. Only 13% had 20 or more books in their childhood home. This paucity of reading material pointed to a strong oral context in their backgrounds.

A further indicator of orality is the fact that 94% had a significant person in their childhood who often told them stories. These were mostly their mothers or fathers, or grandmothers or grandfathers who recounted tales about the forest, or told them religious myths or family stories.

To complicate this mixture of literacy and orality, in their ministries they were targeting people who were largely incapable of understanding literate communication.

The median age of the participants was twenty-eight. A third of them were single (two got married during the program). Half were from Christian homes or came to know the Lord in childhood. Another third came to the Lord as teenagers. Only 16% were converted as adults. Although most of them claimed to have read the entire Bible, few knew more than a handful of verses by memory. All were multilingual. Twenty different languages were spoken altogether; of these, nine were the primary language of one or more participants.

All of the participants were full-time workers who were engaged in evangelization and church-planting efforts, mostly in pioneer areas where few people had heard the gospel; only a handful were serving as pastors of somewhat established churches.

The agency supervises their workers through a leadership accountability structure. Monthly workers' meetings are held in each division where reports are compiled for every worker's activities and productivity. Until recently their work consisted mainly of giving out literature and preaching. Now however, Hindu resistance to traditional ways of evangelistic outreach had increased and violence against Christian workers was commonplace.* One of the strongest arguments for changing to a biblical storytelling model of communicating the gospel was the opposition they were encountering.

Because the organization's aim was to multiply storytellers, they tried to bring candidates from as many different divisions as possible, including more than a dozen who were field leaders. If the leaders had not been included, it is likely they would have been less receptive to the radical new paradigm of ministry that their workers were bringing home from storytelling training. It was also significant that the president of the agency was promoting the project. Especially in a hierarchical society such as India's, a successful conclusion would have been unlikely without the leaders' support for the project.

Stories and Children

My name is Sunil Kumar Sadhu. After I started attending the storytelling training, I would always tell a story to my six-year-old son before going to sleep. He would say, "Daddy, you have

---

* See Appendix B for two accounts of persecution against the workers.

to tell me a story." And every night I would teach him one story. One day at school, some of the other boys beat him up and he was crying. So the other children said to him, "Let's go and complain to the principal." But my son replied, "No, no, no. I will not complain to madam."

Then those children went and told her, "Madam, they beat Sadhu."

So the principal summoned him and asked, "Who beat you? Tell me and I will beat them. I will wear out five switches on them!"

But my son Sadhu said, "No, I will not tell on them, because my Daddy always tells me stories. And he said, "Forgive your enemies; forgive those who are doing the wrong."

My son remembered a story I had told him (Mat. 18:21–35). He told the teacher, "One day there was a man who had borrowed 5,000,000 rupees from a rich man. Then his master forgave him the money he borrowed." He remembered that story and he told it to his teacher. He said, "That man forgave the one who owed him so many rupees. So, in the same way, I will forgive them."

The next time the principal met me she asked, "How are you teaching your children? Sadhu is well disciplined and he's very good in all his activities. He's a very good boy."

A few days later when a teacher was absent, the principal said to my son, "Sadhu, stand up in front of the class and tell a story—whichever story your daddy has told you, tell it to the class. Every day you have to tell a story to the class."

So every day my son is standing and telling the stories to the other school children. And these stories are one way to make the children very good.

Chapter 8

THE STORY TRAINING

I could a tale unfold whose lightest word
Would harrow up thy soul, freeze thy young blood,
Make thy two eyes, like stars, start from their spheres,
Thy knotted and combined locks to part,
And each particular hair to stand on end,
Like quills upon the fretful porpentine.

—WILLIAM SHAKESPEARE

Ideally an equipper of storytellers should serve as a coach instead of a lecturer. To conceptualize this we use the term trainer instead of teacher. In the Oral Bible program, during a typical 10-hour training day, no more than an hour is given to classroom work; even this is often in an interactive format, and not simply lecture. Most of the training time is spent observing the storytellers as they practice individually and in groups, helping them improve their skill level. This entails not only learning the stories, but also knowing how to perform them well.

An important variable in any training program is the level of trainer skills. One program might seem more effective than another, while in reality it may not be the program as much as it is the quality of training provided by a particular trainer. As Mark Naylor points out, "In establishing an experience based cross-cultural training program ... the key factor is the enthusiasm and ability of the mentor to guide the process in the cross-cultural context."[182] Spending time with the students is essential. In this sense, a training program could be compared to evangelism where the most important factor—regardless of which program is being used—has been shown to be the amount of time and intensity of contact that occurs. Without this, no training program will be highly successful. J. Oswald Sanders wrote,

> Leadership training cannot be done on a mass scale. It requires patient, careful instruction and prayerful, personal guidance over a considerable time. Disciples are not manufactured wholesale. They are produced one by one, because someone has taken the pains to discipline, to instruct and enlighten, to nurture and train one that is younger. [183]

It is also important to note the significant differences between teaching children and teaching adults. Malcolm Knowles points out that adults bring a different set of motivations, goals, and expectations to the learning experience than do children—techniques used for teaching adults should reflect these differences.[184] This is particularly true when giving training to those who are already active in ministry, as contrasted to students who are pre-service. Corporate trainer Mel Silberman uses "active training" methods developed while leading business training seminars. He writes,

> "Everything we know about adult learners suggests that participants must be actively engaged during a training program for results to occur.... Active training occurs when participants do most of the work. If you neatly package the information or elegantly demonstrate the skills, you, not the participants, are doing the work...." [185]

A STANDARD DAY

Each training day followed the same general pattern.

Table 4. Sample Training Day Schedule

	Day 1	**Day 2**	**Day 3**	**Day 4**
6:30	Prayer	Prayer	Prayer	Prayer
7:30	Eat			
8:00-8:30	Worship / COMMUNION	Worship (Group A lead) Testimonies	Worship (Group B lead) Testimonies	Worship (Group C lead) Testimonies
8:30-10:30	Learn: Gen. 2:5 to 3:24 (Paul tell)	Genesis 1:1 to 2:4 (Teresa tell)	Gen. 15:1–9,18; 16:1–16 (Teresa tell)	Gen. 25:19–34 (P/T team telling)

	Day 1	Day 2	Day 3	Day 4
11:00	Break			
11:15-1:00	Gen. 4:1–12, 16–17, 25–26 (Teresa tell)	Gen. 11:1–9 (Ismail tell)	Genesis 18:16 to 19:29 (Ismail tell)	Genesis 27 (Nileswar tell)
1:00	Eat			
2:00-3:00	Class (Paul)	Class (Paul)	Class (Paul)	Class (Paul)
3:00-5:00	Genesis 6:5 to 9:29 (Laren tell)	Genesis 12 and 13 (Laren tell)	Gen. 21:1–7; 22:1–19 (Laren tell)	Genesis 28:10–22 (Ismail tell)
5:00	Break			
5:15-7:15	STORY Performance (telling, drama, song)	STORY Performance (telling, drama, song)	STORY Performance (telling, drama, song)	Process stories* COMMUNION (Group A lead)
7:15	Eat			

The number of stories that can be learned in a given amount of time varies. In groups where everyone has at least rudimentary reading skills, it is possible to advance more quickly.† Depending on the length of the story, between one and two hours was adequate for this group of storytellers to learn a new story, including practicing it as drama and composing a story-song.‡ The sequence of learning activities was as follows:

1. The participants first listened to a trainer who told them the story in dramatic fashion using a national language. Listeners sat in a semicircle.§

---

* This included spiritual formation activities like asking the participants, "Through which stories in particular did God speak to you during the training?"

† Since the stories are meant to be passed along to end-users who may not be able to read at all, it is essential to avoid training methods that *depend* on literacy. While groups of literate or semi-literate learners are able to progress faster by reading the stories in their Bibles, non-readers are equally able to learn by just listening to the stories, although at a slower pace.

‡ Toward the end of the course the storytellers became appreciably quicker at mastering the stories. This was undoubtedly because they had become accustomed to learning the stories, but it may have also been partly a result of being more familiar with the material from the Gospels.

§ Linear seating for storytelling should be avoided if possible. Circular seating fosters the power of storytelling and amplifies the intimacy between the teller and the group.

2. Next the 30 participants broke into separate language-centric learning groups.* They began by looking over the story in their Bibles for ten minutes to familiarize themselves with it in their own language.
3. Then they practiced telling the story in pairs or subgroups of no more than 3–4 people so there was opportunity for everyone to tell.
4. After everyone in the subgroups told the story at least once, the full learning group would gather and listen to one or two people tell the story again.
5. Then each learning group composed a story-song and practiced singing it, which took perhaps 30 minutes.
6. If there was time left over, the groups often began working on dramatizing the story, in which they found great delight.

Evenings were given to performing the stories. This included telling, dramatizing and singing them. Normally each of the learning groups performed one story that they had learned during the day. The group would select one of its members to tell the story while the rest presented the story in drama and story-song. Each story was first told, then dramatized and sung.

We found that drama is an effectual tool for learning the stories. It allows the participants to get inside the skins of the Bible characters and walk with them through their experiences. It also lends itself to humor that was in the original story and which is often lost in readings. Dramatization is natural for these Indian storytellers because the Hindu epics are frequently presented publicly in this way. The best dramatizations incorporated the dialogue found in the Scriptural accounts. Overlooked details often showed up in the dramatization of the story which in effect became an oral exegesis of the text.

By the end of the training day, each participant had listened to every story half a dozen times as it was told and performed by others. In addition, everyone had told the stories at least once and had also shared in dramatizing and singing the stories. This story saturation gave them enough confidence to begin telling and perfecting the story in the field during the next six weeks.

---

* The 62 participants in this program each spoke one of nine primary languages. The three learning groups were made up of those who planned to practice the stories in 1) the national language; 2) in a state language that a third of the participants speak; and 3) another learning group for all the other languages.

ACCOUNTABILITY

Accountability is an essential part of training—if no one checks up on assigned tasks, people tend to conclude they are unimportant. An old adage asserts, "Whatever does not cost is often perceived to be without value." Accountability meant that being in the program cost the participants something. It required them to do the work of mastering the stories instead of just sitting through a class.

Compliance was measured in three ways. The primary instrument was the field report.[*] This one-page form listed the stories that were learned in each module with space for the participant to record three occasions where he or she told each of the stories and the number of people who listened.[†] This form had to be completed and returned to the program facilitator at the beginning of the next module. During the second module, students Kuldeep and Rathnadeep were dismissed from the program and Dulji and John were placed on probation because they had not done their assignment. Knowing about this caused the rest of the student body to take their fieldwork more seriously. John repented and eventually became a committed biblical storyteller.

Second, each training module began with a snap quiz on the stories from the previous training. This was done in the individual learning groups. Each participant was called on to tell a particular story (or part of a story if it was a long one). In this way it was easy to see who had been telling the stories and who had not.

Finally, each storyteller was required to train at least one apprentice (disciple) who would be able to tell all of the stories. During the comprehensive final exam, the storytellers brought their apprentices for testing to verify that they had completed this part of the field assignment (see Section III for the exam results of the storytellers and their apprentices).

Despite the hard work that was required, the program proved to be fun for the participants. This agrees with Ong's description of oral learning: "Verbalized learning takes place quite normally in an atmosphere of celebration or play." In oral cultures, learning is often event-oriented, which also emphasizes the celebratory aspect. Ong concludes, "As events, words are more celebrations and less tools than in literate cultures."[186]

Seeing how their listeners frequently responded to the stories in dramatic ways motivated the storytellers to work hard at learning the stories. During each training event, we gave them opportunities to share personal accounts

---

* See Appendix C for a sample field report.
† See Appendix A for a list of the categories of places, people and occasions where the stories were told.

of things that had happened when they told the stories. These reports allowed others to glean new ideas about how to use storytelling and also stimulated them to greater efforts. The trainers in particular welcomed this feedback since we often had no direct contact with the fields where the stories were being used.

LEARNING TO TELL THE STORIES

So far we have discussed a number of important training elements such as praxis, the training schedule, accountability procedures, the use of learning groups instead of academic classes, and the place of drama. Now I will address some other areas that relate specifically to learning to tell and perform the stories.

Story Selection

Obviously it is not possible to include all the stories of the Bible in a single story track. Criteria for deciding which stories to include or exclude may emerge from different perspectives. For instance, selection could be based on the culture of a particular target group, related to their unique worldview. Stories that address particular spiritual barriers in a society or that serve as bridges from indigenous beliefs to Christian truth would be included, while stories that would offend unnecessarily can be left out or postponed. For example, stories about killing cows offend Hindus deeply. Because this is not an essential part of the gospel, such stories may be excluded or told in a way that is less offensive to the listener.

Another perspective is theological. Most missionaries, either explicitly or implicitly, will include some doctrinal criteria when selecting stories, based on the particular spiritual truths they believe are important for their listeners to hear and understand.

A social perspective yields still different criteria: when people are poor, their worldview is different from people who are well-to-do. They need different stories. Stories of God's provision and of his protection for the powerless are very attractive to those who are in poverty. Similarly, there are certain Bible stories that appeal particularly to women and their unique challenges in life.

One important criterion that I used in story selection was that the story should first of all be a good story. Good narrative elements like dialogue, plot, action, conflict, characterization, crisis, climax, and resolution make a story easier to learn and tell, and more attractive for a listener.

I found that the storytellers tended to bog down in the stories of Saul, David and Solomon. So instead of learning all of these stories, I included only the minimum necessary to carry the thread of the macro narrative.*†

Structuring a Story Track

A mental index structure is essential so the storytellers can retrieve the stories as they are needed. Otherwise stories become scattered bits of knowledge with no way to connect or recall them.

It is best if the stories are taught in the same order in which they will be indexed in the students' minds. Several possibilities exist. The stories could be learned topically; for example, stories about sin and judgment could be learned together. This would fit well with a systematic approach to teaching Bible doctrines, However, oral communicators find it difficult to recall information like this. Since they cannot write things down, remembering information categorized in the form of lists is an arduous task.

The stories could also be learned according to a church lectionary. Each season of the year brings its own set of stories: Christmas, Easter, Pentecost, and so forth. In a repeating three year cycle, a large number of stories can be learned in this manner. If the non-Christian calendar were also taken into account, pagan stories that are connected with indigenous festivals could be addressed directly by Christian stories. This may be one of the best possibilities for a congregation to learn a large number of stories in a systematic and useful manner. In the oral Bible project the training was scheduled so the storytellers were practicing Christmas stories during December and Easter stories in April. This was found to be valuable for the learning process. There was not time to fully develop the idea of a lectionary, but it would seem to have significant potential and deserves further study to determine how such a story track could be developed and employed among the churches.

Another option is for the stories to be learned chronologically, that is, in the same order in which they appear in the Bible. This system is used by proponents of Chronological Bible Storying. It has many advantages. However, a Bible chronology can be too extensive for beginning storytellers to master in the time available to them. A chronological track typically includes between 50 and 100 stories. Shorter tracks that focus on only one theme have been developed for use in particular situations. For example, J. O. Terry has developed a story track of "grief" or lamentation

---

* See Appendix D for a list of stories included in the track.
† A subsequent track for advanced storytellers would supplement and fill in the gaps between these initial stories.

stories which has been effective with women of certain communities and in times of disaster.[187]

Finally, story tracks can be organized biographically. In oral societies, stories about people are a traditional way of recalling historical information. The Greek oral epics such as the *Iliad* and the *Odyssey of Homer* were all about early Greek history. In primitive societies, genealogies are typically recounted for many generations. A biographical story track utilizes a relatively small number of Bible characters who succeed one another chronologically as the structure for remembering the stories.

Consider the fact that one can think through most of the stories of the Old Testament by following the lives of no more than a dozen individuals and their families or associates: Adam, Noah, Abraham-Isaac, Jacob, Joseph, Moses, Joshua, Samuel-Saul, David, Solomon, Elijah-Elisha, and Daniel. These 12 cover most of the historical eras of the Old Testament. The Gospels chronicle the life of only one Man (with many supporting characters), and Acts can be told by simply following the experiences of Peter and Paul. If someone were to learn the stories that pertain to these fifteen people, they would have a mastery of a large portion of the Bible.

Of course, not all the Old Testament stories are included in this schema—for example, the books of Judges, Ruth, Nehemiah and Esther are left out. However, once the basic index structure is created in the storytellers' memories, it is relatively easy to place these stories in proper relationship to the others in subsequent continuing education modules.

As storytellers become familiar with the stories through use, cognitive subindexes will be created based on particular situations they encounter repeatedly. In this project, it became common to find thematic groupings of stories about God's judgment on sin, his healing of the sick, provision in times of financial need, and miracle stories like barren women who gave birth or the dead being raised to life. However, the primary biographical index is always available in the storyteller's mind providing access to stories from the entire panorama of the Bible placed in proper relation to one another.*

Remembering the Stories

It is widely believed that nonliterate people have superior memories. For example, in one of his many novels about Africa, Wilbur Smith writes, "Like many illiterate people he had an infallible memory."[188] But the reality is that

---

* The multiple choice portion of the comprehensive final exam required the students to demonstrate their knowledge of the stories in random order (see Appendix L).

their memories are normal, whereas those of us who have learned to rely on the crutch provided by a print system have substandard memories. Plato predicted this millenniums ago when writing was first becoming commonplace. In his discourse, "Phaedrus" (380 B.C.), Plato has the Egyptian king, Thamus, say this about the new invention of writing:

> This discovery of yours will create forgetfulness in the learners' souls, because they will not use their memories; they will trust to the external written characters and not remember of themselves. What you have discovered is an aid not to memory, but to [reminder], and you give your disciples not [wisdom], but only the semblance of [wisdom]; they will be hearers of many things and will have learned nothing; they will appear to be omniscient and will generally know nothing; they will be tiresome company, having the show of wisdom without the reality.[189]

As Plato's words suggest, memory was highly valued in preliterate cultures. The word "mnemonics" is derived from the Greek word *mnemonikos* ("of memory") and refers to the use of an artificial device for aiding in recall. Some of the ancient Greeks used elaborate memory structures. They would imagine a room or even a large house with each idea they wished to remember placed in a particular spot. Then they could walk through their imaginary house and recall what each item stood for as they came to it.[190] Using this memory system, they could even recall lengthy discourses without referring to written notes. However, a mnemonic aid does not have to be complex. It can be as simple as someone tying a string around a finger to jog their memory and remind them to pick up a loaf of bread on the way home.

Preliterate societies have long used mnemonic techniques ranging from prehistoric cave paintings commemorating particular hunts, to beautiful stained glass windows in cathedrals to recall Bible events in medieval times. The Quipu used knotted strings as a memory aid to recount the historical narratives of the Inca. Various North American Indian tribes used pictographs as memory aids. Even writing was originally developed— not to replace memory—but as a mnemonic device. A mnemonic aid does not have to be an object or image; it can be a song, a poem, a chant or even a dance. Grant Lovejoy tells how a group of storytellers he worked with in Africa created a chant that listed the names of 60 Old Testament stories in chronological order and through it were able to maintain the chronological accuracy of the stories.[191]

In India, telling stories with the use of pictures as memory aids started perhaps as early as the sixth century B.C. Itinerant bards with *kalamkari* cloths (picture scrolls and picture sheets) still travel around India today telling the Hindu epics and religious fables. A narrator tells the story, and as the drama progresses an assistant slowly unrolls the scroll event by event, illumining each scene with an oil lamp.[192]

Traditionally the Patua people were the oral newspapers of Indian society. They traveled from village to village singing their own compositions while unrolling hand-painted scrolls featuring current events, stories of Hindu gods and goddesses and Muslim fakirs. Now their scrolls and songs frequently feature issues of worldwide concern, but with a local twist. For example, in one artist's version of the events of 9/11, the son of a rich Bengali gentleman goes to New York, secures a job in the "Oil Trade House" (i.e., World Trade Center), and tragically dies in the terrorist attack along with thousands of Americans.[193]

Several of these talented artist-storytellers attended a biblical storytelling training module that I led. Afterward they commented, "Before we came here this week we did not know very much about the Bible. But after hearing these stories, now we are sure this is the path we want to follow." By the end of the training they had finished a beautiful 7-foot long colored scroll depicting stories from Creation to the Flood, and had also composed a story-song to go with the pictures. Their production was clearly a dynamic expression of their new faith in God, contextualized for their own people.

In the oral Bible project, each story was identified by a mnemonic symbol that served as a "memory peg" on which to hang the story. I found that the work involved in selecting appropriate mnemonic symbols provided opportunities to exegete both the Scriptural story and the storytellers' context. Deciding which symbol was most central to the story and which one would best communicate to the group I was teaching helped me to begin understanding the story in their context. Generally speaking, symbols with minimal cultural content are easier for the story learners to adopt. Drawings, by definition, are more associated with a specific culture than are pictographs. For this reason, symbols are better suited to forming schemata or file folders for holding information or concepts without prejudicing the viewer toward a particular cultural representation.* For example:

---

* See Appendix C for a sample mnemonics sheet. Online resources can be used to develop your own mnemonic symbol sets. For example, search for fonts with names such as Aboriginebats (1 and 2), Fonts of Afrika, Egyptian, Greek1, HF Hobofont SW, Nahkt, Barnyard, Danceman, Handsign, Gallaudet, Glifiknu (Gyptienne), Pharaoh, Meroitic-Hieroglyphics, and Stickmanbats. These and others are easily adapted for use as mnemonic symbol sets.

Figure 7. Mnemonic Symbol: The Flood

When looking at the first symbol—which is obviously not a representation of reality—the learner must search among existing memory bank and schemata for something that is related. This linking or association and the consequent construction of knowledge helps the concept be remembered better than if the mind were trying to recall a drawing of something that is foreign to its experience. Another consideration is that the ability to correctly interpret a three-dimensional drawing indicating perspective is a learned skill that an oral communicator may not have.

Jacob's Dream is another example of a mnemonic symbol (Figure 8). It is distinctive and easy to recognize at a glance and is also easy to reproduce—anyone can draw it with a stick in the sand or a piece of charcoal on an old wooden board:

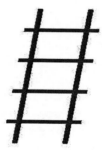

Figure 8. Mnemonic Symbol: Jacob's Dream

In contrast, an artist's rendition of the scene in Genesis 28:10–22 would be much more complex and would be limited to what one person in a particular culture could imagine it to be.

To remind the teller of different episodes or elements of a story, a frame can contain a grouping of symbols. For example, the story of the fall in Genesis 2:5 to 3:24 was represented by these three symbols:

Figure 9. Mnemonic Symbol: The Fall

These mnemonic symbols function in place of written story titles. Instead of having to read a title, the teller identifies the stories by simply glancing at a symbol. Once a particular symbol has been associated with a story, it becomes easy to refer to that symbol both for learning activities and for story selection. In fact, because it bypasses the need for processing data that is inherent in literate representations, the connection between title and story is much faster. Its efficiency lies in the ease with which humans process basic visual information.* But most importantly for our purposes, symbols bypass the twin barriers of illiteracy and language that have often hindered missionary teaching.

One of the learning activities in the oral Bible project was known as the clothesline chronology. In this exercise, a rope was strung across the front of the room, and a large copy of each story symbol was attached to it in chronological order with clothespins. To review the stories, a trainer would go through the symbols in order, reminding the students which story each mnemonic represented. Then the students were called on one by one to do the same. In a second exercise, the story symbols were removed from the clothesline and shuffled. The learning groups then competed to see which group was faster and more accurate at pinning the stories back up correctly. Watching this exercise was humorous, but at the same time it reinforced both the meaning of the symbols and their order in the macro narrative. Most of the storytellers became capable of recreating the entire clothesline chronology in their own minds without looking at a piece of paper.

The mnemonic symbols sometimes gave occasion for a non-Christian to ask to hear the stories. Prashant's Hindu landlady had come to collect the monthly rent. While in the house, she noticed the mnemonic sheets and asked the meaning of the symbols. In response, Prashant's wife told her one

---

* Recognizing this, the U.S. army is now developing electronic battlefield systems that deliver information to soldiers in graphic form allowing for responses that are more instinctive and therefore more rapid. Harold Coyle, *More Than Courage* (New York: Forge, 2003), 275.

of the Bible stories. Consequently the landlady was healed of a migraine, and as a result, she forgave them that month's rent which was past due.* In another instance, John S. told stories and showed the symbols to some Hindus. He reported, "They became very interested by hearing the stories and seeing the pictures." Now two people from different families have been baptized and are attending the church. (January 2007).

Satish made friends with a Hindu man who had been inciting others to violence against Christian workers. After he told the man some of the Bible stories, the man's attitude changed. He even gave Satish money to buy a Bible for him. Satish said, "When I gave him the Bible, then that man started to read all the stories for himself. I gave him all the picture symbols that go with the stories, too." Since the mnemonics sheets have the Scripture references showing where the stories can be found in the Bible, this man was able to use them to find all the stories and read them himself. Now he has been converted and is a member of Satish's church. (October 2006).

This section would be incomplete without mentioning a couple of other points in closing. First, my wife and I both tried unsuccessfully on separate occasions to encourage groups of storytellers to create their own symbols instead of just using symbols that we created for them. The exercise apparently required some cognitive skill that most of them did not have. A second issue was that since each symbol must be unique, eventually the story tracks ran out of symbols to use. The only alternative was to begin using line drawings instead. In practice, both symbols and simple drawings were equally effective as mnemonic devices as long as the graphic was assigned a mutually agreed upon meaning and the learners were clear about what it represented.† To verify their comprehension, it was good to ask questions like, "What is this picture/symbol?" "Why was it chosen to represent this story?" Then the trainer could be sure they had made the connection in their own minds.

Some people have used colored pictures for telling Bible stories. This is different from the use of symbols as a mnemonic. In 1998–1999 Teresa and I trained storytellers in three locations in the use of large, brightly colored, glossy picture books that they displayed to the listeners as they told the stories. These were popular with the storytellers. Nevertheless, we became concerned that the stories were not being internalized adequately. It seemed to us that the stories were still residing in the picture books instead of in the storytellers.

---

* Appendix J:4d.

† The effectiveness of the symbols and drawings was tested at the GEN2 and GEN3 levels, not, however, at the GEN4 level where the storytellers are farther removed from literacy. This should be followed up in future research.

In the summer of 1999, monsoon floods destroyed homes in villages where some of the storytellers lived. After their picture books were lost, they lacked confidence to continue telling the stories. On another occasion, termites built their termite mound in a large supply of picture books that were in storage, ruining them completely.

Because of these experiences we decided to forego the use of story picture books and instead find a way for the storytellers themselves to become the medium of communication. After the books were gone the storytellers were compelled to use their own imaginations to picture the scenes. They began to understand and memorize the stories more adequately, and as a result they became more effective storytellers.

For trainers of oral storytellers, media is not pen and paper or even audio or video recording, but the living hearts and minds of human beings who incarnate the stories into their own lives. The telling of the stories gains tremendous power when this has occurred. Just as important, story replication is not limited by the supply of printed picture books or audio players needed for each new storyteller. Theoretically, at least, the transmission of stories can be infinite.

STORY SCRIPTING

During this project someone asked me, "Are your story scripts straight from the Bible or do you edit them for the telling?" In response, I wrote the following:

> Biblical storytellers do this in different ways. Some hold that word for word reproduction of the text from a particular Bible translation with as little variation as possible is the only acceptable standard. This seems to be best among Muslims, where verbatim memorization of the Quran is typical. Through experience we have found what works well for us. We try to keep several objectives in mind. First of course, is faithfulness to the sense of the original. But in addition, I look for ways to phrase the stories so they will be memorable to the listener like the original was to the original listeners (or at least fresh for those who may have heard the familiar words many times and become immune to them). At the same time, I try to bring the story into the listeners' own context as much as possible. Many people in the present generation do not understand biblical terminology, so we cannot assume this knowledge when we are scripting.

Compare different versions of the Bible as you are scripting. Most are helpful, except for some like the NIV and the Living Bible, which are more suited to personal reading and study than for oral telling. Good versions for scripting for oral performance are the NKJV, New Living, and others. I always start with the NKJV as my base script since it retains some of the orality that was inherent in the English language of an earlier period. Many of the unique ways of phrasing and presentation in the King James Version have to do with the sounds that words make when spoken, not just the ideas they represent in one's mind when reading the Bible alone.*

Furthermore, I may telescope the stories to make them easier to learn and tell, especially the longer Old Testament stories. While not trying to avoid all repetition—repetition is an oral technique—I do trim sometimes. Also, it is common to find material that was relevant for the original audience that is not relevant for our audience today. I tend to avoid obscure place-names when possible, and use a description instead. To make it easier for the listener to keep the story straight, I compound proper names with their titles/roles; for example: King-Ahab, prophet-Elijah, servant-Gehazi, and so forth. Of course as listeners become more familiar with the characters this is not as necessary. Another thing we have found is that as we start telling the stories out loud, the script adapts and begins to sound more oral. All of this is done very intentionally—the Lord has no pleasure in a workman who is sloppy with His Word!

This was good advice for telling the stories in English to English language listeners. But because of the multiple language barriers in the oral Bible project, I quickly found it was necessary to simplify the way the stories were told. After initially endeavoring to retain the charm and memorableness of a well-scripted story, I finally came to the realization that by the time the narrative passed from my English to the translator's broken Hindi to the participants' regional and local languages, little of this would have survived. So it was better to present the story using simplified words that were easiest for the translator to handle, and then trust the indigenous

---

* Shakespeare was so instrumental in the development of the English language that our associations are much more toward Elizabethan English than the word associations the original hearers of Hebrew, Greek or Aramaic may have held. A different approach may be superior for Scripture exegesis, but for story performance the sonorities of language are crucial. For the most accuracy in scripting stories, the NKJV can be compared to other translations that may have a better level of biblical scholarship in regard to particular texts.

storytellers to reconstruct the narratives using their own vernacular and oral communication styles.

Oral literatures are often full of wonderful sounds that are highly memorable and thus ideal for oral learners. In the Scriptural text, many unique ways of phrasing are used because they made "wonderful sounds" in the original language. However it does not follow that they will have the same wonderful sounds in our language. The correct solution is for gifted storytellers to recreate them in the unique style of their own language and culture.

Goody argues that inexact recall can actually be better than verbatim recall because it takes advantage of the process of "recoding" the information; that is, rephrasing the text in the storyteller's own words, which gets it into long-term memory. Instead of repeating the story, people "reconstruct" it.[194] In one example, village storyteller Somarsing rephrased this complex text from 2 Samuel 11:11:

> Uriah said to David, "The ark and Israel and Judah are dwelling in tents, and my lord Joab and the servants of my lord are encamped in the open fields. Shall I then go to my house to eat and drink, and to lie with my wife? As you live, and as your soul lives, I will not do this thing."

In reconstructing the story, Somarsing had Uriah state simply: "My country is more important than my wife."

For a story to be accepted into a culture it must come dressed in native garb, not in foreign attire. No Bible story is truly incarnated into a culture until this happens. The stories in the Bible were crafted to appeal mainly to Jewish people. When a Jewish storyteller said "Abraham," it made immediate positive connections to a vast library of attachments. However, this is not so for most other cultures; for them, Abraham is just another difficult name to learn.

Every language has customary ways of formulating speech, and this is particularly evident in oral cultures. Marcel Jousse pointed out that oral social groups tend to stereotype frequently used ways of expression in traditional oral formulas or clichés.[195] In reconstructing a Bible story, the indigenous storyteller will instinctively choose the formulas that are most familiar to his or her listeners, using words and patterns that are understandable to people in that culture. Susan Wittig notes that formulaic style has value for the listener because it sets up a psychological anticipation that results in more efficient recognition and improved understanding. In terms of its persuasive value, formulaic composition results in a greater likelihood of acceptance and agreement by the listeners.[196] The more that vernacular forms of speech, stock phrases, and formulaic sayings belonging to the local context are included in the warp and the woof of the communication fabric, the more the story will be perceived as part of the culture instead of something that is alien.

My journal recorded my efforts to help sensitize the storytellers to guidelines for bringing a story into their own culture:

> I worked with them on "crafting a story" by telling them the scripted stories while asking them to follow along in their own Bibles, pointing out where I had made changes and why. The two poles are: 1) not changing the meaning, and 2) crafting it so their hearers can understand it in the same way the original hearers did. For example: change Pharisee, Sadducee, scribe, and so forth to "high religious person." (or *pandit*, priest, and so forth, whichever it is in their own context). Also John the Baptist's reference to "sons of Abraham" (Mat. 3:9) was changed to "born a Santal," or "your father was a *pandit*," etc. (Journal notes; January 2003).

Tom Steffen argues that the fundamental nature of communication is one of shared symbols structured in culturally-appropriate and comfortable narrative patterns.[197] Thus we could say that the divine truth tends to be encapsulated in the shared symbols and the narrative elements of a story more than in the individual words that a particular narrator uses to tell it.[*] As an example, the effectiveness of the annual repeating of the Passover story by Jewish families to their children did not depend primarily on the head of household repeating the text word for word, but rather in symbols and actions inherent in the story such as blood sacrifice, bitter herbs, unleavened bread, and so forth.

One of the things that drove us to develop a storytelling model in India is the paucity of words available in our context. In contrast to English, languages like Hindi (and even more, the tribal languages) have insufficient words to express the concepts needed to communicate Bible truths. To greatly compound this difficulty, the interpreters available to us were not proficient in these languages. But even if they had been, the listeners would not have been able to understand the words they used because these are not words that are common in typical village conversations. I concluded that we would never be able to transmit significant amounts of learning under

---

* Even the translators of the revered King James Version text wrote, "Another thing we think good to admonish thee of (gentle Reader) that we have not tied our selves to a uniformity of phrasing, or to an identity of words, as some peradventure would wish that we had done.... For is the kingdom of God become words or syllables? why should we be in bondage to them if we may be free, use one precisely when we may use another no less fit, as commodiously?" (Original Preface to the KJV; spelling modernized for clarity).

these conditions, especially if the goal was for the message to be infinitely reproducible within each people group.

Fortunately, there is a proven technology within oral cultures that bypasses this limitation. In stories the truth is carried not in individual words, but in the story elements themselves such as plot, characterization, dialogue, and so forth. This is essential since oral communicators are largely incapable of finding meaning in solitary words.

LeRon Shults points out that any attempt to use human language to express the characteristics of God must fall short:

> The truly infinite God of Christian faith is beyond all our linguistic grasping, as all the great theologians from Irenaeus to Calvin have insisted, and so the struggle to capture God in our finite propositional structures is nothing short of linguistic idolatry.[198]

Of course there are risks in reliance on symbol and narrative. Tom Steffen addresses this:

> God is a risk taker. Recall the messy nature of symbol and narrative and the freedom to interpret it noted above. It becomes quite obvious that those who wish to deal in symbols and narratives are willing to risk misinterpretation. God as Symboler and Storyteller seems more interested in the recipient's journey to truth than the immediate articulation of the right answers.[199]

New Testament scholar N. T. Wright points out that narratives may actually be one of the best reflections of reality. "A story, with its pattern of problem and conflict, of aborted attempts at resolution, and final result ... [is] universally perceived as the best way of talking about the way the world actually is."[200]

Some have expressed concern with the possibility of heresies arising because of a reliance on stories. They equate the use of indigenous communication forms with an increased danger of syncretism. However, western literate communication forms have not proven to be a safeguard against syncretism, either. Many indigenous Christians who received the gospel through literate means freely mix pagan and Christian practices and beliefs. The solution is not to use formulations that originated in other cultures, but to seek ways in which the Word of God can find vital lodging in people's hearts and minds, thus filling all the voids that their own cultural forms and functions previously occupied.

Because storytelling is art, the particular words, sentence structure, emphases, gestures, tone of voice, facial expression, and other nonverbal communication signals that are used to paint a story on the canvas of a listener's mind and heart will vary from one storyteller to another. The creativity of any artist is mixed into the picture that emerges: his or her own perspective and training, frame of mind, previous experience, medium, and so forth. It is even possible to identify a well-known artist just by looking at a painting he or she has produced. Each has an individual style. Just so, one can hear different storytellers tell the same Bible story and enjoy it more each time.

The fact that stories can be told in different ways is especially relevant when these narratives make their journey across linguistic and cultural lines. One of the first field assignments in the oral Bible project required the students to find a storyteller in their own context and listen to (and then report on) how he or she told stories. Any type of story was admissible: religious, family, or personal. The purpose of this exercise was to impress on the students the viability of storytelling as a medium of communication in their own context and to sensitize them to the unique ways that stories are told there.

For greatest effectiveness, a narrative presentation of a Bible story is best given as an oral paraphrase of the written text, taking advantage of auxiliary communication channels not available to print communicators. For example, a character scratching his head, looking puzzled, saying, "What should I do?", may express exactly the sense of the written text in which a narrator says, "and he did not know what to do." Viggo Søgaard points out that a translation intended for audio presentation should "conform to the features, style, and structure of oral discourse rather than to those of the print medium."[201] These oral techniques are not additions to the text, but rather are similar to the role of paraphrase in writing which is done for clarity or interest. The original narrators who told these stories would certainly have taken advantage of such techniques.

Steffen defines narrative as a picture in the mind of one person transferred to the minds of others through a full-bodied experience that embraces the mind, the imagination, the emotions, and volition.[202] We might ask: if we are addressing only the person's cognitive realm, is this, in fact, an accurate presentation of God's Word? Or is it simply a one-dimensional snapshot without depth or power to transform the hearer? A truly authentic presentation of the Word must impact more than the mind of the listener; it must also affect the emotions, the will, the imagination and even the spirit in order to confront the hearer in the three areas of encounter defined by Kraft as essential to conversion: truth, allegiance, and power.[203]

Kraft cites Bible translator Eugene Nida who popularized the concept of dynamic equivalence translation which is "directed primarily toward equivalence of response rather than equivalence of form."[204] According to Nida,

It would be wrong to think ... that the response of the receptors in the second language is merely in terms of comprehension of the information, for communication is not merely informative. It must also be expressive and imperative if it is to serve the principal purposes of communications such as those found in the Bible. That is to say, a translation of the Bible must not only provide information which people can understand but must present the message in such a way that people can feel its relevance....[205]

Similarly, for a story to be authentic it should be told in a way that seeks a total response equivalent to that elicited from the original audience. This will almost certainly require a different presentation than merely repeating the printed words verbatim. Following Steffen's analogy of transferring a picture from one mind to another, when a foreigner from a modern western city tells a story to a tribal person in a rural village in India or Africa, the picture that is created in the listener's mind will have little resemblance—in most of the details that make it seem authentic—to the picture that was in the mind of the teller. However, it will be a picture that fits its new context and which is able to communicate powerfully with the people who live there.

Dialogue is of great importance to story scripting. Robert Alter is particularly helpful on dialogue:

Everything in the world of Biblical narrative ultimately gravitates toward dialogue— ... It means that quantitatively, a remarkably large part of the narrative is carried by dialogue, the transactions between characters typically unfolding through the words they interchange, with only the most minimal intervention of the narrator. As a rule, when a narrative event in the Bible seems important, the writer will render it mainly through dialogue....[206]

Alter notes that there is surprisingly little direct character description in biblical narrative. Instead, character is revealed through other means. The importance the Bible places on dialogue can be seen in the following observation:

In reliable third person narratives, such as in the Bible, there is a scale of means, in ascending order of explicitness and certainty, for conveying information about the motives, the attitudes, the moral nature of characters. Character can be revealed through the report of actions; through appearance, gestures, posture, costume; through one character's comments on another; through direct speech by the character; through inward speech, either summarized or quoted as interior monologue; or through statements by the narrator about the attitudes and intentions of the personages, which may come either as flat assertions or motivated explanation....[207]

Bluegrass storyteller, Chuck Larkin, stresses the importance of dialogue when he says, "Always substitute at every opportunity Character thinking out loud and Characters in dialogue."[208]

Finally, in most languages there are different words that can mean "story." For instance in English there are fables, myths, epics, narratives, historical accounts, reports, tales and so forth. In India, Brahmin listeners may know the proper Hindi language terms, such as *athyayika*, which denotes a story that is based on historical fact. The one who is telling such a story, who is versed in Sanskrit stories, is called an *akhyanavidah*, while a *pauranika* is a teller of ancient stories called *puranas*.[209] However, few of the village people have a large Hindi vocabulary. For them a story is simply a "*kahani*" which is the Hindi word for fable.[210] A storyteller is a "*kahanikar*," or a teller of fables. Obviously it is not helpful to have the listeners think that what a biblical storyteller is doing is telling fables. So the storytellers were taught to start every Bible story with this formulaic introduction: "This is an old story and a true story. It is in God's book." They liked this so much that some would introduce their story enthusiastically, saying, "This is a very, very, very old and true story!"

PERFORMING THE STORY

It is important to note that verbal communication does not correspond precisely to oral communication. Jousse distinguishes between oral style, spoken style and written style. He defines spoken style as the speech of everyday conversation, whereas oral style speech is designed to be heard, remembered, and transmitted by memory.[211] In western societies verbal communications such as sermons, lectures or speeches are usually simply extensions of print media.

The difference between oral and spoken speech is illustrated by Frederick Buechner's description of how the words of the Bible first came alive for him when he was a student at Union Seminary in New York City during the days of Paul Tillich and H. Richard Niebuhr:

But for me, as for most of us studying there in those days, there was no one on the faculty who left so powerful and lasting an impression as James Muilenburg. He was an angular man with thinning white hair, staring eyes, and a nose and chin which at times seemed so close to touching that they gave him the face of a good witch. In his introductory Old Testament course, the largest lecture hall that Union had was always packed to hear him. Students brought friends. Friends brought friends. People stood in the back when the chairs ran out. Up and down the whole length of the aisle he would stride as he chanted the war songs, the taunt songs, the dirges of ancient Israel. With his body stiff, his knees bent, his arms scarecrowed far to either side, he never merely taught the Old Testament but was the Old Testament. He would be Adam, wide-eyed and halting as he named the beasts— "You are … an elephant … a butterfly … an ostrich!" –or Eve, trembling and afraid in the garden of her lost innocence, would be David sobbing his great lament at the death of Saul and Jonathan, would be Moses coming down from Sinai. His face uptilted and his eyes aghast, he would be Yahweh himself, creating the heavens and the earth, and when he called out, "Let there be light!" there is no way of putting it other than to say that there would be light, great floods of it reflected in the hundreds of faces watching him in that enormous room.[212]

This description of James Muilenburg's performance of the Scriptures shows how oral systems provide a much wider communication spectrum than just the use of one's voice. Herbert Klem cites Ruth Finnegan:

… what in literate culture must be written, explicitly or implicitly into a text can in orally delivered forms be conveyed by more visible means—by the speaker's gestures, expressions, and mimicry. A particular atmosphere—whether of dignity for a king's official poet, … enjoyment … grief … —can be conveyed … by the dress, accoutrements, or observed bearing of the performer. …In these cases the verbal content now represents only one element in an opera-like performance which combines words, music, and dance….[213]

Klem lists eleven different signal systems: verbal, written, pictorial, audio (change of voice), kinetic (gestures), tactile, spatial (moving around), temporal (timing), artifactual (objects), optical and olfactory.[214] Each of these communication channels can carry important information about the story. To an oral communicator, presentations that depend only—or even primarily—on speaking can seem dull and flat. The credibility of a story may even depend most on signals that are least explicit.

For this reason, in the oral Bible project emphasis was given to training the storytellers in story performances that involved the whole body. Four symbols (Figure 10) were routinely used to represent the elements that make a good biblical storyteller; the participants were graded on these four areas in their presentations. The first symbol refers to correspondence to the written text, while the other three refer to "whole body" storytelling, that is, the performance of storytelling.

Figure 10. Four Symbols of Storytelling Competence

The book symbol is a reminder that the told story must be faithful to the Scriptures. Was the story complete? Was it correct? Was the dialogue in the story reproduced as characters speaking and not as prose? Being faithful to the source also means not adding personal commentary or tacking a moral on as part of the story.

The other three symbols pertain to the performance of the story. Presentation is given equal weight with content, since content only matters if it can be understood, learned and reproduced by the listener.

The performance elements are universal although the ways they are expressed can vary greatly from one culture to another. Symbol two represents the use of facial expressions. Is the speaker's face telling the same story as the spoken words? If the storyteller's face does not express the emotions that correspond with what he or she is saying, the story will lack credibility with the listeners. Arthur Burrell, in his 1926 book, *A Guide to Storytelling*, gives an anthropological list compiled by Charles Darwin that describes the physical use of facial features to express a wide variety of emotions.* Burrell

---

* See Appendix E.

suggests that the storyteller should practice in front of a mirror or ask a friend to critique the expressions he or she wishes to convey.

Symbol three represents the use of gestures and body movements. Gestures are a way to say something without speaking. For example, hand movements can clearly communicate yes, no, good-bye, come, go, and so forth without speaking a single word. Burrell gives this advice for learning to use gesture and body movement effectively:

> Gesture should be learned—if learning be necessary—from life rather than from books; from watching people walking, talking, quarreling, in the street. A railway station is an excellent place to study gesture.... The best way to practice is to act the scene or clause with the very thing in your hands to which the story refers. If you want to gesture the sweeping of a room, or mounting a ladder, or the throwing of a bucket of water out the window, or the kissing of a child, or the wearing of a sword, or the turning of someone into the street, just get hold of the broom, ladder, bucket or child, or person to be thrown out and do the thing. After doing it half a dozen times, watch your action and repeat the movement restrainedly without the help of broom, ladder, or bucket.[215]

A word of caution is in order here. There is a distinction between theater of the mind and theater of the stage.[216] In theater of the mind the storyteller stimulates the listener to imagine; that is, there is no direct presentation of images. Generally a storyteller will want to create theater of the mind—thus recreating the scenes inside the mind of the listeners instead of on stage. However, depending on the particular audience (children, for example) and the particular culture, varying degrees of body action, movement and gesture can be appropriate. It is important to note that different cultures have widely differing standards in storytelling. What is appropriate in one culture may cause discomfort to the listeners in another. Furthermore, gestures have no meaning in and of themselves. The only meaning they have is the shared meaning that is assigned to them by a particular culture. Therefore, gestures and their meaning will vary considerably.

The final symbol of Figure 10 refers to the use of the voice. This is not in regard to the particular words that are spoken, but rather to modulation of the teller's voice: loud, soft, fast, slow, high pitch, low pitch, old person, young person, and so forth. The use of different voices is especially helpful in dialogue. Some storytellers have more skill for this than others. However, a monotone presentation will always tend to kill a story.

The participants in the oral Bible project were all ministers who had been trained in Bible schools of varying quality. However, their oratorical style was learned more through their observation of other ministers to whom they had been exposed during their Christian life than through their Bible school experience. Many had developed poor public speaking habits. One frequent error was the use of monotone. Another was that much of the time when preaching they appeared to be angry. Their facial expressions, hand gestures, and shouting all contributed to this effect. In the storytelling training, drama was employed as a culturally acceptable medium that gave the storytellers freedom to explore the performance aspects of storytelling. The hope was that this would transfer to their individual storytelling performances and often that happened.

Asher Korkora tells how he came to realize that his way of speaking had made it seem that he was angry:

In my station I have always conducted Sunday services for the children. But when I would speak to them, my voice and face were stern like I was commanding them. I even gave out chocolate to make them listen to the message. But they still would not sit quietly and behave and listen properly. Some would get up and walk away. And my own son was one of those who was misbehaving. He would be walking out. Or he would be pinching or hitting the other children. He was the pastor's son, but he was misbehaving so much.

But when I attended this storytelling program, I learned that we should have a different attitude when telling the stories. We should be careful to use the right facial expressions, the proper voice, hand and body motions when we are telling the stories to the people. Our voice and face must show a loving attitude and we should also use action, so the people will be attracted to hear the message.

So when I went home, I started telling the stories in this way to my Sunday school. I began telling all the stories we learned here, starting with the story of creation. My voice and face and attitude were different, more loving. So I was telling in this new way and all the children liked it and were eager and ready to sit quietly and listen attentively to the stories. Now they are sitting properly when I am telling the stories. The entire atmosphere has changed totally. One day, one of the children even reminded me, "O, you forgot to tell about how God made the stars!"

Now as I said, I have a three-year-old son, whom I love very much. But even though he is my own son, he never used to sit and listen properly. He would be misbehaving, getting up, walking, going here and there, pushing, hitting, pulling on the other children during children's Sunday school. I know that often the pastor's son is not well-disciplined, but in my heart I had a desire that my two children should be disciplined and should know God. I have been praying for them, "Lord, give my children good knowledge and discipline."

Before that, my son would always fight with a neighbor's son who lives nearby. I thought that was such a bad example, because he is a pastor's son. Then once when I was telling the story of Cain and Abel, both of them were sitting there. And both of them began crying. The tears were running down from my son's eyes. This story really changed them.

So now that I have started telling these stories in this new way, my own son has become so proud of me. He will go and tell so many others, "Come, look. Come and see how my daddy is telling so many stories so nicely." So he will tell them when is the next time they can hear me telling the stories and now he is bringing others to hear the stories. And he is helping me. He is ready to sit quietly and listen whenever I am telling the stories. I am very thankful for this change. (Asher Korkora; March 2006).

On one occasion when we observed the storytellers in a village context and participated in their storytelling event, I had occasion to note how attractive the Bible stories are to people who have never heard them before. I described the event in my journal:

This little church is unusual in that it was built by the believers themselves without mission subsidies. The walls are of wattled mud construction, nicely plastered. The roof is galvanized sheet metal. The floor is made of mud, which is still drying as evidence that the last of the work was only completed the previous day. Teresa and I and other guests have plastic chairs to sit in (there are also a couple of benches), but most of the people sit on mats that have been placed on the floor. The church is decorated with different colored tissue paper with cut-out patterns of crosses, hearts, and stars which hang where a ceiling would normally be.

We begin with about 30 adults present, but as the day goes on the number of people keeps growing. By the end of the day, a hundred villagers are crowded into the little 12 X 25 foot church, with 30–40 more crowding around the door and even the little windows. It is easy to tell that many had never been to a Christian service before. Men came in from the fields and women cheerfully left their housework to stay and listen just as long as someone was willing to tell them stories.

When coming to the end of one Bible story, Teresa asked, "Shall I tell another one?" The answer came right back, "Yes, yes! Another one! Speak!" I was reminded of the old hymn, "We've a Story to Tell to the Nations."

STORY-SONGS

From the beginning of the pilot project in 2001, story-songs quickly became an important part of learning and disseminating the biblical stories. Ballads have always been common in oral societies as a medium for preserving and spreading stories. Many of the early Greek epics were sung as well as told. In the Bible itself, a significant portion of the canon was originally in the form of song. One of the earliest recorded examples is the women's song that was performed on the shores of the Red Sea after the deliverance from the Egyptians (Exodus 15). For Miriam and the other women to perform this impromptu song-dance is witness to the prevalence of story-song in the Hebrew culture of that era.

One of the language groups in the original pilot project were the Santals, who have a common saying, "Where there is a story, there is a song." Almost from birth, a Santal learns how to compose story-songs seemingly on the spur of the moment. These are often accompanied by tribal dances in which women and men face one another in a kind of line dance. The Shadris, another tribal group represented in the pilot project, also create story-songs performed with dance, but their dance is circular. Believers from these tribal communities have been known to dance through the entire night.

So from the beginning of the program, one of the regular training activities was for each learning group to create a song in their own language and distinctive musical style to go with the Bible story they had just learned. Every learning group seemed to have at least one talented individual who was able to compose a song that had more than passing value. Usually 30 minutes would be enough time to complete this activity.

However, some problems also showed up. First, because there were at least five different languages in each training event, it was difficult for the composed songs to be performed adequately, especially since a story-song can be quite long. A few of the songs were composed in the national language and managed to become widely adopted by all the groups. But the majority were in indigenous languages which limited their dissemination to a single ethnic community. Second, as the program grew and we began training multiple story tracks at the same time, it became more and more difficult to focus on anything beyond just teaching them to tell the stories. Training days were few and story tracks were long. So unfortunately, important components such as spiritual formation exercises and the creation of story-songs took secondary place. While these were never dropped entirely, the emphasis became more sporadic.

When the second oral Bible project began in 2006, I recruited three co-trainers, Laren, Nileswar and Ismail, who had learned to tell stories in the original pilot project. Laren insisted that it was important to make story-song a principal activity in the new program. Because of this, even without my full attention, the use of story-songs continued. Because Laren spoke Oriya—the same language as 40% of the new trainees—he could coach them in composing and singing story-songs in their language. Many of these songs were carried back to the field where the storytellers taught them to others along with the Bible stories.*

The use of story-song had a long history in missionary practice. Writing from his experience in India, Bishop Lesslie Newbigin reported, "Even the dullest villagers pick up [the story-songs] quickly and many of the congregations have learned to sing and dance them beautifully.... [They are effective] for printing the Gospel story indelibly on the minds of people who will never learn in any other way."[217]

Having followed the composition and use of story-songs for six years among hundreds of storytellers from dozens of different language groups, I am convinced of its value and highly recommend that any biblical storytelling training program should explore its potential.

---

* Appendix F.

If I believe this, will it happen to me?

Maya's father was a renowned village witch doctor, but by God's grace both Maya and her husband are strong believers. Maya never went to school, but has taught herself to read. Her husband is a government employee; they have three children. Maya's father had four wives. All the children born to Maya's mother became Christian believers in adulthood.

Maya often tells stories in her own village. One morning as she was reading her Bible and praying, a poor illiterate woman from another village came by. This woman was a habitual drunkard whose husband had abandoned her. Seeing Maya with her open Bible, the woman asked what she was doing.

"Are you chanting some mantra? Are you doing magic?"

Maya replied, "No. I would not do anything like that. This is the Book of Life—here you can find out about your life."

The woman asked her, "This Bible is like a magic book?"

After thinking for a minute, Maya answered, "Yes, this Bible is like a magic book. Because if you believe the things that are in it, they can happen to you."

Then Maya told her Jesus' words from Matthew 11:28: "Come to me all who are tired and deeply burdened and I will give you rest."

With a tremor of hope in her voice, the woman responded, "If I believe this thing, will it happen to me?"

Starting with the story of the Creation, Maya told her many stories from the Bible. After several hours, the woman went on her way, but God's stories were now her stories. She could have faith that this God would act toward her in the same way he acted toward Adam and Eve, toward Noah, or toward Abraham and Sarah.

Chapter 9

THE PRODUCT

God made man because he loves stories.

−ELIE WIESEL

The oral Bible project was intended to equip bivocational and full-time Christian workers to share the Bible in ways that oral people can understand and reproduce in order to facilitate the spread of the gospel all the way out to the fringes of each people group regardless of the level of literacy among them. This would occur not only through the efforts of the storytellers, but also by their "downline," that is other individuals who had also become tellers of God's stories through their efforts. Much of the training consisted of the participants practicing what they were learning by telling and teaching it to others.

THE BICULTURE LEARNING MODEL

We will now look at three models that help show how biblical stories were disseminated across cultural barriers in this project: first, Ralph Winter's E-1 to E-3 model; then Eugene Nida's S.M.R. model; and finally, Paul Hiebert's bicultural bridge model. Each of these contributed to the design of the oral Bible project.

At the International Congress on World Evangelization in Lausanne, Switzerland in 1974, Ralph Winter addressed what he considered a critical misunderstanding of the missionary task. Because the church now has a worldwide presence, some groups had begun to suggest there was no longer any need for traditional missionary strategy. Instead local Christians everywhere could finish the job by evangelizing those who lived around them. Winter argued that geographical proximity is not the same as cultural proximity—groups living side by side could be light-years apart culturally. To bridge this cultural distance would always require a special kind of evangelism, one that did not obligate people who wished to follow Christ to become culturally like those who evangelized them.[218]

Winter proposed a new model for discourse about cross-cultural evangelism, one that posited *cultural* distance instead of *geographical* as the focal point. In this scheme, E-1 represents the culture of the messenger while E-2 and E-3 represent the cultures of the receptors (Figure 11).*

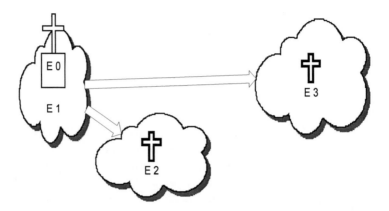

Figure 11. Ralph Winter's E-1 to E-3 Model of Evangelism

E-1 would signify evangelism directed toward people who are much like the church people. For example, a Santal who wins another Santal to Christ would be doing E-1 evangelism. To win a member of the Bodo tribe is not as easy because the language and culture are not the same, and also because in the recent past these two tribes have been at war with one another. This calls for a different kind of evangelism which Winter termed E-2. However for a Santal evangelist to try to win an Indian Muslim to Christ would mean crossing a cultural divide so vast that a

---

* Later, E-0 was added to the model to represent evangelism within the church. For example, for a Santal church to win their own children would be E-0 evangelism.

radically distinct style of evangelism would be needed.* Winter called this E-3 evangelism.†

To win a person at an E-3 distance (or beyond) means someone has to leave the comforts and security of their own culture, learn a new language, learn how to eat unfamiliar foods, learn a different lifestyle, and learn to love people who may appear unlovely, in order to share the gospel with them. Even more significantly, the greater the cultural distance between messenger and receptor the more difficult it is to encode and decode the message accurately.

In many ways this task requires an exceptional person: one who is a gifted linguist, is culturally sensitive, who has a deep commitment to the task, is willing to suffer hardship for long periods of time, and who has an unusual ability to adapt to other cultures personally. Needless to say, individuals who can be effective after crossing multiple cultural barriers are rare. The church has often celebrated their unique ministry.

In contrast, nearly anyone can carry the gospel across one degree of cultural distance. For every gifted person who has been effective at going from E-1 to E-3, there are hundreds who are able to cross from E-1 to E-2 or from E-2 to E-3.

In this project, I adapted Winter's model so it reflects a bridging strategy. Instead of the message having to cross huge cultural distances in one leap, this model allows the journey to take place in steps like a relay race where the baton is handed off to each new runner who in turn carries it to the next stage (Figure 12).

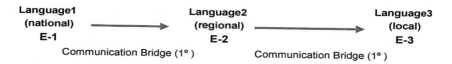

Figure 12. Modified E-1 to E-3 Model

Because of the large number of languages and cultures that exist in geographical proximity to one another in India, people become quite adept at cross-cultural interaction. They often speak several different languages: a birth language, a state or regional language, and a smattering of the national language. In addition they may speak enough words of other nearby local or

* There is a remarkable abhorrence among the Santals of the Muslims whom they call *turuk*, a term which carries a connotation of contempt. J. Troisi, *Tribal Religion: Religious beliefs and practices among the Santals* (New Delhi: Manohar Publishers, 1979), 247.
† In many areas such as India, vast degrees of cultural distance are frequently overlaid in a single geographical location like a giant mosaic.

state languages to get along when necessary. When the gospel is put into a form that transfers easily—such as a story—it becomes simple for it to travel across linguistic and cultural barriers.

For example, Pastor Pangi Jonah Raju gave this account:

> One day a man from a nearby state came to see me. He does not know Telugu but I know a little broken Oriya, so I told him the story about Abraham. This man's wife had left him, and he was very troubled. Only his daughter and son-in-law were living there with him. Then I told him the story of what happened to Job. Job was alone and his friends had also left him. But in the end he got his family back and God really blessed him. Upon hearing the story about Job this man got very excited and interested, and he asked me, "If I go to prayer meetings and church, do you think God will give the same kind of blessings to me?" I told him, "Yes, definitely, if you believe, then God will bless you. Because God is the same. And nothing is impossible with God." So he started coming to prayer meetings and church services. He was constantly coming to church to seek after God. After one month, his wife who had gone away—she came back! And he had not even called her. Now they are both coming to church. This man told me, "I will also become a storyteller. And I will come and tell stories with you." (April 2006).

The second model that contributed to my understanding was the Source, Message, Receptor (S.M.R) communication model originated by Eugene Nida (Figure 13). This model shows that communication happens mainly in areas of shared experience; the more overlap in shared experience, the greater the likelihood the receptor will understand the message as the source intended.[219] David Hesselgrave points out that the word "communication" comes from the Latin word *communis* (common); to have communication it is first necessary to establish a "commonness" with the other person.[220]

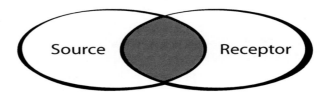

Figure 13. S.M.R. Model:
Communication Depends On Shared Experience

A foundational principle of communication is that a message is what the receptor understands it to be. Charles Kraft addresses this in regard to his theory of "receptor-oriented" communication:

> The understanding that what messages mean is constructed by the receiver rather than inherent in the message is perhaps the single most threatening insight of contemporary communication theory for Christian communicators.... Those who deal with communication from a Christian point of view tend to focus much more strongly on either the source of the message or the message itself than they do on the receptors.[221]

Because messages are decoded based on the receptor's own experience, a large degree of shared experience between source and receptor increases the likelihood for accuracy in decoding the message. Daniel Shaw points out, "In most aspects of daily life, where common knowledge is assumed, effective communication is an expected result." [222] In multicultural contexts this shared experience is often absent, so the potential for misunderstanding a message is increased and communication becomes far less effective.

LaNette Thompson showed that knowledge is stored in the human mind as layer upon layer of schemata. For example, a simple code word or symbolic phrase such as "going shopping" signifies a group of subactivities which differ widely from one context to another. This array of schemata can be characterized as an information processing system.

> In *perception*, schemata assimilate incoming information, working to recognize and process input. In *memory*, schemata provide organization for memory storage.... In *recall*, schemata fill in the blanks of "what probably occurred" when information is missing (Mandler, et al. 1980, 19–20).[223]

This explains why the source and the receptor must have a degree of shared experience for communication to take place. Where there is no shared experience, the receptor will fill in the blanks with information that is accurate according to his or her own context, but which may not reflect the intent of the source.

The S.M.R. model highlights the difficulties inherent in cross-cultural communication. The farther apart the source and the receptor are culturally, the less likely it is for communication to be understood as the messenger intended. In this project, there was no possibility of shared experience with end users who were E-3 and beyond in relation to my own culture. Even for the storytellers themselves, the cultural distance to the receptors was often extreme. Jeetendra described tribal people whom he is trying to reach as having the appearance and character "just like animals." James Korkora told how the people he is working among even "offer human sacrifice in their fields at planting time." Kodanda said, "Where I am working … it is such a place, you can say that it is like Sodom and Gomorra. Even the parents encourage their sons and daughters to do bad things."*

In comments such as these one can perceive the stark cultural divide that separates these messengers from their intended receptors. What was needed was a model that not only diagnoses the problem but also offers a solution. This brings us to the third model, the Bicultural Bridge. Paul Hiebert maintained that the gospel primarily moves from one culture to another through interpersonal relationships. He pictured these relationships as a bicultural bridge. "Communication across the bicultural bridge takes place within the biculture: a new culture that arises in the interaction of people from two different cultural backgrounds."[224] Because it is impossible for either to enter fully into the culture of the other, a kind of halfway culture is created, one in which both can participate. "If communication is to take place between peoples of different cultures, a satisfactory biculture must be worked out in which both sides find a measure of mutual understanding and satisfaction…. It is here that the gospel and church are translated into a new culture."[225] While Hiebert was referring mainly to the relationship between western missionaries and national field leaders, he also seemed to recognize that such bicultures could be formed at different stages of the diffusion process thus creating a series of bicultural bridges.[226]

The oral Bible project was a bicultural training structure in line with Hiebert's model. The central training program itself was the first stage—a limited biculture of people from E-1 and E-2 cultures who were together for a total of 24 training days over 15 months. Through this and subsequent bicultural bridges, the stories were able to quickly move to the intended receptors at E-3 and beyond (Figure 14). These stages are marked GEN1 to GEN4 to represent the transfer of the biblical stories from one generation of learners to the next. At each stage the stories adapted to a new language and culture, but otherwise remained essentially the same.

---

* Oral reports; March 2006.

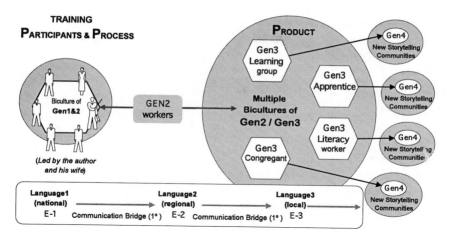

Figure 14. The Biculture Learning Model

There are many advantages to this model. It has the benefit of not extracting people from their own culture. The new village Christians will never have to enter the world of GEN1 that is at an E-3 distance from their own to receive leadership training. The implications are that it will be much easier to find and train people who are above average within their own sphere who might have performed poorly outside it. They will also be free to remain much more as their own people are instead of having to accomplish the extremely difficult task of adapting to a distant culture while remaining true to their own. Instead of extracting them from their network of friends, relatives, and acquaintances (as is the common practice), they learn to pass the gospel on and win others immediately. As more people are converted, the new storyteller naturally tends to become the leader. So this model has enormous potential to raise up new leaders from within the harvest instead of externally.

A major criticism against groups that rely on personal witness to share their faith—for example, the Pentecostals—has been that it tends to produce a weak theology. Hrangkhuma writes,

> Faith is spread through personal witness. However ... this also means that the depth of Christian nurture which should come after conversion may not always be adequate. It is mostly evangelism by the lay people, and although important, something more than this is needed for the deepening of faith and growth in the knowledge of the Word.[227]

Giving new converts biblical stories addresses this problem. Now they no longer have to rely on their testimony alone; instead, through knowing the stories they are also equipped to share significant portions of God's Word with others. In this way, not only the trained leaders, but every believer—from the smallest child right up to the oldest grandmother—can be an effective witness for Christ within their own sphere of influence. Dasrath related an incident that illustrates this:

> Once I visited a Hindu family and spent a long time sharing the creation story with them. I told them the whole story—how God created this universe, how God created human beings and how God blessed them. Because all this was new to them, I wanted to start from the beginning; otherwise they could not understand the stories and all. So I started from the creation story onward. They were very happy to listen. They had been worshipping other gods, but they had never heard a story like this. The story impressed their life so much that the head of that house, Mahrduthi, accepted Jesus Christ as his personal Savior. The next day Mahrduthi went to a tea shop and saw some of his friends gathered there. They were talking about their god Shankar. Mahrduthi listened to everything they were saying, and then he spoke to them like this, "See, you said that Shankar is god. But I want to share a story with you." So Mahrduthi told them the creation story from the Bible. They answered, "We never heard a story like this. It's a wonderful story. From this story, we get a clear idea about the creation of human beings." So they were very impressed by hearing this story and some of them believed that, "This is a true story; this is how God created everything." (January 2008)

This approach also allows the church to take on the cultural characteristics of the people in which it is being planted, instead of being seen as a foreign implant. Donald McGavran argued that most opposition to the gospel is not on theological grounds at all:

> The resistance of most Hindus, Buddhists, and Muslims to the Christian faith does not arise primarily from theological considerations.... Most Hindus are more animist then Hindu; the same may be said for each of the other major religions. Their resistance arises primarily from fear that "becoming a Christian will separate me from my people".

> Most opposition to the Christian religion arises not from theological but from sociological causes. Individuals resist separating themselves

from their own people to join another. This arouses their emotions. They then look around for reasons to back up their feelings of fear and disgust, and announce that they reject Christianity because of some theological weakness in it.... They refuse Christ not for religious reasons, or because they love their sins, but precisely because they love their neighbors.[228]

Because the biculture model allows for adaptation at each stage, when the message arrives at the respondent it does not seem foreign. Thus it minimizes one of the major reasons people may reject Christ.

GENERATION 1

The story chain of transfer began with five trainers: my wife and I, and three Indian nationals: Laren, Nileswar and Ismail. Teresa and I know a little of the national language, Hindi, but our teaching, storytelling and coaching were typically done in English and then translated into other languages by one or more interpreters.

Laren is from the same region as the largest group of storyteller trainees, so he speaks their regional language and understands their culture. This became a significant factor in how well the men from that region performed in the program; their attrition rate was the lowest of any of the learning groups. The other two trainers, Ismail and Nileswar, came from two different tribes in the northeast, and for them the centralized training was a significant cultural/linguistic leap.

Ismail is a young man from the Santal tribe. In the two years he spent at a Bible school, he became competent in English and the Hindi language. Nevertheless, he struggled to make the adjustment to serving as a leader in the oral Bible program. Consequently his learning groups ended up having the most dropouts. Ismail's learning groups were comprised of Hindi-speaking trainees.

Nileswar, who is from the Bodo tribe, is a mature Christian worker in his mid-fifties. Of the three Indian trainers, he had the most difficulty adjusting to the culture. The food at the training location was excessively spicy and greasy, and he was often sick. He had seldom traveled outside his own region before, and struggled to speak the national language. His learning groups were the most difficult linguistically, consisting of trainees who were learning to tell the stories in five different languages. Despite these challenges, Nileswar proved to be an effective trainer. He is a dramatic storyteller; his use of gesture, voice and facial expression added greatly to his storytelling performance. His contribution to the overall program was to model enthusiastic and dramatic storytelling.

GENERATION 2

The GEN2 trainees were described in chapter seven. The 61 men and one woman who attended the training events came from eight different Indian states.* They spoke a total of 20 different languages. Besides tribal and regional languages, most had varying abilities to speak either Hindi or English.

Attending the training modules was difficult because of the huge distances most had to travel. For many it took more than 48 hours each way by bus and train, which meant leaving their families and churches for an entire week. Another difficulty arose because the oral Bible project's duration was extended. Originally planned to last only four training modules (60 stories), this was lengthened to six modules plus a final exam module (100 stories). This meant that instead of a commitment of less than a year, the participants would have to spend almost two years completing the program. Furthermore, in the first year of the program—before it was extended—the rule was that anyone who missed a training module was dropped from the program. This was because each module equated to two months of work which was impossible to make up. In light of this, it was nothing less than remarkable that over half the trainees would eventually complete the training and become competent biblical storytellers.[†] The statistics show some of the variables in a training program such as this. Both trainer skills and composition of the group itself affected outcome (see Table 5):

Table 5. Project attrition rate during the first 14 months

TRAINER:	Laren		Nileswar		Ismail		Batch A	Batch B
BATCH [‡]	Start	Drop	Start	Drop	Start	Drop		
A	13	1	9	2	10	5		
B	14	4	7	3	9	6		
TOTALS	27	5	16	5	19	11		
ATTRITION	18.5%		31.25%		57.9%		25%	41%

---

* The agency's strategy was to train at least two storytellers from every division so they could go back and teach the adult literacy workers to tell the stories (see next section: Generation 3).
† Forty-one storytellers successfully completed the six modules of training. Of these, 33 returned six months later to take the comprehensive exams; 29 received diplomas while three received certificates of completion.
‡ Because of the large number of participants, I divided the trainees into two batches. Every training module was given twice, first for Batch A, then for Batch B, back-to-back. This was a grueling schedule that required the trainers to do 80 hours of training in just nine days time. It was necessary because the trainers themselves came from another part of the country, traveling almost three days each way.

GENERATION 3

The GEN3 storytellers were in two categories. First were the personal storytelling apprentices recruited and trained by each GEN2 storyteller. Every participant was required to train at least one other person as a storyteller. Some trained a family member such as their wife or one of their children. For example, one minister taught the stories to his nonliterate wife as she prepared meals each day. Others trained a member of their own church or even a non-Christian. Much of this training was done in informal ways, such as spending an hour or two together or taking the apprentice along on ministry rounds. Sudhir gave this report:

> After completing the first training module, I went back to my ministry place. There is a family of tribal people living there who has a teenage son named Purushtum. I always used to stop by and take him along. While he was with me, we were always talking, just making conversation about nothing. But slowly, I started to tell him the Bible stories which we learned here.

> After telling all those stories, one day I told him again about the story of Noah. Then I explained a little bit about the story to him: "Just like in this story, the people nowadays are also like this. They are disobedient to God, they are living in worldly pleasure and they are forgetting God. But the judgment of God will come to them at last." So after explaining some things like this out of these stories that youth understood.

> Since he was always coming with me, the two of us became very good friends. His family members were all Hindus so they were not at all happy for their son to go with me. But whenever I went to storytelling ministry, he would faithfully accompany me. Nowadays I have a bicycle, so Purushtum would pedal the bicycle, and I would sit on the back and tell him the stories as we were going here and there, different places. After that, he received Jesus Christ as his personal savior and he took water baptism. And he is my first disciple. (October 2006).

Some storytellers took a more formal approach to setting up a teacher-disciple relationship, much like the Hindu "guru-disciple" model. Sunil Kumar's account illustrates this:

One day I went to a family and told them the Bible stories. There was a woman listening nearby who appeared to be a prostitute. So I told the story about Rahab, and she listened very carefully. Later she came to me and asked, "Pastor, is it true that God likes such people?" I told her, "Yes." She answered, "Now I can understand that God loves everyone. He even loves people like us. God never despises even the sinners."

That woman was from a nominal Christian background. But she was not walking with God and she never attended church. After I told this story, she started coming to the church regularly, and when she became so interested to listen to the Bible stories, I told her other stories, too. I taught her the New Testament story about the woman who was a sinner and whom the people were trying to stone.

One day I asked her, "Now that you have learned the stories and are attending the church regularly, will you tell the stories to others? Do you want to be my storytelling disciple?" And she said, "Yes, I am ready to be a storyteller disciple. And I will tell the stories to others also." Now she is one of my disciples. And for one year she has become a regular attender of my church and is telling the stories to others. (October 2006).

The first training module was given in February 2006. By the third module in October, the 50 storytellers who remained in the program reported a total of 114 new GEN3 storytellers that they were training one-on-one.

A huge advantage of storytelling the Bible is that it immediately equips brand-new believers to be effective witnesses while their relationships with non-Christian friends, relatives, neighbors and business associates are still strong and vital. Donald McGavran called such relationships the "bridges of God" because they allow the gospel to spread throughout a community.[229] By means of these relationship bridges, evangelism can occur out to the fringes of each new believer's social network. Hearing a Bible story, a villager can come to Christ one day, and on the very next day effectively witness to others by simply repeating that same story. Often the new converts will already have been learning the stories even before they were converted. Sekhar Rao tells about a teenage boy named Srabon who became quite popular because of the stories he was telling:

After coming to the first storytelling training, I went back to my village and taught all the stories we had learned here. Before that, I had tried to preach there but preaching did not work. But when I told the stories to one of my ninth grade tutoring students, Srabon, he shared the stories with his parents. His parents said, "It will be very nice if we will learn the stories in between your tutoring classes."

Then Srabon went and shared the stories with many of his friends, and he brought friends to tutoring class to listen to the stories. All of them are Hindu, but they are enjoying learning the stories—they like them. Then Srabon went house to house telling the stories, and other people also called him to come and tell the stories to them.

After seeing this, I feel very happy because I had been trying so hard to preach to them, even though they were not listening. But now through the stories, many people are eager to listen. And that boy wants to come with me. But I am not taking him with me. Whichever stories I am telling, every story I tell, then that boy is telling it to others, and people are inviting him to come. So he is going house to house and he is telling the stories everywhere. (October 2006).

The second category of GEN3 storytellers consisted of 359 literacy workers who, as part of the oral Bible project, were hired to give literacy classes in remote villages. The adult education (AdEd) project was conceived as a way to establish a Christian presence in areas with strong resistance to Christianity, something that is especially prevalent in the Hindu heartland of the country. By providing a service the villagers would consider valuable, it was intended to be a nonthreatening gateway for the gospel.

The AdEd program was done in tandem with the oral Bible project and lasted nine months. The initial goal was to give literacy classes in 500 villages that had high levels of orality. As Hindu or animistic villagers learned the alphabet, little by little they also heard Bible stories that were recounted to them by the literacy workers. By avoiding artifacts associated with Christianity such as Bibles and hymnals, by not preaching or teaching, and through offering a needed service, these workers were able to sidestep much of the usual resistance to traditional evangelistic approaches.* As the literacy workers made friends in the villages through their nonthreatening role and the villagers heard firsthand the stories from the Scriptures unimpeded by their prejudices, many came to faith in Christ and scores of new congregations were the result.

---

* Although often fierce, this persecution is mostly a superficial reaction based on ignorance of what Christianity actually means.

Some of these literacy workers/biblical storytellers were lay Christians recruited from established churches while others were Hindu pre-Christians. All learned the stories together in regional monthly training sessions that lasted two or three days. They were taught by the storytellers who were receiving training in the central oral Bible program. Using identical training techniques of learning groups, drama, story-song and field assignments, a team of several storytellers would teach a group of up to 50 village literacy teachers the stories they had learned themselves.* P. K. Mishal describes how this worked in his division:

> I am thankful that our division is much blessed through this storytelling program. Four of us who are in this storytelling program are training 50 AdEd teachers. We divide them to give 12 students to each of these four storytellers. Not only that, each of us is also personally making one-on-one disciples. Those disciples also are learning from us and when they go back to their homes, they are telling the stories to others also. (October 2006).

Luke Kumar also told about his AdEd program:

> I have 35 storytelling disciples. I always teach them the stories with action and songs for three days during our monthly meetings. Nearly every person that I taught has also taught the stories to another. One of the disciples is conducting adult education classes near our church where he is telling the stories to more than 15 older men and women who are non-Christians. There are also about 30 children in that class, from both believing and nonbelieving backgrounds. (October 2006).

A last example is from Benjamin Pani. He reported,

> I told the stories to three women in a mountain area. After hearing these stories, they came and gave me money to buy a Bible for them. Before that they had no Bible. But when I told them these stories, now they are asking me for a Bible, because they are very eager to learn the word of God. One day I mentioned to my field leader that there were three women who wanted to teach the Bible stories to others. He told me to immediately appoint them as literacy workers

---

* Besides sharing the teaching load, team teaching has the added benefit of providing encouragement and motivation and of keeping the told stories accurate in a community of storytellers. The fact that the central training was structured to be led by a team of trainers instead of just one person modeled team teaching for the storytellers.

so they will tell the stories as well as teach literacy in the AdEd centers. Now after six months, they are serving as adult education teachers and they are strong in their faith and have also taken water baptism. Previously in that mountain area our church only had 12 believers. But now because of this storytelling program 40 people are attending our Sunday services. (October 2006).

Most of the married storytellers told the stories to their own families, and often their family members also learned to tell them. For example, Sunil Kumar said, "Again and again, I have been learning these Bible stories during these training events. When I go back home the first thing I do is tell all the stories to my wife and my two children." (January 2007). In the storytellers' accounts of divine provision for their financial needs, it is especially evident that story took center place in the discipling of the minister's family.* By the final training module, the participants reported that they had taught their wives to tell an average of 28 of the stories they had learned in training.

GENERATION 4

Even in the relatively short time frame of this project, it was possible to document many results that occurred at a GEN4 distance. Among these were many conversions and the creation of new storytellers and biblical storytelling communities. The diffusion of stories was happening in many different ways. Perhaps the best way to get a glimpse of the broad spectrum of these results is to offer reports from the storytellers themselves. Pitambar gives an example of how his storytelling resulted in three new GEN4 storytellers through his GEN3 disciple Naalini:

When I am going to make disciples, when I am telling stories, I look to see those who are listening and giving attention to me. Also, I am studying whether they are persevering. If so, then I can make them a disciple. Even when I am telling stories to non-Christian people, I am alert to see if I can make any disciples from among those nonbelievers.

Once when I was telling a story in a village, I noticed an 18 year old girl who was listening to the stories. Naalini became my disciple and I taught her all 27 of the stories.† I found that she is active and always

---

* See Appendix J:1b, 4a-4c.
† At this point in the course, the participants had finished the Old Testament portion of the story track and were just starting to learn the New Testament stories.

ready to tell stories. When I am speaking or sharing stories, she is always listening attentively and she is courageous to share the stories with other people. The disciples tell stories to both Christian and Gentile [non-Christian] people. When Naalini is telling a story, the Gentile people are eagerly coming and sitting together and listening and observing what God has done. Then those who are seeking to know the stories can also tell the stories to their own people. When she goes to tell the stories, my disciple Naalini also selects people to make into disciples. She has made three disciples from the tribal people. One is Porja, one is from the Bhatra people, and the other is a Harijan. (October 2006).

Phelemon tells how a GEN4 storyteller in his downline started a new congregation:

After I told the story of Naaman in my church, a believer who was there went and told that Naaman story to a woman in his village. Her name is Mahade. She was sick and very weak and was suffering much pain. As he shared the story, he told her, "God will heal you." After telling the story, he prayed for her. Then she was able to get healed and after that she started coming to church. Next she told the story to another man nearby, and after sharing this story, they started a church. (February 2007).

Ramesh's wife was one of his GEN3 storyteller disciples. He explains how she made GEN4 storytellers of children in their Sunday School:

I made another disciple who is my wife. Many children come to our Sunday worship. During the preaching time I ask her to take the children to the other side of the church where she teaches them the stories. Now my wife has already formed a small group who are going and telling the stories door-to-door. (October 2006).

There were instances of children hearing the stories and going home and telling the stories to their parents. Ramesh gives one example:

My ministry is mostly among tribal people. Their language is different and they are totally illiterate. Once a week I visit a village where I conduct a Christian worship service. Some of the tribal families there worship the god Shiva. When we conduct the worship, those people never come. When I told the stories to the children of the believers, the Hindu children also started coming to listen. At first, the Shiva worshipping parents strictly forbad their children from going to the storytelling program. But some of them were attending the children's group anyway. After listening to my stories, these children went back and started telling the stories to their parents. Then their parents called for me to come to their homes and they started listening to the stories from me. They have not yet come to faith, but I believe in coming days they will. (October 2006).

In another instance, Prakash relates how a story that was carried home by children transformed a family:

I am ministering in a village where most of the people are rigid Hindu people. They are not at all believing in Jesus and they are not ready to take his name, and they oppose Christians. I started conducting a small tutoring class to help the children with their schoolwork. I shared the story of Cain and Abel with them, and that story really touched their hearts. So after that, the children went home and told that story to their own families.

Now there was a man living there who had two wives. His grown children were always fighting and arguing over how his land was going to be divided among them. So there was no peace or joy in that family. The next day, two women from that family came to my home and asked me to tell them that story. So I went with them and shared the story of Cain and Abel in their home. And God did a work in their lives, because that story really touched their hearts. And they started to think and discuss among themselves, "Every day, we are quarreling and arguing over this land. And there is no peace and joy in our lives."

So the next day, they came to me and said, "We don't want this land; let them take it. But we want peace and joy in our family." There are many brothers in that family. One of those brothers is named Govind Bagh; he and his family have now started attending my church. There are five people in his family and now all five are ready to take baptism. (April 2006).

Often, seemingly spectacular results occurred among GEN4 hearers. Bibhuti tells of a dramatic encounter in which one of his GEN3 storytelling disciples won an entire village to the Lord:

After learning the Bible stories, I went back to my field and taught them to some new storytellers I am training there. One of my storyteller disciples is a man named Podunga. One day he went to a village where there is an old shrine the villagers had made for themselves out of stones placed together. They worshipped at that shrine—the goddesses were staying there. This was making trouble for the whole village so they had no peace and comfort.

Now when this man Podunga (who had learned the stories from me) saw the situation, he called to one of the men and said, "Brother, can you listen to me? If so, then I will tell you a story." The man was eager to hear it. (The village people love to listen to stories). So Podunga told him the story from 1 Kings 18 about Elijah and the challenge of the idol priests at Mount Carmel. He told how God answered with fire and afterward Elijah tore down the pagan altars. As the villagers listened to the story, faith came to them. And so they asked Podunga, "Can you do this?" He answered, "Yes, I can do it, if you will help me."

A family was staying near that shrine and taking care of it. But the children in that family were dying one after the other. They were eager to agree because they wanted deliverance from that problem. So they told Podunga to do it. They helped him tear the shrine down—together they tore it down completely. Afterward it was reported that the villagers saw a woman going away from the village and she was weeping as she went. She was not someone from that village—the villagers say she was the ghost of that shrine.

After that, Podunga prayed for all of them. Twenty-five families there came to faith in Christ. Recently my coordinator came to baptize them. I praise God that through the stories, God can do this kind of thing also. There are about 120 people living in that village, about 25 families. So nearly the entire village came to the Lord. (January 2007).

THE ADULT EDUCATION COMPONENT

Most of the previous examples relate to storytelling that took place in the normal context of ministry and life. The second leg of this project was the AdEd program. As was mentioned earlier, adult education classes were held in 359 locations during the oral Bible project. Many were in unreached villages known to be resistant to traditional evangelism. Classes were held three nights a week for at least an hour. As the illiterate village people learned to write the alphabet, they also listened to storytellers recount the mighty works of a God of love unlike any god they had ever known. As a result, over nine months 34 new churches were planted, each having at least seven newly baptized members (some were much larger). But beyond that, 182 other new congregations were also started. These were groups that did not yet have enough baptized members to be considered an official church.* Also, 28 new full-time workers were selected from the best of the adult education teachers and sent for Bible training. It was expected that afterward they will return to lead some of the new congregations.

This impossible thing—who did this thing?

My name is Bhibuti. Once I went to a village where no one knows Christ at all. There was no one there to listen to me, only a small girl from that village who came to listen. I began to tell her the stories that I learned here. And then I shared the story about Sarah, how she had been barren, but finally had a child called Isaac at the age of 90 years.

This was amazing to the little girl who was listening to me, because at this age, no one can give birth to a son or daughter.

She asked, "This impossible thing—who did this thing?"

So I slowly shared with her that only Christ can do this; no other person can do these things. So she told me to tell something more about Christ. So I shared with her, and ultimately, she came to accept Jesus as her personal Savior. The girl's name is Payanti.

---

* This data is conservative. The report from which it was taken included the results from only 14 divisions. Four other divisions where AdEd programs were being conducted in at least 58 villages were inadvertently left out of the report. By extrapolation, the above statistics could be as much as 16% more than is reflected in this data.

Section Three

FINDINGS FROM THE RESEARCH

Chapter 10

OUTCOMES THAT EMERGED FROM THE PROGRAM

All human beings have an innate
need to hear and tell stories and
to have a story to live by.

–HARVEY COX

In this section we will look specifically at findings from three research instruments that address the project's primary objective of using biblical storytelling for knowledge transfer among peoples of oral cultures.

The first instrument is a database comprised of verbatim reports collected from the GEN2 storytellers. More than 250 pages were digitally recorded, translated and transcribed. From these, I identified and coded 50 themes, of which a number have been selected for in-depth treatment in this book. The second research instrument is a follow-up questionnaire that was submitted to 54 agency field leaders in 18 divisions where this project was applied. A third set of research findings was gathered during the comprehensive exams that were administered to thirty-three of the storytellers and twenty-two of their apprentices at the end of the program.

VERBATIM REPORTS FROM THE PARTICIPANTS

Two or three times during each training module opportunities were given for telling "personal faith stories" about specific events that had occurred because of telling the biblical stories during the previous weeks. Some of the participants were eager to share during every training module; all eventually contributed at least one account of something that had resulted from telling a Bible story. The storytellers would give the account in a regional language and afterward it would be translated into Hindi and then into English; 166 of these verbatims were recorded and transcribed.

Since these reports were collected during class time as public testimonies, they are far from comprehensive. Language barriers also hindered us from getting as deep a description as I wished. Nevertheless the accounts provided a remarkable window into how biblical stories functioned in the areas where the storytellers lived and ministered. My belief is that the applications, responses and themes that they revealed are representative of what follows the telling and hearing of biblical stories in these contexts.

After coding the entire database of reports, I first tried to discern the main theme/themes in each account by asking myself, "What story was this participant telling?" When several accounts were told together (which happened fairly often), each incident was treated as a separate narrative. In this way each theme could be tabulated by the number of narratives that focused on that category. Categories that I judged to be extraneous were not included in this first tabulation. The results are shown in Table 6.*

Table 6
Coded Themes by Number of Accounts

THEME	CODE	Number of Times
Adult education program	ADED	19
Church growth / church multiplication results	CHGR	32
Comparing storytelling with more conventional approaches to ministry	PRCH	18
Conversion results	CNVR	45
Family of the storyteller	FMLY	12
Felt need: for physical healing	FLHL	26
Felt need: for finances	FLT$	16
Felt need: childlessness	FCHD	15
Felt need: for peace in human relationships	FGHT	12

---

* Since many accounts had more than one theme, the total exceeds the number of accounts. See Appendix I for explanations of each of the themes that were coded.

THEME	CODE	Number of Times
Felt need: people raised from the dead	FDTH	3
Felt need: instances of demonic presence in a home/village	FDMN	3
Felt need: for help with school (final/placement exams)	FXAM	1
Felt need: fear (in this case, of a demonic presence in the home)	FLFR	1
Felt need: witchcraft curse *	FWTC	0
Felt need: other (water, food, protection, abandonment, and a sick cow)	FOTR	5
Judgment stories (instances of telling stories of God's judgment on sin)	JUDG	10
Making new storytellers	CHEL	25
Money (storytelling that led to monetary offerings for the storyteller)	$$$$	5
Personal application by storyteller (healing, forgiveness, encouragement, etc.)	PRSNL	14
Resistance to the gospel (that was overcome by biblical storytelling)	RSIS	20
Telling to children	CHLD	8
Transformed individuals or families	TRSF	7

In addition to those listed above, some themes were important to the transfer and functioning of the biblical stories at a GEN3 and GEN4 level. I will treat some of these below. Appendix J provides other relevant examples and more instances. †

Application of Story

Application of story was mentioned 45 times. It was seen mainly in two types of interactions: a) what the storyteller said after telling the story, or b) what the listener understood it to mean. Often this took the form of concrete

---

* Despite the fact that witchcraft curses did not appear in the verbatims of the oral Bible project, it is a common belief that when there is misfortune it is because someone paid a witch to put a curse on one's family or oneself. Many women (and some men) in India are killed each year after being accused of being witches. This was more evident in the research done during the pilot project when lay people including women and teens were in the program.
† See also Index of Verbatims.

comparisons: "In the same way …" or, "We should be like …" or, "We should not be like …"

Some members of Arepally's congregation presented a dramatization of the Hannah story (1 Sam. 1, 2), and many people from the village came to watch. One man had gone to witch doctors many times because he and his wife were barren; he had magic amulets tied around his neck, his waist, and his hands. He and his wife, Vanitha, had been married for seven years without being able to have children. After hearing the Hannah story they said to Arepally:

> Sir, now we have believed in Jesus Christ. We had wandered to so many doctors and witch doctors. But we could not find any serenity in our life. And no one could give us any children. But today we have really recognized how God gave a child to Hannah. And we believe God will make a miracle in every life. So like that we believe just like the story of Hannah. We believe just like Hannah believed. Since we have heard and seen these stories from you, from now on we will not go anywhere else. We will no longer go to the witch doctors, nor to the hospitals, nor to the doctors. Because now we believe in Jesus Christ. So we will pray to Him for a child like Hannah. (January 2007).*

Simon Pargi's accounts seem to point to a high degree of intentional story selection that matched application to specific needs. Where there was a sick water *buffalo* he told the story of Jacob's flocks (Gen. 30:29ff); where a person had died he told stories about people who had been raised from the dead (1 Kings 17; 2 Kings 4; Luke 16:19–31); where there was a problem getting water he told the story of Isaac's wells (Gen. 26).† This use of story also connects with the related theme of felt need.

A storyteller may recognize a need of which a listener is unaware, especially if the storyteller has had a similar experience. This could also be a prophetic function which manifests itself as a denunciation of evil practices. For instance, Bibhuti recounted this story about his disciple, Patras, who told the Abraham/Lot story (Gen. 13:2–18) to some idolaters:

> He told them that Abraham was not getting the blessings from God because he never left behind the former things. "When God spoke to Abraham he made it clear that unless you will leave the former

---

* Two months after hearing this story and placing their faith in Christ, Vanitha and her husband became pregnant with their first child.

† See Appendix J:1a for the complete account of these incidents.

ways, such as the worship of idols and your nephew, you cannot receive God's blessings. Because," he told them, "the former things such as idolatry are a hindrance to God. You will not be able to receive the blessings of God unless you leave those ways behind." So all those people believed. Now they have left those former practices behind, and these 10 to 15 people are coming to church. (January 2007).

A biblical story becomes a basis for faith. Much as a literate Christian might quote a favorite promise, the storytellers tell a favorite Bible story. For them, a conceptual statement does not carry the same power as a story which shows by example what God will do in a particular situation. Prashant was teaching the stories to an illiterate well-digger named Champala. One day while Champala was laying brick on an open well that he had been digging, he slipped. As he was falling 30 feet to the bottom, a Bible story flashed into his mind—he remembered how Joseph's brothers threw Joseph into a well (Genesis 37). Instantly he prayed, "Lord, just like you protected Joseph, you can protect me!" Miraculously when he hit the bottom of the well, he was not killed; in fact, he was not injured at all. (February 2007). A catalog of Bible stories that are instantly accessible no matter the time of day or night or the severity of the situation, equips believers to respond effectively to opportunities, challenges and dangers.

The manner in which the storytellers applied the biblical texts concurs with Ong's description of one of the characteristics of thought and expression of oral people: thought is conceptualized and then expressed in ways that are "close to the human lifeworld, assimilating the alien, objective world to the more immediate, familiar interaction of human beings." [230] A mark of oral learners is that they do not trust conclusions based on abstract or propositional statements. It is firsthand experience—either personal or vicarious—that makes something concrete, hence trustworthy. N. T. Wright would categorize their approach to understanding the stories as either pre-critical or one of naive realism because through the stories they believe they are gaining access to the actual event itself. [231] A common question from first-time listeners of a Bible story, was, "Is this a real story?" Once they are satisfied that it is a real story they are comfortable identifying with the character or characters and believing that this God could do something similar for them.

In contrast to scholarly hermeneutics based on detailed grammatical analysis of the texts in their original historical contexts, oral culture believers typically follow a common sense or plain meanings approach to interpreting the Scriptures. Mark Ellingsen asserts that an approach free of an "alien interpretive framework of preunderstanding" is the best way to let the biblical stories speak to us:

> To insist that narrative texts have an autonomous meaning, not contingent upon the interpreter's perspective is ... a way of guaranteeing the public character of theology and preaching. On such grounds, all persons, regardless of their view of Christian faith, are equally qualified to enter into the dialogue to identify the meaning of Scripture. The biblical narrative model aims to proclaim an intelligible, publicly accessible Word.[232]

In fact, in light of the down-to-earth nature of the Scriptures, the common man is perhaps the one best fitted to interpret them. It is the practical experience and exposure to the forge of everyday life in a specific context that produces the tensions in which theology must be formed to be truly relevant and meaningful to those who live there. The unschooled believer who is familiar with his or her own culture will often have a better sense for the meaning of the Biblical text within that culture than even the best-trained outsider. The deep spiritual insights of even new converts on the mission field bear witness to this.

Comparisons of Storytelling with Other Methods

In oral contexts, conventional ways of teaching the Bible have often proven inadequate. Some of the more serious drawbacks include incongruence with local learning styles and consequent lack of comprehension and reproducibility. Language barriers may be a significant deterrent to the use of written training materials compounded by the need for a high level of literacy. Furthermore, particular teaching methods can cause resistance simply because of their foreignness.

Storyteller Sudhir had studied for two years in Bible School before entering the oral Bible program. He gave the following account of the contrast between the two approaches:

> Most of the people in my church are uneducated. Whenever I preached, they could not understand; some would get bored. But when I came back from the story program, I began to tell them the stories and they listened with great interest. One evening I was conducting a cottage meeting at a home. It was mostly adults who were there. After worship I asked them, "Now I will preach—or shall I tell a story?" And they all shouted, "No, no, no! Now, you can tell the story." They are very happy to hear the stories. After I tell the story, if I ask them, "How was it today?" They say, "Today the story was very nice, very wonderful.

We understand it." And they are also telling it to others.

During the rainy season, when the tribal people go to the rice fields to work, sometimes I go and speak to them. The people gather and eagerly listen to my words as I share stories with them. Sometimes I just stand there and talk with them. Then they say, "Sir, please tell us those stories again, those stories which you shared with us before, last week or some day before. We are really touched by them." (January 2008).

Upakari is from an area with very low literacy. After attending Bible school for three years, he started an outreach to a village by trying to reach the children. He told how storytelling is transforming his ministry.

When I began I was not in this Bible story program. I was thinking, "Through these children we can reach the parents." I even gave them some toys. At first 10 to 15 children came to hear me. I took my Bible, I read my Bible and I started to talk to them from the Bible. Afterward the village people were asking the children, "That new fellow, what was he telling you?" The children answered, "He took his black book, a big book, he read from it and he started talking." Now after telling their parents this, the children stopped coming to my house. After some time, I became discouraged thinking that what I had felt in my heart would not happen after all.

Some time later my coordinator called me and said, "You have to go for storytelling training." So I came and joined this program. After finishing the training last time, I went back to that village. I was thinking to myself, "How can I tell these stories to the children? I cannot invite them to my home. If I invite the children to my house, their parents will scold me and make me leave the village."

So I went to an athletic field where some people were playing sports and the children were watching. I sat with the children and started to speak with them. Slowly I began to share a small story. Suddenly the people who were watching the game stopped watching and came towards me. So I quickly finished the story and went home. That evening I was out, but the next morning when I awoke from my sleep some children came to me saying, "Oh, yesterday evening we came to your house. Uncle, where had you gone?" And I said, "You children, why did you come to my house?" They answered, "We wanted to listen to the same story you told us at the athletic field!"

Now every day the people come. They are not my church members—
they are Gentiles [non-believers]. But every day up to 20 of these
children gather to listen to the stories. So every day I tell the stories
and the children like them very much. And some of them are already
telling the stories to their parents. (March 2008).

Following are two lists that present unsolicited comparisons between
storytelling and other Christian methods such as preaching, teaching,
tracts, films, witnessing and Bible reading. These descriptions by 27 different
storytellers establish a strong rationale for the use of storytelling in place of
more commonly accepted methods. The summaries are compiled from the
storytellers' observations and comments.*

The subjects have an average of 13 years of formal education, so they
can speak authoritatively about the relative effectiveness of literate methods
in their own contexts. The fact that preaching was the main focus of their
comparison is to be expected because preaching is a verbal presentation
of the gospel that, on the surface at least, corresponds more directly to
storytelling than other methods mentioned here. These testimonials show
the power of stories in transcending barriers of orality, language, and
religious resistance.

Disadvantages of Conventional Methods in Oral Contexts

1. In many areas religious resistance to Christian preaching is strong.
    People reject tracts and preaching. Carrying a Bible or using it to
    preach is a red flag for anti-Christian groups.
2. People who are unaccustomed to reading find preaching
    uninteresting. They do not like listening to it. They cannot
    understand sermons that use abstract or propositional
    terminology such as is taught in Bible school. This can cause
    Christian workers to become discouraged. "People would come
    for worship and then leave when the sermon started. But after I
    started telling the Bible stories, everyone began to stay and listen.
    In fact, now they are so eager to learn the latest story (and story-
    song) that they come an hour early!"
3. Sermons are difficult to recall and repeat. One pastor testified
    that even after hearing an excellent sermon he would be unable

---

* See Appendix H for the actual verbatims and summaries from which these two lists were
compiled.

to remember it later when he needed it. "Those messages were not working in my heart. But whenever I am going through a problem, then I am reminded of the stories and this gives me courage and brings faith in my heart."

4. Among lifelong Christians, there is often a bias in favor of preaching.* However new believers often find sermons baffling. The resulting boredom and lack of interest can cause them to stop attending the church.

5. Literate forms of communication enjoy a high degree of status. Since nonliterate communication is commonly associated with the poor and uneducated, one reason that ministers may be slow to embrace storytelling is a fear of what other Christians will think.

6. A literate model of worship causes uneducated believers to feel shamed. By not being able to read they are disenfranchised and unable to fully take part in the life of the church.†

7. In areas with multiple languages, vocabulary in common use is limited to words related to familiar everyday activities. Consequently, the reservoir of words that can be understood by an average listener is small. Languages like Hindi and even more so, the tribal languages, have insufficient words to express theological concepts. This makes it particularly difficult to preach a sermon. But because story does not depend on individual words but on a structure built from elements such as plot, action, dialogue, characterization, crisis and resolution, stories are simple to articulate and easily transfer from language to language even with limited vocabulary.

8. Ministers can be very intense and may even shout and use forceful gestures when preaching. Sometimes it seems to listeners that they are angry. Storytelling draws on a different set of skills, so it is easier to speak in a way that is attractive to listeners.

Advantages of Storytelling in Oral Contexts

1. Biblical storytellers have no need to carry their Bibles because the stories are in their hearts. So they are welcomed even in places where religious resistance to Christians is strong.

2. Storytelling attracts people to the church regardless of their religious

---

* This does not necessarily mean they are able to understand, remember and repeat the sermons. Rather it is akin to the preference for the Latin mass among older Catholics. Sermons are a comforting religious form identified through centuries as the "correct" way to do church.

† See Appendix J:9b

affiliation. They attend regularly and listen with much interest. Stories are particularly attractive to people of low literacy. "Before this when I was just preaching, the people from outside were not listening. But when I started to tell the stories, Hindu people also came to listen."

3. Storytelling is an excellent way to communicate the Bible to both Christians and non-Christians. Ministers often fail to realize the degree to which preaching has become an elite medium. It has its own unique vocabulary, hermeneutics, and presuppositions making it largely incomprehensible to the uninitiated. In contrast, a Bible story told using the vernacular is a communication form that anyone can understand.

4. Storytelling helps people recall what was taught. They can easily remember the stories including all the details. "When I started learning the stories, the first thing that happened was a miracle that took place in my own life. All those chapters and things which we have been learning, they have all been printed in my mind."

5. One of storytelling's strongest dynamics is its unique ability to foster relationships between Christians and non-Christians. These friendships become bridges between unchurched people and the Christian community. "Many times I went there and shared the gospel. But they are very new people so I had not talked much with them. But through telling them these stories, now I am getting to know the people very well."

6. Storytelling is an excellent way to center conversations around the Bible and spiritual things instead of just making "small talk," thereby redeeming the time.

7. Storytelling is highly effective for enfolding and discipling new believers. It is easy for them to tell the stories in turn to their own network of acquaintances and family. Even little children can take the stories home and tell them to their parents and siblings, awakening their interest in the Bible as well.

8. Storytelling is an excellent way for a pastor to help his own wife and children learn the Bible.

9. Storytelling enables the biblical storyteller to understand the passage deeply and communicate it well

10. Storytelling equips new leaders effectively even in low-literacy contexts. Regardless of their reading level, they can lead the church by telling selected biblical stories.

11. Storytelling enables every church member to know the Bible. Even nonliterate people can understand deep spiritual truths and grow spiritually through the stories.
12. Church members who cannot get anything from sermons are able to easily understand the biblical stories and can then go out and tell them to others.
13. Storytelling makes it possible for readers and nonreaders alike to fully participate in the life of the church. This attracts nonliterate people to the church. One pastor uses an interactive format to encourage listeners to talk about the story—some members are literate and others are not, but the story method makes it possible for everyone to take part.
14. Storytelling makes it easy for lay believers to carry on the ministry when the pastor is away. Sermon preparation is a specialized skill, but telling stories is something all are capable of doing well.
15. Storytelling promotes church multiplication through the spontaneous development of new home groups and church plants.
16. Storytelling has power to bring about personal transformation in ways that sermons do not.[*]
17. People who have never responded to witnessing respond to stories.
18. Through hearing the Bible stories, believers who previously had little interest in reading the Bible begin to discuss it and read it for themselves.
19. Telling and listening to a story from God's Word can become a sacramental moment in which the reality of God's presence is experienced in a very real way. One pastor remarked, "When my wife tells the stories in Sunday School, then the children are very happy, as they are in the presence of God then." Another said, "After that Christmas storytelling program, four new families have been coming to church to sit in the presence of the Lord."
20. In these contexts, good storytelling can even compete with films. When storytellers told biblical stories during a Jesus film showing, they found that some people liked the storytelling even better than the film.

---

[*] See example in Appendix J:7b.

The Interface of Orality and Literacy

Few Bible storying projects work in a purely oral culture in which there is a complete absence of literacy.* Most oral societies have at least a few members who can read to some degree. Walter Ong speaks of levels of orality within cultures:

> Long after the invention of script and even of print, distinctively oral forms of thought and expression linger, competing with the fo.ms introduced with script and print. Cultures in which this is the case can be referred to as radically oral, largely oral, residually oral, and so on through various degrees ... of orality.[233]

Jack Goody believes that nearly all cultures have been affected by writing in one way or another; that is, historically, or through a religion of the Book (Islam, Christianity), or through a literate-based religion such as India's which allows a greater ordering of the world.† Modern schooling has also influenced many societies even where it has not made them literate.

Scholars like Ruth Finnegan, Catherine Hezser and Susan Niditch have cautioned against approaches that treat orality and literacy as systems that are separate and apart. Niditch writes, "We err if we view oral and written cultures, oral and written literatures, as incompatible.... Literacy ... must be understood in terms of its continuity and interaction with the oral world."[234] This is true for many traditional cultures today.

An oral Bible training project can (and should) legitimately interact with the literacy available to it, by using the written text of the Bible as the authoritative guide to keep oral expression faithful to the original. Some of the *midrashim* are examples of the wild fancifulness that can happen when there is no authoritative source in the oral transmission of narratives.[235]

Even though the oral Bible project was set in an overwhelmingly oral context, there are a number of ways that it interfaced with literacy. These are not easy to categorize; the field where the two technologies compete is as disorganized as a battlefield. First were instances in the verbatims showing how storytelling led to an interest in Bible reading for both Christians and non-Christians. For example, Benjamin Pani said, "I told the stories to

---

* This is particularly true where there are established churches, since Christian communities tend to have a higher literacy rate than non-Christians. Even in a radically oral culture, the fact that there is a single printed corpus signifies that what is being taught is not oral but written. Goody, 110f.

† Goody, xiv, 187. Goody's chapter about the effect of the Hindu scriptures being written, even though most people were forbidden to read them, is pertinent, 110f.

three Hindu women. After hearing these stories, they came and bought a Bible from me because they are very eager to learn the word of God from the Bible." (April 2006). Satish reported, "Little by little I told a fanatical anti-Christian man the stories, and now he is so eager to read the Bible. He even gave me money to buy him a Hindi language Bible. When I gave him the Bible, he started to read all the stories himself." (September 2006). Phelemon Kawade told how he went to a Hindu ashram as part of his first field assignment:

> Uncle had given us a homework assignment to observe a storyteller in our village. I knew where there was a Hindu ashram. So I went there and heard a man who is a storyteller and a teacher at this Hindu ashram. After listening to him, I told him the story of Adam and Eve including the Fall—all the way through the part where God drove them out of the garden. This story really touched that man's heart. I gave him my address, and the next day this Hindu teacher visited my house.

> He said, "Pastor, yesterday you told that story. How can I get that storybook?" I replied, "No, we do not have a storybook like that. But we do have the Bible. All the stories are in the Bible. So if you are willing to take a Bible, you can take it." So he bought a Bible and took it and went back to his house. And he began reading the Bible. (April 2006).

Christians also sometimes became more motivated to read the Bible after hearing its stories. Pedapalliwar tells of his experience:

> After learning these stories, I went back to my field and began telling them in cottage meetings and at church. Before that, the people were not very interested in the Word of God. But after sharing these stories, I encouraged them to read the Bible and tell Bible stories to others. So they enjoyed these stories very much. As I was visiting in their homes, now I have noticed that they are very interested to read the Bible and are wanting to discuss God's word. (April 2006).

Similarly Sangram reported, "This storytelling program has helped and blessed me very much. Before, the people in my church would not read the Bible, even though they did own Bibles. And they were not able to understand or remember the things I was teaching them." (September 2006). People with minimal literacy often lack motivation to read (this may be the Achilles heel of many excellent literacy programs). But when believers experience a hunger for the Bible, they become highly motivated to read and consequently their reading skills begin to increase.

Hearing the Bible stories told is fascinating to people in ways that Bible reading is not. Sunil described how his church services have changed since he started telling Bible stories:

> Most of the people in my church have attended school. When I used to preach they could understand. But even so, after I started sharing the stories, they were very interested to learn the story and they listened very carefully and are really blessed by the stories. After I tell the story, I ask them, "How is this story today? Do you like it? Do you understand it? Did that story touch you or not?" All these questions I would ask them after finishing our worship. And they are answering me, "Today, what you were preaching, along with that you shared a story. The stories are touching us and really we are blessed by God. We understand very clearly and for remembering, the stories are very nice for us." (April 2006).

Another way that literacy came into play was when the storytellers would read their Bibles to prepare for a story performance or to gain courage or strength. Sangram gives an example of this in regard to the Elijah/Elisha stories: "After telling these stories two or three times, I came back home and I started to read this story portion again. God was speaking to me through this story, because in those days I was going through a financial crisis." (September 2006).

A third way literacy was mentioned was when storytellers thanked God that they knew the stories by heart so they did not have to read from their Bibles in order to talk to others about Christ. Two comments are typical: "By the grace of God, as we learned these stories, without carrying our Bible we are going and sharing those stories and we are reaching the Hindu people through the stories." (James Korkora; February 2007). "I thank God that I now know these Bible stories so that I can share the Bible stories with other people without needing to first open and read from my Bible." (Sangram; January 2007).

One reason it was important to them to be able to share the Word of God without having to open their Bible is that in Hindu India the Bible has become a lightning rod that attracts the attention of anti-Christians. Sometimes fanatical Hindus will beat the Christian workers and tear up the Bibles they are carrying. However, a less obvious reason is that for oral communicators authenticity is in inverse proportion to reading. For instance, the Santals have a saying, "A mouth is better than a book." [236]

The Santals have no recorded history and all that is known of them has come down by word of mouth handed down from generation to generation. They consider written history as unreliable and therefore depend on their oral traditions. This is expressed in their proverb: *Puthi reak' khon tuthi reak' sorosa* (memory is superior to books or the mouth is our printed book).[237]

For literate people, seeing something in print affirms its authenticity, whereas for an oral learner, communication that is authoritative is connected with the person who is speaking the message. The credibility of the message is linked to the credibility of the speaker. The person who brings the message is always a part of the message. Hence his or her character speaks as loudly as the words themselves, perhaps more so.

For oral learners, reading is also perceived as less user-friendly than oral communication. This bias can provoke a negative preconception when someone opens the Bible to read to them.

During the oral Bible pilot project, Maya had opportunity to tell the Christmas story to a large group of people in a village near her home. Afterward the villagers told her, "We have heard this from many people, but now when you were telling us, it was very interesting because you did not even open the Bible to tell us about it." (January 2004). Maya described with tears how being able to tell the stories had changed her and given her confidence to speak the Word of God:

> Before entering this oral Bible program, I had no confidence—not even in a women's group—because I could not read well and I had very little education. But now through hearing and memorizing these stories, I can stand anywhere anytime and tell the stories, even without first reading them or having to open the Bible. This is a big help for me. It has given me confidence, boldness and joy, and has also increased my faith. (February 2004).

Identification with Bible Characters

Another area that turned out to be significant in the verbatims was identification with Bible characters. A friend in the U.S. describes how, through the stories that her father told her as a child, she came to know people she had never met:

> I come from a family of storytellers. Some of my earliest memories are of my dad telling me of his life adventures. I have come to know

and cherish family members that were gone long before my birth, and World War II comrades that shared a very special part of my dad's life. I know that when I walk in heaven, and I see them, I will know them, and I will smile because of my dad's stories. His stories are real, they are moving and they are powerful. They have always transported me to a place and time that I would have never experienced without hearing them.[238]

When a listener or teller begins to identify with a Bible character, it can become a powerful influence in the individual's life. In effect, even though the characters are historical figures who are long dead, they can become mentors to the storyteller. What was told and written about them and the things that they said become part of the fabric of the storyteller's life. The storyteller, in turn, often urges others to learn from these characters, especially in circumstances of crisis.

It is even possible to "consult" with a beloved Bible character, asking how he or she would respond or act or speak in a given situation. An ancient saying in the Babylonian Talmud reads: "When the dead are quoted, their lips move." [239]

In the movie, "I Am Sam," the main protagonist, Sam, is a mentally challenged man who is fighting for the custody of his daughter. Sam makes all his important decisions by thinking about what one of the Beatles might have done in a similar situation. By internalizing all of their songs, stories and movies, no matter the dilemma he could always find a parallel and thus know what course to follow.[240] The story of "The Great Stone Face" by Nathaniel Hawthorne (1851) is a similar tale.

These examples express wonderfully how people who think in story can make decisions about their lives without resorting to handling truth propositionally as we are taught to do. Another example is found in future chess master Bruce Pandolfini who marinated in the "texts" of past chess games to achieve a winning sense of the game. Determined to improve on his natural talent for the game, Pandolfini bought a two-volume set (in Russian) of the 500 games played by Soviet chess master Mikhail Botvinnik. He spent a year studying these games, and then decided to commit to memory 60 games, move for move. He said:

I lost a position in my mind, which was quite common at first, I started again from the first move. To remember the moves I would create a story line that tied all the logic of the game together.... And then you develop an intuitive sense of how to handle similar positions, and your moves flow naturally.[241]

In the same way, internalizing the biblical stories can become an unconscious guide for life's daily decisions.

In oral cultures, stories are a way to keep the people who are important to a family or to a community alive and real. They live through the stories that are told about them. As long as the stories are told, that person keeps participating in the community. Once the stories are no longer told, the person is relegated to the archives of history. We might ask what this says about our own Christian community which no longer tells stories about the people who are most foundational to us as a community—biblical characters certainly, but also others. The African-American community is an exception in one sense at least. The constant telling and retelling of the stories about Martin Luther King keep Dr. King and his ideals alive within the community.

Certain Bible characters became very important to some of the storytellers. They often based their faith not on one story alone, but upon the entire life of a faithful story character like Abraham or Elijah. On one occasion Prabash Kumar was unable to get a train ticket to come to the storytelling training module because all the trains were full. He said later, "I was not worrying because I believed that, 'The God of Elijah is with me.' " He traveled part of the way by bus to another city where by chance he met three other storytellers who were also coming for training. They happened to have an unused train ticket that they gave him. (February 2007).

Rajat's supervisor ordered him to transfer to another district which turned out to be the same one where Australian missionary Graham Staines and his two sons were burned and killed by the Hindus not long before. When Rajat found out that he and his family had to move there, he said to himself, "My God, the God of Elijah, is with me, and he will help me. So I will go there." (October 2007).

When the time came for Sangram's wife to deliver, the doctor told them she needed a cesarean section surgery but they had no money. Because Sangram had learned the stories of Abraham and Elijah he was able to have faith to receive provision from God. He said,

> I had faith because I learned the stories here. So I believed in the story of Abraham and Elijah, and I was believing how both of them had faith in God and received provision and blessing from God. I prayed saying, "You are the God of Abraham and the God of Elijah, so please also provide for me."

Through several unexpected gifts, Sangram and his wife received the full amount that was needed for her surgery.

Similarly, the faith displayed in the lives of certain Bible characters became foundational for Sabat:

> I told my family, "Believe in God and he will provide for you." I am always telling them these stories, such as the stories about the faith of Abraham.... I told my wife, "Our God will provide it...." Afterward I reminded her, "Our God provided it."

Sabat's statements of faith echo the words of Abraham in Genesis 22:8, 14.[*]

After going through an especially difficult financial period, Sunil said to his wife: "You see, our God of Elijah has provided us with everything we needed." [†]

Faith

A similar theme was that individual Bible stories served to amplify personal faith. For example, Bibhuti Digal told the story of the paralyzed man from John chapter five to a sick woman. As she heard the story she began to cry. He encouraged her to believe, saying, "Have courage. See, God is doing many miracles through the stories. This is not a story made by man. It is the true story that took place 2000 years ago." The woman believed and was healed. (March 2007).

Kakasheb's father became seriously ill. The doctor prescribed a CAT scan and some expensive medicine. Kakasheb told the doctor the story of the paralyzed man from Mark chapter two. He said, "I believe that same God will heal my father too." His father got well and didn't need any of the treatment. (February 2007).

A believer from Phelemon's church told the story of the woman with the issue of blood to her brother who had been diagnosed with throat cancer. Upon hearing the story, he said, "I am feeling that somebody has touched me. I do believe that God will heal me." (February 2007).

Prabash often experienced stomach pain and had blood in his urine. When he came for the storytelling training, he was ill. But as he took part in the Eucharist (with the telling of the story) he immediately felt that he was being healed. Since then he has had no recurrence of this sickness. He said, "Through this storytelling program, God is giving me more faith and helping me in my ministry." (January 2007).

---

* See Appendix J:4c for Sabat's complete account.
† See Appendix J:1b for Sunil's complete account.

Rajeth told the story of Joseph to a non-Christian family who had financial problems. "I told them how Joseph had a vision from God and how his vision was fulfilled. I said, 'You also need to see the vision concerning your family. Have faith in God. One day your vision will be fulfilled.' " He encouraged them to believe like Joseph. Soon after that their son got a job as a driver. Now the mother recognizes that God is at work in their family. (September 2006).

Sabat told a ladies group the story of Abraham's call, focusing on his faith. After hearing that story they believed, "Nothing is impossible for God." As they remembered the story, their faith increased. Afterward one of those women told the story to a non-Christian pregnant woman who was very fearful about her delivery.[*] They brought her to Sabat's house where he prayed for her. Sabat said, "She got faith and did not have a difficult delivery as she had feared. Now three new people are coming to listen to the stories and they bring the woman's new baby with them." (April 2006).

When Sangram first heard the story of God's provision of a ram for Abraham (Gen. 22:1–19), he identified with Abraham in his need. He began praying, concentrating on the stories while he prayed. As a result, faith increased in his heart for God's provision. A short time later when he was visiting another city, a woman gave him a monetary gift of enough money to live on for four months.

A new believer in Sangram's church who was a Muslim convert became very ill. The doctor said he had to be admitted to the hospital for at least a week. But the family was very poor and could not afford the medical bills. So Sangram told them the story of the paralyzed man from Mark chapter two. Sangram noted, "Because they had no money, they had no other way except to believe." Within two days the man was well, and in a week he was back at work again earning money to feed his family.

Finally, in cultures like these it is common to find objects that are empowered through religious veneration or witchcraft. Part of the worldview of these societies is that spiritual power for good or evil can reside in particular objects or words. So it is a small step for them to believe that God's power resides in his stories as they are being told. Sanjeeb gave this account:

I made one storytelling disciple who is illiterate and does not know how to read at all. The new name we gave him is Moses. Before sharing these stories, I told him, "The stories I am telling you, there

---

[*] In the year 2000, India accounted for one quarter of all maternal deaths worldwide. Today in India, one woman dies every seven minutes from a pregnancy related cause, which is an improvement over the last five years. It is estimated that pregnancy-related deaths account for one-quarter of all fatalities among Indian women aged 15 to 29.

is a power in them. If you tell them to other people, then definitely God will work through them." So he started to share the stories with other tribal people and many sick people started coming to him. Now he is like the tribal doctor. Through these stories, many people are getting healed through him. (September 2006).

Ong has a passage that addresses the power of spoken words in oral cultures:

For anyone who has a sense of what words are in a primary oral culture ... it is not surprising that the Hebrew term *dabar* means 'word' and 'event'. Malinowski (1923, pp. 451, 470–81) has made the point that among 'primitive' (oral) peoples generally language is a mode of action and not simply a countersign of thought, ... Neither is it surprising that oral peoples commonly, and probably universally, consider words to have great power....

Deeply typographic folk forget to think of words as primarily oral, as events, and hence as necessarily powered: for them, words tend rather to be assimilated to things, ... Such 'things' are not so readily associated with magic, for they are not actions, but are in a radical sense dead, though subject to dynamic resurrection.[242]

The sense of stories as empowered words may be one reason there were many healings and other supernatural results that consistently followed the telling of the biblical stories. Bilion Soren put it this way: "We told them stories of Jesus Christ, the powerful stories, the healing stories. And they believed."*

Felt Needs

Felt needs are human beings' most basic concrete needs for material supply, food, clothing, shelter, protection, healing from sickness and so forth. In impoverished cultures there is no social net to fall back on in time of need, so these are constant concerns for most people. Survival is a precarious endeavor requiring each member of the family to work every day to have food and shelter for that day. If a family member becomes ill or there are unexpected expenses, no safety margin exists. In such circumstances, God often shows His deep love to people by caring for their needs. In this way they can begin to understand the good news of God's redemption in a personal way and

---

* See Chapter 11 for Bilion's story.

understand that God has their best interests at heart; that he is on their side and against anything that might cause them harm.

The Burning Bus

During one of the training events in the pilot project, the storytellers learned to tell Psalm 91. It was quite difficult for them since this genre of Scripture has no plot or other narrative elements to aid recall. However, they worked with it each day during the morning devotional time, and by the end of the training event most were able to tell it fairly well.

The next day as one of the groups was traveling back to their home state, a frightening bus accident provided an immediate opportunity to apply this Psalm to their felt need for protection from danger. Emily, a pastor's wife, was with her husband and two of their teenage children on the bus. She describes what happened:

> When we finished our storytelling training and were going home, on the way we met with an accident. And we four were very afraid, thinking we were going to die. Suddenly I remembered Psalm 91 and I got peace in my heart. What happened is, they had many goods loaded on top of the bus. When we went underneath an electrical wire over the road, the bus caught fire and started burning. The bus was fully packed and there was only one door so we could not get out. We saw from the window that there was much fire and we felt very afraid. When we finally were able to come out, we saw that the fire was really, really big. We were all very frightened. In my life, I had not had such a frightening experience. But I remembered according to Psalm 91 how God is faithful and I felt very relaxed in my heart, and I thank God for taking care of us.

Her husband, Santosh, added, "Because Sir had taught us Psalm 91, only because of this we were able to have peace in the midst of this accident." Later when their teenage daughter, Roslen, would think of traveling on another bus she would become afraid. "Whenever I thought, 'I have to go for the training program,' then I remembered the accident on that same road, and I was afraid. But then I think of Psalm 91 and I have peace in my heart." Another storyteller who was on the bus that day was Somarsing. He said,

> I also felt that Psalm 91 was so important. It was just because of us that nothing worse happened to that vehicle, because we are God's people. When I reached home I told my family that they also should

learn Psalm 91 so they will know how faithful God is. I taught everyone in my home to memorize that Psalm.*

The power of this Psalm continued to meet the felt need for physical protection in Santosh and Emily's family. Their daughter, Roslen, recounted another frightening experience that happened not long after.

> One day as I was sweeping my room, a big cobra snake was hiding under a bowl beneath the bed. Uncle and Auntie had taught us to always tell Psalm 91 to ourselves. So that day also, I had said that Psalm to myself. Then I started working and sweeping the house in the morning and even though I touched that cobra, it did not harm me. Then I remembered where it is written in this psalm, "Even the cobra and lion you will trample on them, but they will never be able to harm you." That same thing had just happened in my own life, otherwise that cobra would surely have bitten me. But instead the snake hid its head and did not stand up and bite. When we had killed it, we saw that it was a very large cobra. But it did not bite. Then I recognized that really, God's word is very powerful, and that even the cobra was kept silent before a child of God. Because of that, I am alive and I am still continuing to learn the Bible stories.

Other Felt Needs

There were never-ending opportunities for applying the biblical stories to felt needs both personally and in the lives of others whom the storytellers encountered day by day. My research identified many of these. Table 7 lists some of the most significant felt needs and the number of verbatims that pertained to each.

---

* Somarsing is a former alcoholic who was converted through the storytelling, and who then entered the training himself. See Chapter 11 for his story.

Table 7. Felt Needs

Felt Need	Number of Times
Physical healing	26
Finances	16
Childlessness	15
Peace in human relationships	12
People raised from the dead	3
Instances of demonic presence	3
Help with school studies	1
Fear	1
Other	5

To be effective at matching biblical stories with felt needs, proficiency in a broad range of stories is needed. One might ask if there is a Bible story suitable for every human need. Teresa found that the Santal women would often look at the underlying emotions brought forth by a particular need and then select an appropriate story to tell. For example, a woman who was accused of being a witch was made to feel terribly ashamed. So the Santal storyteller would think of a biblical story about a woman who was ashamed, perhaps telling the story of the woman with the issue of blood (Mark 5:24–34).

In other instances, in the absence of a focused parallel story, the storytellers would often simply tell any faith-building story. The dramatic case stories in chapter 11 show graphically how felt needs can bring people to Christ.

Field Leaders' Questionnaire

During the agency's semiannual leaders meeting, a questionnaire was administered inviting the field leaders' feedback and their advice about the oral Bible program. Only leaders who had personal knowledge of the program in their own divisions were asked to respond. Of the 130 junior and senior leaders present, 54 completed the questionnaire.* Of those, eleven (18.5%) had completed at least part of the oral Bible training themselves.

The responders were generally positive in their assessment of the program with a median response of 78.2%. Those who knew most about the program rated it higher than those who knew least (a mean of 81.5% compared to 71.7%). Two of the questions solicited written responses:

A. Please give your opinion (please be honest) about this program?
B. Would you like this program to continue? If yes, do you have any suggestions for us to improve/change it to be more effective?

I later organized their responses into 13 broad categories:

1. *LEARN BIBLE*
2. *UNDERSTAND*
3. *EXPAND*
4. *SPIRITUAL RESULTS*
5. *ATTRACTIVE*
6. *EVANGELISM*
7. *CHURCH GROWTH/ MULTIPLICATION*
8. *PICTURES, BOOKS, MATERIALS*
9. *ADULT EDUCATION PROGRAM*
10. *SCHEDULING AND LOCATION*
11. *URBAN MINISTRY*
12. *OTHER SUGGESTIONS*
13. *GENERAL COMMENTS*

Below I give composite summaries of their statements for each category followed by my comments.†

1. LEARN BIBLE

SUMMARY of leaders' responses:
This method is a good way to learn large amounts of Bible text and be able to keep it in one's heart. Learning the Bible as a story in an orderly [chronological] way is very helpful. Both the evangelist/worker and the people he is leading can learn to know the Bible this way.

---

* A senior leader is normally supervisor of 30 to 40 ministers and a junior leader supervises seven to 12 ministers.

† The questionnaire and verbatim responses from the leaders can be found in my D.Min. thesis: "Telling God's Stories with Power: Biblical Storytelling in Oral Cultures" (United Theological Seminary, Dayton, OH, 2007), 269.

INTERACTION by author:

The respondents tended to agree that the oral Bible program improved the biblical knowledge of the storytellers. The rating for parallel question 2, "Did the storytelling program improve the Biblical knowledge of the storytellers?" was 83%. On the other hand, they expressed some doubt about question 4c: "Is the audience able to share the gospel with others through the storytelling?" giving it a rating of only 64%.* Apparently they were not as sure the listeners would be able to repeat the stories to others. This element showed mixed results in the pilot project. For example, one storyteller said that after he tells a story just once, his listeners are able to go home and repeat it to their families. However, another successful storyteller said that almost none of his congregants learned to tell the stories. This is an area that needs further study to ensure that the gospel can be spread by every believer, not just the pastor. This response may also reflect some pessimism by ministers who through long experience have come to believe that their congregants are unable of sharing the Bible with others effectively.

2. UNDERSTAND

SUMMARY of leaders' responses:

Storytelling makes it easy to understand the Bible. All ages—children, youth, and older people—can easily grasp the Word of God. It is especially helpful for unschooled [nonliterate] people. They are able to both learn the Bible and teach it to others by sharing the gospel in story. This is a method that fits the Indian culture where religious books traditionally communicate through story and song.

INTERACTION:

The parallel question 4b, "Is the audience able to learn/understand/ remember the Bible through the storytelling?" earned a rating of 81%. In counterpoint one respondent said, "Sometimes [it is] very hard to understand the meaning of the story." It is true that some Bible stories can be more difficult to understand either because of their content or perhaps because of some unfamiliar wording or circumstance. However, while some unpacking of the story may be helpful—especially if an interactive approach is used—the storytellers should be careful not to leave the impression that a story can have only one particular application, or that the pastor is the only one qualified to interpret its meaning. Any story can have within it diverse messages that speak to the listeners in distinct ways according

---

* Those who knew most about the program rated this 72%, while those who knew least rated it 55%.

to their needs. Often the story itself is the message; an explanation may simply weaken its impact.

3. EXPAND THE PROGRAM

SUMMARY of leaders' responses:
Seven respondents recommended that the program be expanded; they wrote: it should be started division-wise ... to other divisions also ... it could be used for an entire region ... it should be told to everybody in all the different languages. "Do this storytelling in all villages. Please take it seriously," one begged. Others pointed to the need to prepare more trainers for the program.

INTERACTION:
Indian trainers will be essential to the long-term success of the project, so preparation should begin as soon as possible. Beyond the agency's standard qualifications for leadership, these should be individuals who 1) are gifted storytellers, 2) have a commitment to storytelling as a methodology, 3) tell the Bible stories accurately and with enthusiasm, 4) have a gift of leadership, and 5) are able to develop others by coaching them in the same way the central training program does.

Some thought should be given to developing the role of a biblical storytelling coordinator who travels to all the divisions to encourage, teach and model storytelling. This traveling storyteller would encourage local sub-divisions to sponsor storytelling festivals and other cooperative outreaches, and assist them in carrying it out. The coordinator would also lead short-term storytelling training events in regional areas to equip grassroots workers with new biblical stories. Ideally one such coordinator would be appointed for each language area. Of course, these must be people who have been trained in the biblical storytelling program, having proven themselves as committed and gifted storytellers.

Perhaps the best way to develop trainers is to assign them to serve in the centralized training program for a time, coaching groups of new storytellers and being mentored by the program facilitators.

4. SPIRITUAL RESULTS

SUMMARY of leaders' responses:
According to five respondents, the storytelling program can bring increased faith, newness to ministry, and spiritual awakening to a village. It can lead to spiritual breakthroughs for the church. It is also good for unity.

INTERACTION:

As the stories spread throughout the village from person to person, so also does the power of God to change lives in response to the faith of those who hear the stories. Stories are good for unity for several reasons. First, storytelling the Word of God unites the community of believers because all ages and education levels can take part in telling and hearing the stories. Ong points out that while writing and print isolate, "… the spoken word forms human beings into close-knit groups." [243] It also unites because biblical stories are transformative. Believers who may have wrong attitudes toward others are brought under conviction. Perhaps most importantly, the stories produce unity because they instill common values and create a worldview that is shared by all members of the community.

5. ATTRACTIVE

SUMMARY of leaders' responses:

Everyone likes to listen to stories. They like this program—they think it is good.

INTERACTION:

In many areas, religious resistance to Christian preaching is strong, but not so for storytelling. As one storyteller testified, "With storytelling it is very easy to make friends with non-Christians. Everyone—the young and the old, even high caste people—likes to listen to stories. This makes it very easy to approach them and tell them stories from the Bible." Parallel question 4a ("Did the storytelling program bring more attention among the audience to hear the gospel than the traditional method?") was given an 83% rating, echoing this assessment.

6. EVANGELISM

SUMMARY of leaders' responses:

Sixteen respondents wrote that this is a very good program to present the Gospel. They said that storytelling is the best way to reach the unreached people—through it many people are being converted from Hinduism. It is helpful when evangelizing new villages, especially wherever there is opposition. It is the best way to share the Gospel among unschooled and tribal people. Storytelling is also very effective at bringing children to the church and for use in the Sunday School. It is good for gospel preaching and for propagating the gospel.

INTERACTION:

This point had the highest number of responses, all enthusiastic. Parallel question 1, "How effective do you think the storytelling program has been to share the gospel?" rated an 84%. Question 8, "Could you reach those villages / people, which were considered to be anti-Christians, after the implementation of the storytelling program?" rated somewhat lower at 72%. On question 5, "Do you think the storytelling program along with the literacy program has been a helpful tool for outreach?" the leaders responded with a resounding 89%.

7. CHURCH GROWTH AND CHURCH MULTIPLICATION

SUMMARY of leaders' responses:

The respondents wrote that the storytelling program helped their missionaries to develop a mission station . . . it helps the growth of the church . . . their people benefited and learned more stories from the Bible ... more and more people are joining and their ministry is growing through storytelling.

INTERACTION:

If a mission agency's structure is designed to accommodate "normal" church growth, when fast growth begins to happen it will stress the system making it difficult to assimilate all the new churches and believers. This agency is accustomed to training all of their workers externally to the church planting process; that is, pulling them away from their context and sending them off to one, two or four years of training. This way of training could prove too slow if rapid church growth starts happening in an area. The agency is already facing a serious shortfall of leaders needed for the 216 new congregations that were formed in just 15 months through the combined oral Bible and AdEd programs. One solution is for leaders to develop from within the church-planting process itself. The storytelling program is particularly suited for this because new believers can be equipped for ministry just by learning and telling the Bible stories.* Storytelling equips new ministers effectively even in low-literacy contexts. Regardless of their reading skills, they can lead the church by telling biblical stories. Benjamin Pani reported:

Dayalusun is the elder of our church. He was not knowing anything, but because of that he was listening carefully to everything. He was only able to read and write a very little, but I did tell him the stories. After

---

* See Chapter 11 for the stories of Mangal and Bilion, two tribal men who were trained for ministry in the O.B. pilot project.

learning all the stories, he is leading our church by just telling the stories. And through this way, the believers are coming up into Christ. Every one of the church people knows the stories. (January 2007).

8. REQUESTS FOR PICTURES, BOOKS, MATERIALS

SUMMARY of leaders' responses:
Eight of the respondents suggested using pictures, visual aids, books and other materials to supplement the storytelling.

INTERACTION:
Before my wife and I began to develop the oral Bible training program, we had tried a similar storytelling program in which we provided picture books for each of the storytellers. Several drawbacks were found to the use of visual aids for storytelling.

First, visual aids are susceptible to damage through normal wear and tear, as well as destruction by insects and monsoons. Second, the requirement that each storyteller have a picture book limited the spread of the stories.

Perhaps more importantly, the storytellers tended to become dependent on the picture books, so they did not feel a need to learn the stories well. The stories were external to them in the pictures they pointed to during the telling, so they did not internalize the stories deeply.

Other possible significant issues apply to how oral learners see pictures. These have to do with perspective (three-dimension vs. two-dimension), colors, partial figures, ethnic depictions and so forth.[244]

A final point is that when a storyteller or evangelist brings external artifacts such as pictures or books, it is easy for the villagers to identify that person as a Christian worker. This becomes a lightning rod for religious opposition which may take the form of destroying the materials and beating and expelling the evangelist from the village.

9. ADULT EDUCATION PROGRAM

SUMMARY of leaders' responses:
Two respondents mentioned the adult education program. One said the storytelling is very helpful with the AdEd classes. The other suggested providing materials such as books, chalk, and gaslight or lantern for the literacy classes. Parallel question 5, "Do you think the storytelling program along with the literacy program has been a helpful tool for outreach?" rated an 89%, the highest score for any of the responses.

INTERACTION:

Although the AdEd program was greatly used of God to provide access to hundreds of resistant villages, it was not administered as well as it could have been. Part of the reason was that the man hired by the agency to oversee the program proved to be unsuitable for the job and was removed. Afterward his role was never filled and every division leader did what he thought was best which usually amounted to just teaching the village people to read the alphabet. It would not be difficult to upgrade this part of the program in any future cycle of training. This is important to answer critics who could claim that the storytellers are only doing this to convert people. Any literacy project should be done with excellence as a witness to Christ. Also, if new believers in a village can begin to learn to read, it will help them in their Christian walk.

10. SCHEDULING AND LOCATION

SUMMARY of leaders' responses:

Three of the respondents suggested changes in timing or location for the training.

INTERACTION:

The oral Bible program, as it has been taught, is a long-term effort needing almost two years just to finish the basic track of 100 stories. The 240 hours of training, plus the required fieldwork is equal to six postgraduate level seminary courses. This level of training is appropriate to equip ministers as competent biblical storytellers. Because it is an in-service program, no time is lost from ministry as is the case with residential training programs.

But there is also a place for shorter courses for those who are unable to give enough time to complete an entire basic track of stories. Shorter tracks like the Acts stories can be offered. This should be taken under consideration in future planning. Ideally, if the storytelling model of training is adopted for workers and churches, it should be seen as a lifelong learning model instead of simply an academic degree to be completed. New stories can continually be taught both in training courses as well as other events. There are perhaps more than 500 stories in the Bible so the supply of biblical stories will not be quickly exhausted. Beyond the pure story genre, other texts such as the book of Revelation would be ideal for storytellers to learn to tell as well.

11. URBAN MINISTRY

SUMMARY of leaders' responses:
Three of the respondents agreed that the biblical storytelling program was ideal for villages. But they requested that something else should be developed that fits urban ministries that are trying to reach educated people and modern youth.

INTERACTION:

The oral Bible program was developed mainly to reach low-literacy people, many of whom live in rural areas. This is majority India as it exists today and will continue to be for the foreseeable future. The church has largely failed in its attempts to use literate methods to reach and disciple these people, which is why this program was developed. However, storytelling has great power even for literate people. Take, for example, the huge number of films produced by Bollywood. These are popular not only among illiterate people—everyone likes a good story. Another example is that of the Hindu epics which are still popular among Indians of many educational levels.

If biblical storytelling were adapted to an urban context it could perhaps become an important tool for evangelization and discipling. The biblical stories are at least as exciting as the Hindu epics. Christians who have been in the church for many years regard preaching as a more adult form of communication and have come to think of stories as suitable only for children in Sunday School. So storytelling probably would not be as well received in established churches or among lifelong Christians. Instead, if storytelling were used to reach out to Hindu people who have recently migrated to the cities from villages, especially those who have low literacy, it could become a powerful tool for new church plants.

I recommended that when the agency begins a new cycle of oral Bible training they should enroll several workers who are targeting such people in the cities. Then the method can be tested to find out if it works in urban areas as well as rural. Low literacy communities in the cities may also welcome the adult education literacy program together with biblical storytelling.

12. OTHER SUGGESTIONS

SUMMARY of leaders' responses:
One respondent suggested producing a group skit (drama) program for the villages. Another recommended developing the storytelling program in more languages. And a third liked the innovative nature of the program, saying "If we will use more new methods it will be more effective."

INTERACTION:

The idea of developing a traveling drama/storytelling team to present the biblical stories has merit. Drama teams that present the Hindu epics have always been popular in this culture. Bible school students could do this during the time they are not in school. Local churches could also develop dramas as a way of outreach to their non-Christian neighbors. These dramas should present biblical stories, not modern ones, so the audience will be transformed by the Word of God and so they will learn the Bible.

Regarding the request for more languages, it is simple for storytelling to travel from one language to another because story does not depend on individual words but on a structure built from elements such as plot, action, dialogue, characterization, crisis and resolution. The language barrier is also minimized because there are no printed materials in the oral Bible program. Each story is represented by a symbol so no written words are used. However, to address the respondent's concern, it would be good to develop oral Bible trainers who are fluent in other languages besides the two or three major languages that have been used so far.

13. GENERAL COMMENTS

- "This program is good. It is an encouragement." (respondent #28).
- "This program is very best. Continue this program." (respondent #29).
- "It is a very good program. But in my station we could not start it because we do not have a storyteller to train others. In our village there is so much opposition for preaching the Gospel. So maybe it will not work out. Yes, we want it to be continued." (respondent #32).
- "Totally new, but appreciatable. Very helpful to fulfill the agency's vision." (respondent #34).
- "Very, very good. One successful program and project." (respondent #39).
- "Realize it is very, very good program. Thank you." (respondent #47).
- "This program is very good. . . . Good running in our area. . . . Effective for ministry." (respondent #50).
- "Very good program. In our villages this program is still going on." (respondent #51).

COMPREHENSIVE EXAMINATIONS

A comprehensive examination was given to the storytellers six months after the final training module. They spent the intervening months preparing for the exam by telling all 100 of the stories at least two times and training an apprentice to tell the stories.

There were two primary criteria for designing an appropriate examination instrument: first, the exam should be limited to the skill areas that were taught in the course; and second, testing exercises should be presented in ways that were familiar to the candidates and in accord with their oral learning styles. I began by asking, "What were the storytellers expected to learn in this course?" It would seem obvious that testing should cover the areas of learning the students were supposed to master. However, I've found it is easy to slip into testing for things that were not part of the learning experience. For example, analytical questions about the stories are unsuitable because oral communicators are used to thinking holistically.

I determined that learning was in at least the following four areas:

1. The stories: Is this student able to tell the stories completely and correctly? Was anything left out, or told wrong?
2. Performance skills: the use of the voice, facial expression and body to tell the story. In other words, how well can the student use other communication channels besides simply repeating the words of the story?
3. Chronological order: can the storyteller place each story in its correct order in relation to the other stories he or she has learned?
4. Training others: each storyteller was required to train at least one apprentice who could also tell the stories. These apprentices must be tested to measure this aspect of the storyteller's learning experience.

I identified two other parameters that limited the design of the examination instruments. First, since the training was aimed at end users who are assumed to be nonliterate, an ability to read and write could not be a condition for taking the exam. This precluded many of the written examination instruments that are common in educational systems worldwide. Second, since the storytellers are from different language groups, each should be tested in the language that he or she normally uses to tell the stories, if possible.

The Exam

The program began in February 2006 with 62 students. After 240 "classroom" hours of work—and many more hours than that of fieldwork—41 workers completed the program in March 2007. Thirty-three of these came to be tested in October; 22 brought an apprentice storyteller that they had trained.*

Testing was done sequentially in two batches: a single-language batch (Oriya), and then a mixed language batch (Telugu, Hindi, Kannada and Marathi). Four days were needed to test each group. The exams were fairly comprehensive, having six elements of equal weight:

1. First was a multiple-choice exam of 108 statements covering every story learned in the course.† The statement was read aloud in the respective language and students then circled one of four story symbols. I made these intentionally confusing so the answer could not be guessed simply by looking at the symbol. Five examinees achieved perfect scores on this segment—four were GEN2 storytellers and one was a GEN3 apprentice who had never been in the central training (see Appendix K: Comprehensive Exam Scores).

2. An oral telling of a randomly selected Old Testament story.‡

3. An oral telling of a randomly selected New Testament story.

4. An oral telling of a story selected by random from Old and New Testaments together.

5. An Old Testament chronology of stories; this component required the storytellers to put the 38 Old Testament stories in correct chronological order. To do this, the examinees placed the representative story symbols in square sleeves on transparent vinyl slide pages that I obtained from a photo supply store.

6. The final component was the score earned by testing each storyteller's GEN3 apprentice (the apprentice's test consisted of two random oral tellings plus the multiple-choice exam). The eleven storytellers who did not bring an apprentice were given a score of "0" in this column causing a 16.5% penalty against their final grade. (See Appendix K).

The exams were administered by Bible school faculty members who have degrees from recognized schools and who are fluent in the languages used for testing. One teacher commented that the multiple-choice component was "not an easy exam"; several asked for copies of the exam as a model to help in designing their own testing instruments. Two of those

---

* We learned later that one qualified storyteller did not attend the exam because he was flat on his back with malaria for several weeks.

† See Appendix L for samples of the multiple choice questions.

‡ For the first two tellings, the storytellers drew three stories and told one of them. For the final oral telling test, they were required to choose between only two randomly selected stories.

who helped administer the testing assessed the program afterward. Bipin Kishore (B.Th.) wrote:

> I thank God for the privilege to enjoy the storytelling program. It was a blessing to me. As we participated in this, we could understand that it is a wonderful way of communicating the gospel to different categories of people. Since the storyteller includes his emotions and feelings to share the story culturally, it is an elegant and explicit way to listen and understand. I believe it will surely impact the lives of many and bring them to the kingdom of God.

Teacher David Isaac (M.Div.) wrote:

> I thank God and it is my privilege to participate in your storytelling program. It was a wonderful program. These simple stories can help people make sense of what's happening around [them], especially when we take Bible readings and when we narrate them in a systematic story form, they can provide incredible insights to the listeners. While judging the participants, as I heard the narrated stories from the storytellers, it was really encouraging to me personally. It is essential in the rural area especially in India, where majority of villagers are illiterate. Without reading any Scripture portion, even village pastors can narrate these stories and can win many souls for Christ. May God bless you abundantly to train many storytellers in order to extend His kingdom in this earth.

I treasure these strong affirmations for the program from men who are part of the academic environment of a Bible School and Seminary.

Because the mixed language group needed parallel testing venues for the various languages, the oral testing was completed more quickly than for batch A. So in the time remaining I assigned the storytellers and their apprentices the task of learning five stories from Daniel 1–6, which they did with relative ease.[*]

Findings

1. The mnemonic symbols are an adequate and effective means of remembering the stories in this context. This was shown beyond any

---

[*] The Daniel stories were included on the field assignment sheets in the Old Testament track, but because of insufficient training time had never been required learning. However, we discovered that a number of the storytellers as well as their apprentices had learned these stories and had been telling them anyway.

doubt through the dual instruments of the chronology exam and the multiple-choice exam. It was even demonstrated to extend to the GEN3 apprentices, some of whom had become so familiar with the symbols they were able to place all of them in order, including symbols for stories that had not been formally required.

2. Transfer: the exam proved the effectiveness of story transfer to subsequent generations of tellers. I expected transfer with some loss (see chapter 5, Fig. 5). As it turned out, 6 out of the 22 apprentices scored higher on the composite exam than their GEN2 teachers. Some were clearly better storytellers: Anil Gaikwad, Jagnath Nag, Pataras Ranbi, Balmik Kumar Digal, Joseph Kumar Lima, and Premsilo Suna all exceeded their teachers on their oral tellings scores. Another four apprentices effectively equaled the scores their teachers made on the oral tellings. This means that 45% of the apprentices who came to the exam equaled or exceeded their teachers on the oral tellings. Some of these apprentices are clearly dynamic storytellers who are able to tell with great accuracy and who seemed to have learned the entire track of stories even without attending the central training. (See Appendix K).

3. Multiplication: the eleven GEN3 apprentices brought by batch A claimed they themselves were training fourteen GEN4 storyteller apprentices; the 11 apprentices brought by batch B claimed 15 GEN4 apprentices. This is a total of 29 new GEN4 storytellers just within the testing body. Of course it was not possible to test them. However, if the performance of the GEN3 apprentices is any indication, some of these downline storytellers would also prove to be well-equipped storytellers.

4. The exam: the testing instruments designed for this exam were shown to function adequately, with one exception. I originally included a case instance component in which an examiner posed a case instance and the storyteller was asked to respond by saying which story he would tell and why. This did not seem to yield definitive results so I did not test the second batch with this component. I surmise there may have been several reasons for the seeming inadequacy of this instrument:

    a. It was too abstract/ artificial, in the sense that the examinees were being confronted with hypothetical or contrived cases. Perhaps this could be improved on by using role play.

    b. The storytellers had not been familiarized with this type of learning activity in the course.

    c. The examiners chose to posit some case situations that were more suited to an academic Bible School environment than to a realistic village context. In the future, cases should be developed as much as possible from actual situations the storytellers have faced in the field. *

d. Despite the shortcomings, one finding was that in the absence of a focused parallel story, the storytellers would often simply tell any faith-building story. Based on the reports they give, this practice seems to yield effective results in their field contexts.

Conclusion

Beyond the stated results from the exam, perhaps the most convincing proof of the effectiveness of the program was found in the reproduction of storytelling in the GEN3 apprentices, and in listening to the storytellers as they recounted 25 new reports about their use of the Bible stories in the field.

Vijaypal's apprentice, Vishwas, reported that he had told some Bible stories to a village family who were Hindus. Consequently Gautum, the head of that family, came to believe in Christ. Among the stories that they had listened to was the "Daniel and the lions" story.

Late one night as Gautum and a friend were walking through the forest going back to their village, they were suddenly confronted with a lion standing in their path. The friend was struck speechless with terror, but Gautum instantly remembered the Daniel story, and prayed aloud: "The one who delivered Daniel from the lions' mouth is able to deliver us also." Then they both turned and ran as fast as they could. Amazingly the lion did not chase them. When they tried to pass through later, the lion was no longer there.

An even more current report happened on the train as they were coming to the exam. Some of the storytellers and their apprentices were traveling on a train filled with young Buddhist pilgrims on their way to an initiation ceremony. Satish had fallen asleep. When he awoke, he saw his apprentice, Anil, engaged in telling the Bible stories to a group of Buddhists sitting near them. Satish quickly went and brought the other storytellers and their apprentices to help. As a result, four of the young Buddhist pilgrims made professions of faith in Christ. The Creation story especially seemed to have great impact for these Buddhists.†

These and other similar reports were convincing testimony that the storytellers had learned the stories in ways that were both usable and reproducible in their own contexts.

---

* In *Case Studies in Missions,* Paul Hiebert gives many true life examples that could be helpful in developing such case instances.
† See Chapter 11 for Anil's story.

Chapter 11

CASE STUDIES

It is easy to forget how mysterious and mighty stories are.
They do their work in silence, invisibly. They work
with all the internal materials of the mind and self.
They become part of you while changing you.
Beware the stories you read or tell: subtly, at night,
beneath the waters of consciousness,
they are altering your world.

–BEN OKRI

There is perhaps no better way of gauging the potential of a training program than to listen to the stories of those who have been changed by it. In this chapter, five storytellers relate how their lives were transformed through the oral Bible project.

FELT NEEDS LEADING TO CONVERSION

Mangal Kisku and Bilion Soren are two Santal men who learned storytelling in the pilot project. Now both are full-time Christian workers. Neither attended a formal Bible school, so they are examples of ministers who received only storytelling training. The deep descriptions in their stories provide a window into the life of a village person, above all their fear of displeasing the spirits.

MANGAL KISKU

Storyteller Mangal Kisku was 33 years old, and had been a Christian for 13 years when he enrolled in the pilot project to learn Biblical storytelling. His parents named him Mangal because he was born on a Tuesday which is *Mangalvar* in their language. As a child, he attended public school for four years, so he can read a little, although neither his mother nor his wife can read. During his storytelling training he lived and ministered in a refugee camp where many thousands of individuals from his people group sought safety from the tribal warfare that destroyed their villages. Mangal and his wife have six children.

The Kisku clan historically was the royal clan of the tribe's kings. His father was the tribal priest of the village, and since the office was hereditary Mangal always knew he would be the next priest. The priest was responsible for all the spirit ceremonies, sacrificing in the holy groves to placate evil spirits (*bongas*) and to get help from the good ones.

In his story (below), Mangal tells how he was converted and received a call into the ministry. Since he didn't know the Bible, no one would listen to him. But when he joined the original class of storytellers in 2001, he learned to tell large portions of the Bible in 130 stories, and he became a highly effective evangelist. In 2005 he was the number one soul-winner for his agency in his state, having significant success planting churches in a forest reserve area that has many new villages.

Mangal's Personal Story

> I greet you in the name of Jesus Christ. My name is Pastor Mangal Kisku. I was born and brought up in a non-Christian family. My whole family background was immersed in our tribal religion. From the very beginning, we had a duty among our people to do the work of priesthood. My grandfather was doing the priestly work, my father did it in his turn, and this priestly duty came to me finally. According to my childhood memories, our household was large and we had many servants. My three older sisters were there, and also my grandfather and grandmother. My mother died while I was young. I was the youngest one, younger than my three sisters.

> As I remember it now, there was no lack in our family. Everything was very good. My sisters were working and we ha d male and female servants who were also working there in our house. Our relatives used to come every week, sometimes twice or even thrice. And there

was so much peace in our family. Of course, whenever guests would come to visit, then there would be drinking and all.

But when I became a little older, a terrible sickness came into our family. And this sickness was very terrible. Everyone in my family became deathly ill. Only my grandfather and I were safe from this sickness. All the others became sick. So we called all our relatives and the village people and they gathered at our house. And we called the *ojhas* (witch doctors). And they did according to their power. They told us, "The *bongas* are eating you. So you have to give a sacrifice to them." They told my grandfather, "Before, you gave a lamb to the *bongas*. Now you have to give another lamb, otherwise you all will die."

So my grandfather begged the village people, "Please help me. You sacrifice the lamb on behalf of us to our *bongas*. You do the priestly rituals to sacrifice to the *bongas*." Then the village people said, "We cannot do this. We have already been sacrificing on your behalf, but it is not working. You must do the sacrifice to your *bongas* yourself."

There is one *bonga* that is named the Abge Bonga.* My grandfather called that Abge Bonga and told him, "I will give this much sacrifice to you." Then the Abge Bonga asked him, "How much are you willing to give?" He replied, "One, two, three, four, five— even ten lambs," and still the Abge Bonga was not happy and he did not bless us. That Abge Bonga did not even accept the ten lambs from us. From that day onward the people in my family began to die. On the first day, two of us died. And just like that, one day after the other, body after body was being taken out from my home. The village people would take one dead body to bury it and when they came back from burying that one, then they would see there was another dead body. And it kept happening like that. One after the other, all the people in my family started to die. My grandfather was so full of sorrow. Even though he was the priest

---

* The *abge bongas* are secret spirits that are proprietary to a subclan. They are considered to be the most sacred and the most guarded household spirits and are said to give earthly blessings and to save in time of danger. In the case of disease and distress within a household, the Santals appeal to them, believing that once this is done the disease will suddenly disappear. Their names are known only by the head of household who keeps them secret until just before his death when he whispers them to his eldest son, who can solemnize the sacrifice to the *abge bongas* only after he has learned their names. (Troisi, 88).

in his clan, he was powerless to do anything. Of all those people in our household, only three survived: my grandfather, my older sister and I. All the others died.

Then my sister got married and she left our home. So after that only my grandfather and I were left. I was going here and there with my grandfather and I was also studying in primary school. Later my grandfather also died. So then I was all alone.

When my grandfather died, the village people gave all our property to my relatives. I started living with my uncle. And that priestly duty which had been done by my grandfather and father, it was given to me by the village people. Although I had no knowledge of how to sacrifice to the *bongas*, still they had given me that duty. So I was doing everything according to their suggestions.

I was not happy living with my uncle's family, so I went away to work as a servant in someone else's house. I was going back and forth and I was doing the priestly work in my village. After doing this for many days, I finally released my priestly duties to the village headman.

While I was there working as a servant, one night I had a dream. A man was standing behind me and saying to me, "You are an orphan. And you do not have any relatives. So what will happen to you in later days? If you believe in Jesus Christ and come to the Lord, then you will be saved and your life will be very good." That man in the dream told me, "You do not know anything and you are sacrificing chickens to the gods. This is not a good work which you are doing. So leave all of that and come to the Lord, and you will be saved and God will help you."

When I woke up in the morning, I clearly remembered the dream. I thought, "What is that? This man in the dream was telling me everything that has happened to me. So what is this?" I was surprised and wondering about this dream, what it meant, and what to do. I thought, "It is real. See, this man told me the truth that I do not have anyone to help me. I am on my own and there is no one with me. I am staying here as a servant. So that man told me the truth. He told me to come to the Lord and he will help me. So I should do this." So I decided to obey that dream.

I got married and we came back to our home where my uncle was living. I tried to find some *ojha* to call our *bongas* again so the *bongas* might tell us something. But there was no reply from the *bongas* for us. I went everywhere to find an *ojha*. At last I found an *ojha* in another village. And that *ojha* had a signboard on his home where it was written *dun guru*, which means the witchcraft chief or head. I went there and he told me about all the things that had happened in our family before. He told me everything. I was surprised and wondering, "Who told him?"

Finally I thought, "It is impossible for me to control the *bongas*. I will not be able to satisfy these *bongas* and I will die." So I made the decision to leave all these *bongas* and come to the Lord. I went back to my home and told all of this to my wife.

I told her, "We cannot live with these *bongas* and we cannot worship them. We cannot control them. So please, let us go and become Christians. Let us go to the Lord and worship the living God." I called all my relatives and the village people and I told them, "We are no longer staying in this *bonga* worship belief. I will become a Christian. And I will no longer do any priestly work." They told me, "From the beginning your family and clan has been doing the priest's work. So who will do it?" I said, "You do it. I am free from it and I will not do it anymore. I am not able to control these *bongas*. I cannot do this work."

So we made a firm decision that day and we went to a Christian pastor who was living near us, and we told him everything about us. We told him that we cannot be "Hindus" any longer. That means we cannot continue with this worship of the *bongas*. We want to be Christians instead. So the pastor told us about Jesus Christ and about God and he made us understand. And on that day he prayed for us and we accepted Jesus Christ in our lives.

After we became Christians, we started to pray more and more because we were afraid that after having left, all the *bongas* might come to harm us. So we stayed strong in prayer. And Pastor was teaching us some words about God and Jesus Christ. But then Pastor moved to another town and left us there.

Then another servant of God came; his name was John Soren. He helped us to become strong in the Lord. We attended a Lutheran church. But when John Soren came, he made us understand more about the word of God, and later we took water baptism in the Dhardhora River.

So we were very happy in the Lord. We were praying more, and we were so enthusiastic to tell others about Jesus Christ. We were preaching to nearby families and in neighboring villages and we won another family in our village to Christ. We prayed together and little by little we won yet another family. Then we started a fellowship there and later, with the help of Pastor John, a church. From 1992, Pastor John Soren told us to work together for the Lord. So in this way we were going into the ministry. We had so much peace in our family and my children were hardly ever sick. If any sickness was coming, then we prayed so that sickness left our bodies. In this way, we were doing the work of God, and little by little, many families started to come to our church.

But then there was the riot [the time of trouble in 1996], the fighting between the Santals and the Bodos. Pastor John Soren was killed by the terrorists, and we all had to flee to a refugee camp. In the relief camp we continued to gather and worship the Lord and work together.*

A Bible storytelling program was starting at that time in a city eight hours away, so two of us enrolled. After several years, I completed the storytelling training and received a certificate.

At the end of each training module, Uncle† would give us a blank field report form and tell us, "Go back to your village and wherever you go, tell these Bible stories to others." I was so happy to be telling the Bible stories. I would call the people in one place to tell them the stories, and they were listening—our Santal people love to hear stories.

---

* This fellowship was made up of believers from three different Pentecostal churches which had been started by Pastor John, Mangal and others, whose members were in the relief camp.
† The term "Uncle" refers to the author.

Even the "Hindu" people (non-Christians) were very interested to hear the stories. At nighttime, I would gather the people in one household and tell them the Bible stories. So this is how I was telling the stories and people were listening and enjoying it.

During this time I was doing day labor work in the field in Serfanguri. Many people would work together in the field squatting in lines while we cleaned the rows of jute grass. It takes all day to do the work. So while we were working together, I was telling them the Bible stories and they were listening and laughing. The people there did not know the word of God, so these stories from the Bible were new to them. They would hear the stories in the field during the days, and at nighttime we would get together and learn the story-songs. They enjoyed those stories and they learned them. When we were working, wherever I would go, then this group of people would also go with me, because they liked the stories that I was telling. So while I was working I was also telling those stories, sometimes healing stories, miracle stories, so many kinds of stories.

One day one family asked me, "See brother, you are telling such healing stories. We have a two year old daughter but she is not walking yet. She is like a lame person. Will you do something for us? You told us about the God in those stories. Can that God heal my daughter?" So I told them, "If you believe in this God, then your daughter will be healed." They agreed and said to me, "Yes, we will receive and worship that God."

So at evening time, when I would go there and tell them stories, I prayed for that girl. She became healed and the whole family accepted Jesus Christ as their Savior. I called my supervisor and they took water baptism. Over time, two or three other families came to the Lord, so we started a fellowship there.

So through these stories I have established two or three churches so far. Because of that I love the stories very much. Those stories are made by God only. They are powerful and people are hearing them and believing, and their lives are changing. Because of that, nowadays I am only telling stories, I am not telling anything else. I am only doing storytelling. Through the stories the work of God is going on and growing fast. I have won many souls. I have been teaching my believers those stories, and they are learning them. I am so happy to tell the stories. I love the stories, because stories are loved by everybody, whether animist or Christian. Nobody denies the stories. And through the stories, the word of God is very easy to share, to do the ministry and to bring the people to Christ.

This is my prayer that in the area where I am staying now, the [government forest] reserve, that God may bring great revival through the storytelling program. Because it is a new area, the people are unable to sacrifice to the *bongas* because their *ojhas* are not there. So they are coming to Christ, and are being set free from the *bongas*. In our village also there are some people who were disturbed by the *bongas* and they were going through different kinds of sicknesses but were not receiving any healing in their bodies. They were helpless. Now those people are coming to Christ and their lives are shining and their families are now doing very good. So I can testify that God is blessing them and God is with us. He is among us. The word of God is growing very fast.

Now I want to do the hard work. I will go to every village and tell the stories of God. We have set a goal to start at least three more new churches in the forest reserve area, because there are so many people who are illiterate, not knowing how to read and write. But they can learn the Bible stories and hide the word of God in their heart. Because it is the true word of God.

Nowadays in our family there is much peace and we can sense the blessing of God. All of us together are working for the Lord; my wife and my children are helping me in my ministry. My daughters have learned the songs which were made from the Bible stories. Whenever we go to visit the animist families, we tell the stories from the Bible and we sing the story-songs. God is working among them through us and people are coming to Christ. So my whole family is fully involved in the ministry.

Wherever we go, this is what I tell people: If you come to Christ then you will be saved. So please come to Christ and pay heed to the stories and be a changed person in your society and in your nation. Do not believe in the *bongas* because the *bongas* cannot do anything for us. They will always put you in trouble and they will kill and destroy you. They will make demands of you, and they cannot help you in any way. They have no mercy, no kindness. But there is a living God who is a merciful God. He loves us and he never wants anything from us. He does not want any money. But he helps us in our problems and difficulties. That God can give you peace and joy in your life just like he changed us. Before, we were living with so much fear and poverty, but now God is providing for us and giving us peace and joy in our lives. See, because we became Christian, from my family, my own children, no one has died. All of them are still alive. They are growing in the Lord and they have a good, sound physical life. My children pray every day, early in the morning. They praise God every day. And wherever a service is held, they are attending and praising God. So I can tell you the *bongas* cannot do anything. They are powerless to a believer in Christ.[*]

Supplemental Report about Mangal Kisku: [†]

People loved Mangal's ministry so much, after the first family came to Christ, altogether they became more than five or six families of believers. Every day they would invite him to eat lunch with a different family—they would even fight over whose turn it was to have the pastor come to eat with them and listen to his stories! In all the villages where he went, because of the stories he told, young people and children came to know him and considered him to be their friend.

Another group started in the village where Mangal's wife was from. Her brother-in-law was suffering intense stomach pain. He had sought medical treatment from a doctor and also went to a witch doctor for treatment, but his condition did not improve. When Mangal went there to visit his relatives, he heard that his brother-in-law was sick, so he told them stories from the Gospels about Jesus healing sick people. Through hearing these stories, the brother-in-law who was sick with stomach pain believed, and after several visits of listening to the stories he began to improve. In only a couple of weeks he was completely well! This village was totally non-Christian, but because of this miracle they allowed Mangal to tell the Bible stories every day, and little by little, people began to believe in Jesus Christ. They understood the love of God in the stories of the Bible when God healed them. Now half a dozen families there are Christian believers. They even have their own church now, and their own pastor.

The *manjhi*, headman of that same village, was also a witch doctor who talked with the spirits. His eldest son was possessed by evil spirits. So when

---

[*] Video interview November 2006; translated into English by Ismail Hembrom.

[†] Gathered from various sources by Ismail Hembrom. (November 2005).

they heard that Mangal was telling Bible stories and praying for sick people, they brought this young man to him for prayer. When Mangal looked at him, he discerned that it was the work of an evil spirit. So to make them understand that God would come and deliver this man, he told them a Bible story about deliverance (Mark 5:1–20). As they listened to this story, both the father and mother believed and asked Mangal to pray for their son. When Mangal prayed, that young man got delivered! Now he is a strong believer in Christ. He has also learned many of the Bible stories and tells them himself. So many people were inviting Mangal to come tell Bible stories in various villages that he did not have time to go to all the places. Because of Mangal's training in the storytelling program, whenever he preached he could bring all the passages together and knew them well. Even young ministers who had a Bible school degree were saying, "This man is unschooled, he doesn't even know Hindi; how does he know all these stories and is preaching like a Bible School graduate?" Bible School graduates know theological ideas, but Mangal knows the Bible itself. He can tell the Bible itself, through the many stories that he knows.

BILION SOREN

Bilion is a fierce-looking man, the kind you would not want to run into in a dark alley. He was originally from a different village. But the war between the two tribes was everywhere and he and his wife and little children had to leave their home and their land and run away for fear of their lives. They too came to the refugee camp. They had nothing; no money, no clothing, not even any firewood to cook their food. And then their real ordeal began. Spirits began to torment them unceasingly:

> We did not know from where this evil spirit came. When the daylight had gone and the dark came, we were unable to go outside our home because we felt so much fear. Even in our dreams, we saw so many *bongas* that were coming. Some did not have any head, legs, or eyes, and they had big teeth. There were so many of these *bongas* in our dreams. Other *bongas* were sticking their big tongues out, showing their tongues to us.

Tragically, a few days later Bilion's young wife became desperately ill and then died in childbirth. The baby also died. Bilion was left with his two young daughters, Sohagini, and Sonamuni. One day a tribal witch doctor came by: "What is going on with you?" that witchcraft man said. "Your grandmother and grandfather were worshipping the *bongas*, these goddesses. But you are not worshipping them and they want to come to you. That is why your wife died. And still they are on the way to come to your family. So you have to worship them, or else you will all die."

Bilion asked him, "What do I have to do?"

The witch doctor replied, "If you don't give them a sacrifice and satisfy them they are going to finish you off."

Bilion became very frightened. How could he appease these horrible spirits? Suddenly he remembered something his father had told him when he was a boy:

> My grandmother had told my father, "You see all these *bongas*? They are very strong. Through them you can do many great, great things. But if you are not able to control them, they may finish you off. So if you find you cannot control them, you must become a Christian." My father had asked, "Then why, Mommy, have you not become a Christian?" She said, "You see, I am able to control them. That's why."

Bilion tells the rest of the story:

> Then I became full of fear. Now I knew that it was these *bongas* that were destroying us and that my wife had died because of them. What should I do? I was in great difficulty. Then I remembered the things that Pastor had told me, the stories from the Bible. Suddenly I took a decision and I cried out to God. I said, "O Lord God, I don't know anything. I only know that you are there, a Creator and I know of Jesus Christ. But I don't know what to do. So You help me. Should I serve all these *bongas* or what should I do? I don't know. You tell me." And then I prayed with tears.

> For two or three days I had been praying like this. I did not know how to pray, but simply from a broken heart and full of faith. While I was praying and crying, then I got peace of mind, and suddenly light came into my heart. Then I saw that the word of God is powerful and I gave my life to Jesus Christ. That was on October 13, 2001. Then I took water baptism and started to live a good Christian life, full of joy, and I started attending the church. From that day, there has not been any kind of sound or disturbance or bad dream in my family or home. Nothing bad has happened to us.

Soon after, Bilion enrolled in the oral Bible pilot project and began to learn the Bible stories:

I had never learned the word of God, I did not even have a Bible, I did not know how to pray. But when Pastor enrolled me in the Bible storytelling program, suddenly I could learn so many Bible stories— so many wonderful stories from the Bible. And my life was touched and deeply changed by those stories. I became a storyteller of the Bible. From that time, while we were learning the stories, I started to tell these stories to others. Because the stories helped me in my own life, I was so interested to tell them to others, because I could explain the answer of the living God. Jesus is really there, always with me, and He wants everybody to know Him.

Over several years, Bilion faithfully attended all the oral Bible pilot project training events and was diligent to complete his field assignments. In March 2005, he graduated second in his class. During this time, he also served his pastor in the local church. Then an opportunity came that he had been longing for, the chance to pastor a church. Every week he would get on his beat-up old bicycle and ride 20 miles each way to the village of Matiapara:

There were a few backslidden Christians in that village, and they were helpless. While I was telling them the stories, they became happy and invited me to come to that place and tell them the stories of the Bible and have fellowship with them. So I got a wonderful opportunity to do God's work. By telling the stories every day with the people in that village, now many people have come to faith in Jesus Christ, and we have established a church there.

In the evening Bilion calls the people together in one place and tells them the stories, and also sings the songs that are related to that story. Bilion describes his communication style:

I was never able to go to Bible School to learn how to preach, or even what the principles of preaching are. All I knew was how to tell a story. So instead of preaching like others, I just simply told the stories whenever I got a chance. I told the stories of the Old Testament, about the lives of Old Testament people, and how God was in the Old Testament. And how Jesus came to this world, and what he did for all of us. Now many people have believed in Jesus Christ and have taken water baptism and there is a good church of around 13 or 14 families there (when I started there were only four families). And people are still coming to Christ through this storytelling.*

---

* When I last saw him, Bilion was preparing to baptize 26 more new converts.

Bilion's felt need for a Savior who could deliver him from the torment of the *bongas* drove him to Christ. Many others are coming in the same way:

> One day a man from another town came to my village looking for an *ojha* (witch doctor). He asked me, "Brother, do you know where that *ojha* lives? We came to see him because we are in such a bad condition. The *bongas* are disturbing us, and we need the *ojha* to find the problem and know what the *bongas* want from us so we can make a sacrifice to them."

Bilion shared his own story with the man, how Christ had set him free from the *bongas*. So instead of going to the *ojha*'s house, they asked Bilion to go back to their village with them:

> They decided, "We will take Bilion, because he shared his testimony of what happened in his own life. It is true—we believe him; so we will take him to our home."

> So I went with them. Their brother was sick; he was in the hospital. I did not get a chance to tell him a story; I just prayed for him and came back home. But I sent word to Pastor and the next day both of us went there and we both told the stories of Jesus Christ, the powerful stories, the healing stories. And they all believed. Again we prayed for them, and slowly that brother was healed and they were set free. Now sometimes when I go to visit them, they say, "It is because of Bilion's story that we changed from nominal Christians."*

After Ismail Hembrom visited Bilion in December 2005, he reported:

> Bilion took me to a family where there was a man possessed by an evil spirit. Bilion told them the Bible story of the man who lived among the tombs (Mark 5:1–20). He also shared other examples to help them understand, and they heard and believed the stories. We both prayed for that demon-possessed man and he began to receive healing and deliverance. That man and his family were all from a non-Christian background. They were Santals who were also doing Hindu worship practices. When they saw that the man was getting some healing, they believed and they asked us, "Come again and tell

---

* This report was compiled primarily from an interview that was recorded on digital video in Gossaigon, Assam (Oct 2006); translated into English by Ismail Hembrom.

us the stories and pray for us. We will believe in Jesus Christ. We are ready to accept Jesus Christ." A week later when Bilion visited them again, that demon-possessed man became totally free. Now that family has taken water baptism and they are believers and attend Bilion's church. This was such a powerful testimony that another family also came to Christ after seeing how that demon-possessed man was healed.

Ismail concludes with this observation about felt needs:

> I have seen that the most effective Bible stories are stories about healing and deliverance. People are coming to Christ because they have these same needs. It is because they are in such a pathetic condition that they are willing to come to Christ. If they have enough money and have all they need, then they do not have a desire to experience or even understand the blessing of God in their life. But if they are desperate and have no other hope and have tried many things, such as medicine and doctors, and religious rites and magic, then at last they will come and try the Christian way. There is only one way to bring them to Christ, and that is either healing or deliverance.

TRANSFORMED LIVES

What do a village drunk, a terrorist and a young man dying of HIV have in common? For each, the power of God's stories—in combination with prayer—was amazingly transformative.

Somarsing's Story

When a storyteller began visiting his home, Somarsing was a hopeless village drunk who spent every cent he could earn on hard liquor. Occasionally he would listen as the stories from the Bible were told to his family. After many visits, Somarsing finally gave his heart to the Lord and was gloriously transformed. Soon he enrolled in the Oral Bible training and over several years learned to tell many stories from the Bible himself. Recently Somarsing was asked to become the pastor of the same church that won him to the Lord. Here is his story:

My name is Somarsing Narjanary. I was born in a Hindu family. When I grew up and got married, we were living near the state border where there was a customs checkpost. I was working there and earning good money. Together with my friends, we were drinking and eating meat and simply enjoying life like anything. But "today a little, tomorrow a little," like that, slowly I started to drink too much and my body deteriorated. Then my family, my marriage became broken down, and even my land was lost to the moneylender. Because of my drinking, I even had to sell the good house I had built. I destroyed everything and abused my family. Finally my wife and children were living in poverty, not having anything because I could not provide for them. There was no peace and everything was unsettled. Everything in my family was ruined; there was no care for anyone and we did not even have any proper clothing to wear. I was drinking like anything, and I was not even aware of where I was sleeping at night or what I was eating. I was unconscious. Sometimes I used to sleep on the roadway and sometimes in the jungle.

Seeing all the destitution of my family, a Christian minister of God, Phulen Bosumatary, came to my home and told me the Bible stories. He was trying to make me understand how to leave the wine behind and live a good life. They spent so much time on me. Every day, twice, or thrice, they used to come and tell me the stories and counsel me. But I was not hearing much, and they were unable to make me understand. But they kept coming to my home for more than one month. At that time I hated Christ and the Christian people; that is why I was not able to hear and to understand. Because these people were always coming, this is what I would do: early in the morning I would wake up and have something to eat, and then I would run away from my home and not come back for the whole day.

So my elder son and my family members and these pastors, they forced me too much to come to the church. Slowly we began attending, and I understood a little bit and tried to change my life. I became a Christian and I was attending the church. After a few months, they brought me to a Bible storytelling program and enrolled me into that program. There also, I was not ready, but they forced me to join. From every angle, I was trying to run away from this. When I came to the storytelling program, I knew nothing about the Bible. I did not know what was in it or any of the Bible stories. I did not even know which was the top or the bottom of the Bible. I had only been with Christian people for one month when they put a Bible in my hand. I did not know what to do with it. But they were telling me to tell the stories from the Bible. So in this way, after one day, two days, three days, I learned a Bible story one by one. Every month and every year I have been continuing. Now I have learned so many stories from the Bible, and now I could know God and I could understand the truth. After I completed three years of the Bible storytelling program, I received the certificate. After finishing that, I have been pastoring a church.

Nowadays the neighboring village people and the Christian people are very surprised to see me, this drunkard who became a pastor in a church. What a wonderful thing that God can do this in a life. Everyone knew me. Before they did not like me because I was a drunkard. People who would never talk to me or be seen with me now talk with me; they greet me. So I feel very happy and am full of joy. My neighbors and my relatives are all happy to see my life has changed and how my family has changed and everything is good with me now. Now I am pastoring over a hundred believers. What a wonderful thing that God has given me such a privilege. Because of that I am so happy, and I am praising God for that. Now I am a worker of the mission—I am a servant of God.

Now even my relatives and others are coming to me, and I am able to lead them to Christ because my life was changed. I even got my land back from the moneylender. All my land and every family member is saved because I accepted Jesus Christ. I am so proud and happy because God has done a great thing in my life and in my family. Now every old thing is passed away and I am a new creation in the Lord. Hallelujah.

What are the things I have learned from this? I have learned the stories well. Slowly, slowly, slowly, because of those stories, that is how I learned everything: what to do, how to live, how to obey God. And slowly, my life was totally changed. I cannot even imagine how I was before, a drunkard and who I am now. I cannot even imagine that I have experienced such a great amount of change. I can say now that I was foolish. I was misusing and wasting lots of money, only for drinking. But God saved me from such a condition, and oh, how greatly my life was changed. People are surprised to see me because I was dead. But God gave me life. The people were so surprised they used to exclaim, "See how your life has changed nowadays. Before there was no peace in your family. But now there is peace and joy in your children's lives, and in your wife's life and in your life!"

And I was in such a condition. But God lifted me. Though I was an ordinary man, God made me out of nothing and he made me into something. Now I myself am teaching the people who are in such a condition, and I am leading the church. That is a great miracle in my life.*

Somarsing recounts a ministry experience:

There was a poor person in my village who couldn't ride a bicycle. He asked me, "Please take me to town on your cycle." After we arrived, I met an old woman there who had known me before. She knew I had come to Christ so she took me along to the house of another elderly woman who had been sick for a long time. Although her family members had taken her to the hospital in Vellore, she didn't get any better. When we arrived, her whole family was there with her. I thought, "This is a Hindu's house. How will I pray here?" So I asked them, "Can I pray?" and they gave permission. I went over to the sick woman and prayed. Her hands and legs were stiff and rigid, like they were stuck in one position. When I prayed, suddenly she opened her eyes wide and started looking at me. Her hands and legs became free. I became frightened because this was my first miracle that I had ever seen. I was thinking, "Now what will I do? Oh, look at the way she is looking at me like this!" I stepped away from her to another corner of the room. I was so frightened, I started praying by myself there. When her family members saw her, they also became frightened just like I was. I prayed, "God save me." They demanded, "What did you do?" I told them, "I didn't do anything. God did it!" Everybody was amazed. Even the old woman who had asked me to come was amazed. Then I told the sick person, "Now you sleep," and she slept. Nobody in that house (except me) was a believer.†

---

* Video interview October 31, 2006; translated by Ismail Hembrom
† Video interview January 4, 2005; translated by Ismail Hembrom.

Somarsing's Story Told by Phulen Bosumatary

When I came into the oral Bible program and I learned the stories, God helped me to tell the stories in my village. There is a man there whose name is Somarsing; he used to drink heavily. But God spoke in my heart to go to this man and tell him the stories from the Bible. So I went and I told his wife, "Since your husband is drunken every day, because of this you became very poor. If you believe in the Lord, God can change your situation and your condition." His wife agreed with me and we prayed for her husband. I went to their house many times, and told them many stories from the Bible. Most of the time I told Somarsing the story of the Prodigal Son. As I continued telling this same story again and again, God started to work in his heart. He changed and started to leave his drunkenness and other bad habits.

People were saying, "He will never be able to stay away from these things." I told them, "He has changed by God's power and he is not going back again." But the people of his village were mocking him, "You cannot change. You cannot live a Christian life. We know you. You have been a drunkard for a long time every day." I would take Somarsing with me like a disciple wherever I went to a meeting, and I taught him more and more of the stories.

Slowly Somarsing's faith in Jesus Christ began growing, and he decided to be baptized in water. He became a regular church-attender, seldom missing a meeting. And whenever programs were being done in my church he was always first in line to help me. Not only that, he also became a disciple of mine in the Bible story program. Now God has blessed them abundantly in their family; now they are not poverty-stricken any longer. Unlike before, instead of fighting and drunkenness, now he's living a gentle good life with his wife and children. I believe that only because of this story program could I have won the heart of Somarsing. And in the same way that I brought him into Christ, he himself is bringing more people to the Lord.[*]

Supplementary report by Ismail Hembrom

When Phulen first brought Somarsing to the storytelling program, he was so new to the Lord that his eyes were still red and he looked cruel. But slowly

---

[*] Report given November 2005; recorded on digital video; translated by Ismail Hembrom.

as he learned the Bible he became so different looking. I was there and I saw it myself. At first I was thinking, "What kind of a man is this? Maybe he is a drunkard, and maybe he is mean. Even his teeth were red because he was still chewing tobacco." Somarsing had just begun the storytelling program and he was unable to read or remember much in those early days. But God can change such a man. What a miracle! So many pastors and others had tried to bring him into the right behavior, to make him leave all the bad habits behind. He was drinking so much; and he was beating his wife and children and others whenever he got drunk. That was before. But God did his work in him. And now he is a very good man.

INTERVIEW (CONDUCTED BY ISMAIL HEMBROM):

Q. I asked Somarsing about his oral context.
A. He told me, "I am not much educated. But I used to read magazines and some stories also. My wife cannot read. But my children are studying in school and they can read. There are not many books in my home, only a few."

Q. Describe your Christian experience.
A. Through the story of the Prodigal Son, God spoke to me and spoke into my life, and my life became changed. I confessed my sin and accepted Jesus Christ. My family and my relatives became Christians. Through me, my wife and daughter were influenced to start telling the stories of the Bible. Now they can tell 20 or 30 stories by themselves.

Q. I asked Somarsing about his use of the oral Bible.
A. I usually share two stories each time. The people like to listen to these stories. I often tell them the story about not worrying (Mat. 6:25–33).
Ismail: He quoted the verses exactly without even looking at the Bible. He has them memorized perfectly, because this is one of the stories he learned in the oral Bible program.

Q. Talk about any struggles you had while doing biblical storytelling.
A. In my place, I cannot conduct the storytelling program outside the church. Because of that, I have not had much success in multiplying storyteller disciples. But, I can tell stories among believers and their families, and some of my own relatives have become believers because I told the stories to them.
Ismail interjects, "The reason why Somarsing cannot conduct the storytelling program outside the church is because his tribe opposes Christianity. If someone comes to Christ, they will make them pay a Rs.10,000 fine. This is paid to the headman

of that village and goes into the society fund for that village. Then they will make them leave their village and go somewhere else. Otherwise, they will beat them over and over; they will quarrel with them. They may even try to kill them, so they would have to leave the village. That is the rule among the non-Christian Bodos.

Q. What were your religious experiences and beliefs before becoming a Christian?
A. Before I worshipped goddesses. I used to hate the Christian people; I was so fanatical that I would beat them. I was totally against all Christians.

Q. Talk about your childhood and your family.
A. Up to age 15, I was living in a rural area. My mother and father used to take me to the Hindu religious places and festivals, because they were Hindu. They believed that Hinduism is the great religion, so they told everyone else to be a Hindu also. Before I came to Christ, I was only a nominal Hindu. But if I heard a Christian, I would become angry against them.

Q. What does conversion mean to you?
A. My conversion happened in 2002, in my old age, after I had already had five children. According to me, conversion means this: You must leave every bad habit behind, turn away from all those old ways, accept Jesus Christ, live a good moral life and serve the Lord.

- Prayer is: asking God to supply anything. When I pray, I pray for every one of the needs.
- About religion: to obey the commandment of God and love my neighbor. God is my Creator and He is everything for me. He is my loving father and he is my need supplier.
- How God functions in my life: He is working every day. Whenever I pray, God hears my prayer and answers me. The most religious acts one can perform: to serve the Lord, to worship, to preach the good news and lead others to Christ. According to me, murder is the greatest sin one can commit in the world. Also, coveting money is a great evil and we should overcome that.
- My idea of the afterlife is eternal life with Christ the Lord.
- Favorite stories: the story of Noah and the Flood and the story of the Tower of Babel.
- Favorite Bible verse: 2 Corinthians 5:17, that "whoever is in Christ is a new creation."
- Favorite Bible character: life of Joseph.

- Three wishes from God: God may keep me away from every problem; I may be His faithful servant; our family may serve the Lord.*

RUBILAL'S STORY

About 7:30 one evening in December a knock came on the door of Santosh and Emily, two of the storytellers in the oral Bible pilot project. It was a messenger from a group of young terrorists hiding in a nearby forest. Would Pastor Santosh please come and help them?

One of the terrorists, a young man who had already brutally killed at least eight people during his career, had become critically ill, crying day and night from the unbearable pain. The terrorists' cook, who is from a nominal Christian family, had told the sick man about a pastor who "tells Bible stories and prays for the sick." Finally the terrorist told the cook, "Go and tell your pastor to come."

When the knock came on their door that evening, Santosh and Emily knew it was dangerous to go to such a place. But after prayer, Santosh accompanied the cook on foot to the terrorists' hideout. When he got there, he told them many Bible stories, especially the stories about Jesus' power to heal the sick; then he prayed with the sick man. By early the next morning, the sick terrorist, who had been unable even to stand, was so much better that he walked to Santosh' and Emily's home. Soon he started coming every day to listen to their stories. Over time he also told them his story. As he recounted the many bad things he had done, he was crying. "No one told me how God is such a great healer. Why was I doing those things? Because I was not knowing about God. I never knew Jesus before." As a sign of his repentance and faith in Christ, he asked to be baptized.

Rubilal had done many dangerous and violent crimes, raping and killing and destroying government properties. Some might ask if God can truly forgive someone who tasted the blood of his victims by licking it off the knife he had used to kill them. It would be difficult for any human being to forgive such horrific acts, but amazingly God's grace and forgiveness extends to anyone who puts his or her faith in Jesus Christ. By his own testimony, the Apostle Paul was such a man. There are indications that even among the 12 disciples chosen by Jesus, some were former terrorists, for instance the man called Simon the Zealot (Luke 6:15). The wonderful old hymn, "Amazing Grace," was written by a former slave trader, John Newton, as his personal testimony to God's power to forgive and transform: "Amazing grace! how sweet the sound, that saved a wretch like me!" It is evident that God saves the worst as well as the best among us.

---

* January 10, 2006.

Here are three accounts of this story: first, by Rubilal himself, then by Pastor Santosh, and finally by Santosh's wife, Emily. It is interesting to note how the stories differ as well as how they agree. Here is Rubilal's story: *

My name is Rubilal Marandi. I was born and brought up in an animist family. I did not know about Jesus Christ. When I was 15, in May 1996, there was fighting between my tribe, the Santals, and the Bodo tribe. To protect our people, I joined a terrorist group. I became a violent man and I killed men and women. With the other terrorists, I destroyed many things belonging to the government. I became skilled in the use of weapons such as guns and long knives.

But after eight years, God caught me, and I became sick. My body became infested with cancer. I went to many different doctors for treatment, but I did not get well. All the doctors told me the same thing: "You are not going to live—you will die from this sickness, because inside your body there are so many wounds." My body was failing and even the smell of death was coming out from me. I was crying out in pain, unable to sleep at night. I thought, "Now I am going to die. There is no medicine that can heal me." I was just trying to enjoy the day, because I expected to die after one or two days. I did not know there is a God who has power to heal me, but I was crying out to get healing from somewhere.

One of my friends told me about a pastor who tells stories from the Bible and prays for the sick. "If you go to him he may pray for you and you might be healed." So I sent for that pastor, and I explained everything to him about my life. He told me stories from the Bible about healing and the love of God and eternal life. I believed in the stories I heard, and I asked the pastor to pray for me. He told me about repentance—I did repent and confessed all of my sins. Then Pastor prayed for me and he went back to his home. I could feel God's healing in my body, and the next morning I went to the pastor's home. I told him, "I am healed!" I was able to understand that God forgave me and healed me; to know that the love of God is there for everyone of us even though I was a great sinner. I understood that God's stories that are written in the Bible are true.

---

* Document written by Rubilal Marandi; translated into English by Ismail Hembrom.

Day after day I kept going to the pastor's house to listen to the stories again and again, so my faith would grow strong. Before long I started attending church services every Sunday, and I learned more about Jesus Christ. Later I was baptized in water. Now I am so happy and joyful living the Christian life. Now God is helping me in every detail of my life. I have started telling God's stories in my own village where there was not even one single Christian believer.*

Rubilal's Story Told by Pastor Santosh Soren

A young man named Rubilal Marandi who was a terrorist was sick with cancer in his male organ. He had gone to many doctors and spent a lot of money on treatments. All the doctors told him that he was not going to get well because the cancer had spread throughout his body. Afterward he was so discouraged and he was staying with the rest of the terrorist gang in the forest. Unable to sleep at night, he was crying out in pain. At last he thought, "I'm going to die. There is no medicine that can heal me." Then Rubilal sent one of his friends to my house. They only knew that I was a pastor who tells Bible stories and that "he is a servant of God, and he could pray for you."

Rubilal had done many dangerous and violent crimes, raping and killing and destroying government properties. I went to see him around nine at night. The first time I saw him he was so seriously ill I could not even fully share the stories from the Bible. All I could do then was to pray for him. I anointed him with oil and gave him some to apply on himself. I told him, "Starting tomorrow you come to my home every day." He agreed and the next morning there he was in front of my door. He was already feeling a little better after the prayer the night before. So I started telling him the Bible stories about having faith in Jesus Christ. I told stories about healing like the story of Jairus' daughter, and the woman who had the issue of blood; how she was going through that sickness for 12 years and she was not cured, but when she touched the garment of Jesus Christ, then she received healing in her body. I told about the Canaanite woman whose daughter was sick. And I told him many other healing stories, and he believed. I told him, "If you really believe in these stories or in God, then you will receive healing in your body." That

---

* About this same time, the government instituted a cease fire and provided means for amnesty and rehabilitation for the terrorists. Through Rubilal's testimony and through the Bible stories, other young men who were terrorists are coming to faith in Jesus Christ.

day that boy believed in Jesus Christ and he accepted Jesus Christ as his personal savior. That night, he was able to receive the healing touch of Jesus Christ in his body. From then on, every day I would tell him new stories, healing stories, powerful stories from the Bible.

After listening to all these stories, then he was able to confess, "Jesus is going to heal me," and believe that He would do it. He had never had a Bible and had never been to church. All I did was tell him stories from the Bible over and over. He accepted Jesus Christ as his Savior, and he was totally healed. He continued attending the church and learned many things through listening to the Bible stories. After one full year, he asked to be baptized in water. I continued to encourage this young man, telling him the stories. Now he has a strong faith in Jesus Christ. He is telling the stories to his family and even his fellow terrorists. There is now a government cease-fire with the terrorists, so he has surrendered to God and to the government. Now he has started a cell group in his village, and he is an evangelist telling the stories with power and boldness wherever he goes, because he has experienced God's power in his life. *

Rubilal's Story Told by Santosh's wife, Emily

One evening, two men came to our home and asked me, "Where is the pastor?" I replied, "Pastor went to the market." Then I sent my son to call him from the market to come home. The two men told my husband, "Pastor, please come to help us; there is a boy who is going through such a sickness. You have to come there." But it is a difficult and dangerous place to go, because only extremists are staying there. So this was a dangerous situation and he was not ready to go there. But I told my husband, "You go there. If you have a problem, then we will come help you." (the terrorist camp was near our home).

When the Pastor got there, he saw a young man lying on his bed; he was in a very terrible condition of pain and sickness. He had been examined by many different doctors, but they had all sent him back, saying, "You will not be cured by medicine." The doctors had told him, "You are not going to be healed or cured. You will die from this condition." It may have been the last night for him to live, and he was crying like anything. He was crying uncontrollably, because he was in

---

* Report given November 2005; recorded on digital video.

so much pain. He had asked his friends to call some Christian pastor or believer to come and pray for him so he could receive healing in his body. That was when they called my husband and he went and prayed for him. The young man was from a non-Christian background. He told my husband, "Uncle, if you pray for me and I receive healing in my body, then I will worship your god; I will worship Jesus and receive Jesus Christ in my life. And I will become a Christian." So Pastor told him a faith story about Jesus, and he believed. He prayed for him and also prayed over the oil and the water, so they could apply it to him during the night. By the next day, the young man had begun to experience the healing touch in his body, and he was so happy. He accepted Jesus Christ, and was full of faith.

That first night the pastor visited him, but the next day when God had healed Rubilal a little, then this young man came to the pastor's house; he walked there by himself. Now he has become a Christian; he accepted Jesus Christ and took water baptism. Besides that, his own mother was paralyzed at that time. When Rubilal received the healing touch of Jesus Christ, he told her, "Jesus healed me and he will also heal you." So because of Rubilal's faith, his mother also came to faith in Jesus Christ, and she has also received healing in her body. Now all of that family, they are in Christ. By seeing these things, people from the neighbor's house are also coming to Jesus. Recently another family received Jesus Christ and took water baptism.

These stories are working in people's lives. Whatever story is written in the Bible, those stories are powerful and are giving life and hope in people's lives. They are changing people's lives and bringing them peace. These are the true stories. Whoever believes in these stories will never be ashamed and their lives will never be the same again. *

ANIL'S STORY

To fulfill the requirements of the Oral Bible course, storyteller Satish had been training an apprentice. At the last minute, his apprentice moved away to the city to find work. So with only two months left before the exam, Satish began to disciple a new believer named Anil, teaching him to tell the stories. Anil is 26 years old. Here is his story:

---

* Report given January 24, 2005; recorded on digital video.

I was born and raised in a Hindu family; all my family members are Hindus. When I was seven years old, I started drinking. I became an alcoholic and for 18 years, I continued in that condition, addicted to alcohol.

In the meantime, I got a very serious sickness [HIV]. At the end my family concluded that there was no hope for me, so they got ready to take me to the hospital. Meanwhile, Pastor Satish came to my home. While I was lying sick in my bed, he shared the Bible stories with me, and I accepted Jesus. But even though I had accepted Christ, my condition became worse and worse every day.

So finally my family took me to one of the better hospitals in our city. The doctors who examined me told my parents, "There is no hope for him." A well-known specialist examined me and said the same thing.

Even so, my parents admitted me to the hospital anyway. For one month I was in my bed, often unconscious in a coma, on the third floor of the hospital. But during that entire month, I always felt Jesus was there in that room with me. My parents, my relatives and everyone thought, "There is no hope at all." (Anil began to cry as he told this part of the story).

Even though the doctors had given me intravenous feeding and all kinds of other treatments, it did no good, because my body could not absorb anything. I had become completely weak; I was so thin that I looked like skin and bones. And everyone told my parents that I would die.

One day I also felt, "I am going to die." I heard the doctors come into my room and tell my mother, "There is no hope for him; he is going to die—he has become infected with HIV." So my family and friends all came to know that I had HIV. The doctor said to my mother, "You can take him home or you can leave him here. It does not matter—he will die either way."

Finally, my mother said, "We will take him home. If he is going to die, at least he can die there at home with us."

But after they took me home, Pastor Satish and others came and started to pray; and they prayed and cried like anything and they asked God for my healing. A few days later a really tremendous change started happening. My body began to grow and put on flesh and live again, and I began to gain weight. Even though I was as good as dead, and I was about to die, God gave me a second chance.

The doctors were amazed. Eight days after coming home, I was totally healed—I was totally healed on that day, and I am totally healed now.

Not long after God healed me, I had a vision. I saw a map of my home state, and I came to know that God had called me to serve him. My ambition now is this: I want to share his stories throughout my state. I thank God and uncle and auntie for this storytelling program and I am so thankful for Pastor Satish because he shared these wonderful stories with me. (October 2007).

By the time of the exams, Anil had become familiar with 90 stories.* Soon afterward, he moved to a primitive tribal area where human sacrifice is still practiced. Less than six months later Anil reported that he had already won 60 people to the Lord by telling the Bible stories there.

---

* Anil achieved a 79 on his exam. See Appendix K.

Chapter 12

CONCLUSION

*A good story is still a good story to
anyone who hasn't heard it.*

—DESMOND BAGLEY

The main purpose of this project was two-fold: first, to focus on how
biblical storytelling can be used to spread knowledge of specific Bible
texts among groups of oral learners; and second, to discover how biblical
storytellers can be multiplied through intentional training.

Missionaries are now beginning to recognize that the learning style of
oral communicators differs in many ways from that of print learners. Yet
most Christian workers still use predominantly literate methods even when
working in overwhelmingly oral contexts. As awareness of this problem began
to surface over the past two decades, biblical storytelling was proposed as a
solution. Since then, significant fieldwork has been done by missionaries who
have used storytelling to evangelize and plant churches. But relatively few
have tried to set up formal training programs designed to equip indigenous
people as effective biblical storytellers.

THE ORAL BIBLE PROJECT

In 2001 I began a pilot project that over a four-year period trained 56 biblical
storytellers. Building on this experience, I started a new training program
in 2006 in a different part of the country. Sixty-two storytellers enrolled
in this program; 14 months later, 41 of these participants completed the
program having learned to tell 100 stories from the Old and New Testaments
in chronological order.

The participants in the program were all full-time workers who were active in evangelism and church-planting activities. They learned to tell from 12 to 17 stories during each of six four-day training modules. Between training events they practiced telling the stories over and over in their own village contexts, bringing many people to Christ and starting more than 200 new congregations.

Because storytelling is easily replicable, many of those who heard the stories also began to tell them. In some cases the stories were relayed to as many as five successive generations of hearers. Some of these downline storytellers were trained intentionally through initiative-driven satellite programs that mirrored the central training model, but in other cases listeners simply heard the stories and then began repeating them. The stories were able to cross barriers of language and culture with relative ease, even finding their way to remote people whom the storytellers described as "living like animals."

A Look Back

In general, the project fulfilled my expectations and in some ways surpassed them. A training model was developed that was demonstrably more effective in transferring Bible knowledge than literate communication forms had been. Not only were the participants able to learn the stories; they also passed them along to others, showing that this model promotes relayed transmission of Bible knowledge beyond the original learner.

Because I have been a cross-cultural church-planter throughout my ministry, an unspoken aspiration was for this project to result in new congregations. Even though this was not included in the stated goals of the project, it turned out that the model led to many new churches being planted. For me (and for the agency), this was the most reliable confirmation the biblical story training had been successful.

From the beginning of the project, God often gave supernatural confirmations of the Divine imprimatur on the told stories through physical healing, provision, conception, protection, and the restoration of human relationships. This demonstration of God's power on behalf of needy people spoke clearly of his love for them. The amazing stories that resulted often reminded me of the community of believers in the New Testament. The dichotomy between the natural and the supernatural that is common in western contexts was absent. For these storytellers and their listeners, God's intervention appeared to be a normal result of telling and hearing the Bible stories. Faith that God would do for them what he had done for others seemed to come quite naturally.

Of course there were also disappointments. During the library research phase in 2000, it would have seemed impossible that six years would pass before the project could be broadly implemented. The final two years before the breakout were especially difficult as the pilot project was winding down without any indication that a next phase would occur. I struggled with doubts and frequently thought of starting the project over in another place like southern Mexico, where my Spanish would be useful. The only word heard from the Lord during this time was, "Wait." The lesson was that God is always working on the big picture; sometimes nothing can be done because God is working on someone else. In this case, the oral Bible project could not move ahead until the agency had completed its period of leadership transition. Once that was in place, the new door opened almost immediately.

A second disappointment was in regard to the young tribal man who I recruited to serve as my research assistant. When H. enrolled in the oral Bible pilot project in 2001, he had been a Christian only a short time. He learned to tell a hundred Bible stories and then left the program to attend the agency's central Bible school for two years. When he graduated (having done his program in English) I requested that he be assigned to the oral Bible project for 18 months as a research assistant and field coordinator. I provided funds for H.'s support and field travel, and for learning the computer and internet in order to communicate with me by e-mail. Although in many ways H. was very gifted, he seemed unable to carry out his assignments satisfactorily. Despite this, he eventually collected a large percentage of the village level research that found its way into this book. He also was the translator for many of the verbatims that were collected. Still, I was often frustrated at my own inability to help H. overcome his dysfunctions and continue to develop as a leader in the oral Bible program, and because much added valuable field research could have been collected if H. had undertaken it in a conscientious manner.

A LOOK TO THE FUTURE

After verifying the results of the program, the agency asked me to repeat it with a new cycle of training that began in January 2008. Since the program had now gone through two developmental cycles, only minor changes in the training method were expected. The training assistants (T. A.'s) who had helped to lead the earlier project were not able to continue in the new program. New T. A.'s had to be selected from the program graduates and carefully mentored to lead the learning groups.

Gifted trainers are essential to any successful training program, and this study clearly showed the important role the T. A.'s have in retaining students. It is a challenge to identify, recruit and train such individuals, but Indian trainers are essential to the long-term success of this project. We were fortunate to find several among the graduates who are deeply committed to the program, and who were eager to serve in this capacity in the new training cycle.

A second area of challenge was financial. The first project was funded by a special donation the agency had received. I only had to cover my personal expenses and a subsidy for each of the six training modules. During subsequent training cycles, I would have to raise the entire budget for the program.

A third challenge is to discover if the results that were achieved are replicable. Is it reasonable to expect that hundreds of new congregations can be started in previously resistant villages in a relatively short period of time through a biblical storytelling training program like this one?

There are also various opportunities to increase the depth of the program by promoting biblical storytelling at the local church level. For instance, a story calendar (similar to a lectionary) could be developed and tested. A three-year story cycle that focuses on one or two stories each week would ensure that the congregants are learning a broad range of stories. This oral "lectionary" should be created with oral learners in mind. By using mnemonic symbols to represent the stories, even non-readers could participate. In this way, faith communities could be led by their natural leaders instead of having to seek literate leaders from outside the community.

Periodic storytelling festivals for evangelism and story-learning should become an integral part of the field-level fabric of a story-based church. Congregations that are in close proximity should work together to host story festivals in nearby villages with the dual purpose of edifying the believers and reaching out to the non-Christian community. Such celebrations follow the model of the *katha* performances that are popular in the Indian context. To prepare for a storytelling festival, each participating congregation would equip its own members to tell certain biblical stories which would be woven together into an epic presentation. A featured storyteller could be brought in from outside to expand the community's repertoire of stories and to model good storytelling practices. Story-songs, group interactive storytelling and indigenous art could all be utilized. Dressing the presentation of biblical stories in festival clothes makes it culturally appropriate, entertaining and exciting for Christians and non-Christians alike.

One issue standing in the way of story festivals is the cost. In impoverished communities, many people live on a day-to-day basis. To sponsor a festival means they would have to provide food or refreshments for the people who attend. This is a significant challenge, but it has been shown that it can be done through cooperative effort. When a group of local churches becomes motivated to believe God for such an outreach, they can work in concert to plan the event and collect the needed resources ahead of time. In noncash societies, contributions of food and material are often more appropriate than money. Successful completion of such a project can significantly increase the faith level of the congregations, and can lead to increased giving and greater effectiveness.

Another area that needs attention is the development of leaders who will focus their efforts on storytelling. To start with, regional storytelling coordinators should be appointed and given responsibility for promoting storytelling in each particular language area where there is high orality. These leaders would be responsible for vision-casting, leading storytelling training events, and coordinating story festivals and outreaches.

AREAS FOR FURTHER RESEARCH

There are several areas where further research would bear fruit. The effects of many promising training programs are barely discernible beyond the end of the training. A longitudinal study of the storytellers who were trained in this program would be helpful. For instance, how many of the graduates have continued using biblical storytelling? If so, in which ways have their ministries changed?

Congregational Research

Studies are also needed to learn more about the new congregations that were planted. For example, have the stories become part of the canon of the local churches? Are new converts continuing to be won to Christ or did church growth stagnate at the end of the formal program? What relationship do the churches have with their non-Christian neighbors? Have natural leaders been allowed to develop? What are their roles? What place does literacy have in these oral ecclesiastical contexts? What kinds of theology have these churches developed? What percentage of the congregants can tell the stories?

Back translations of the stories would help discover the degree of correspondence between the told stories and the Scriptural text, and would also serve to discover ways the stories were incorporated into the vernacular. Case studies of several of these congregations would add greatly to the body of knowledge regarding how biblical storytelling can be best utilized.

Researchers should be aware that although anecdotal evidence can be obtained without too much difficulty, gathering comprehensive research would be much more challenging, since the multiple barriers of language, orality and culture are nearly impenetrable for a foreigner.

Ethnomusicology

Another area of potential research relates to the role of indigenous art forms as a vehicle for spreading the biblical stories. This includes creative expressions such as dance, drama, poetry and song. Missionary ethnomusicologists have shown interest in such research. This would be an excellent subject for a future doctoral project in ethnomusicology.

A strong thread of the research should focus on the indigenous music forms that already exist in that culture. Through this understanding it can be shown how these forms are being adapted to Christian usage. For example, which type does each song represent in the pre-Christian culture? Are they harvest songs, hunting songs, women's songs, or something else? What connotation is associated with each of these distinct music styles in the original culture? Are they styles that have connections to unwholesome activities, making them of doubtful value for use in Christian worship?

The researcher should also seek to discover the various ways that these songs incorporate the text and/or themes of the biblical stories. Do the songs carry parts of the Scriptural text itself either as ballad or refrain, or are the lyrics mainly applications extracted from the story? Which theological doctrines are found in the songs?

The researcher should also ask how the songs are composed. Is composition mostly done by one or two gifted individuals or are there many different people who make and perform story-songs?

Many such questions could be answered through appropriate research. A cautionary note is that the primary purpose of the researcher is to gather information, not to take the place that rightly belongs to the indigenous composers who, as cultural insiders, are in the position of knowing things that an outsider would never understand. A trained worker from outside the culture may have a greater knowledge of the Bible or music theory, but he or she will never have the understanding of the culture that an insider does. This includes knowing what people are thinking, awareness of subliminal story connections, and the barriers and bridges to acceptance of the gospel.

Finally, a study in this area should seek to identify and affirm oral/aural transmission of the songs instead of proposing to make recordings for distribution through devices that belong to technologically (and financially) advanced cultures.

ISSUES TO BE RESOLVED

On the plain where literacy and orality meet, the two competing technologies of learning joust for preeminence. This was true in Plato's time, and it is true today.

An Oral Theology

In the western tradition of spirituality, the definition, statement and acknowledgment of theological doctrines is of great importance. Such theologies follow a conceptual framework and are usually expressed as abstract declarations that follow rules of logic. In oral contexts, western missionaries may interpret the absence of definition of doctrines (according to western categories) as a lack of doctrinal understanding. It should be kept in mind that widely varying methods have been used both culturally and throughout history to develop theological frameworks. Each culture and each people deserves the right to formulate a theology that flows from their own experience of applying the scriptures in their context, since ideally doctrinal understandings are a part of life, not separate from it. For oral communicators, this can best happen through the telling and recalling of biblical stories.

It is certain that oral learners understand more theological truths than a literate style assessment would suggest. What is needed are ways to assess their system of beliefs from their own perspective, not from ours. A discipline of oral theology may need to develop before this will become evident. In the same way that ethnotheology deals with the influence of culture on theologizing, the study of oral theology would take into account the influence of orality on the development of theology. Although we may not be able to predict what this theology would look like, it will undoubtedly be quite distinctive from the propositional and systematic theologies whose development was based on literate ways of thinking.

It is unlikely that oral learners will ever be able to express abstract doctrinal truths in the ways that literate thinkers do. However, if one were to look at the songs they sing, the stories they tell and their behavioral norms—seen in contrast to those of their non-Christian neighbors—it would become clearer that they do have a grasp of doctrinal truths in a form that is suitable for their context.

Research over time will be needed to confirm this. It took the literate church centuries to develop systematic theologies that fit the literate context. Theology appropriate to oral learners will also take time, and will have to be developed mainly by oral learners themselves.

I am aware that this answer will not satisfy many who are committed to more conventional approaches such as doctrinal teaching in formal school settings. In response, it is only fair to recognize that this approach has proven ineffective for many oral learners.

It is urgent for those who are focusing their efforts on literate training approaches in oral cultures to begin to discover their own paradigm shift to oral learning styles. If oral learners are won and discipled through learning the stories of the Bible, they themselves will develop methods fitted to their context which can serve to thoroughly equip oral people with Scriptural understandings. This will not happen overnight, but as it does it will be built on a foundation that reflects the ways that oral communicators approach learning and knowledge and which match the challenges they face in their own cultures.

Institutional Schooling or the Oral Bible Model?

The training provided by Bible schools and seminaries belongs to a literate way of thinking. Books, lectures, libraries and sermons are all a part of print culture. In such programs, learning is equated with schooling and knowledge transfer is assumed to take place in classrooms from teacher to student. Does this approach work? David Kornfield writes:

> An emphasis on content through the lecture method has left the vast majority of Christians unsure of what they believe. Perhaps the men who have been trained [in seminaries] are fairly well grounded in their knowledge of the faith, but they have been unable to transfer this knowledge to their local congregations. Transfer is one of the most crucial learning outcomes in any school setting.[245]

Few institutions have shown interest in adapting their training to fit the contexts their graduates will face in ministry. Because of the inadequacy of such literate forms of training for those who minister in oral cultures, these institutions need to learn from this project and seek ways to integrate major parts of it into their own model.

Practically speaking, this may be difficult to do. The oral Bible training is an in-service model that relies on students telling the stories extensively in their own contexts between training modules. The academic schedules of residential training institutions generally provide little room for praxis. However, Bible school students can be encouraged to take oral Bible training in another program after finishing their degree, preferably as an in-service course of study as they begin their field assignment. Applying the stories as they are learning them will deepen their knowledge of the Bible and multiply their effectiveness in field ministry.

The combination of the two types of training would provide a better foundation for ministry than Bible school alone. The strengths of institutional training are found in the disciplines of study, prayer, corporate worship, a strict authority structure and spiritual formation activities. These can be helpful for developing younger ministers especially. Bible school students are also taught a wider spectrum of knowledge about the Bible. This can enhance their use of stories and improve their storytelling practice.

There are also disadvantages. Bible schools model ways of thinking, learning and communicating that are counterproductive in oral contexts. Having achieved the difficult shift to literate culture, some students will be unable or unwilling to change back because of a fear of losing the perceived status granted by literacy. Resistance can arise from literate pastors who want to discuss their favorite doctrines and display the wealth of their Bible school knowledge, or who honestly feel the oral Bible model does not include enough doctrinal teaching (even though the participants who come out of the storytelling training know far more of the Bible by heart than the schooled students).

Another issue pertaining to ministerial preparation is that individuals who are superb candidates for church leadership in their own context often find it unimaginably difficult to navigate the literate training required by an institution. Culture, orality, language, age and family responsibilities all work against their successful completion of a degree program. In the eyes of the agency, this inability to master print culture disqualifies them for ministry, even though in their own oral context they are highly qualified leaders.

One of the most urgent needs in areas of rapid church growth is for gifted, biblically trained grass roots leaders who are equipped to lead their congregations. The oral Bible program has shown that it can provide such training and can easily be adapted to fit diverse local conditions, needs and constraints.

If, on the other hand, the new churches that have been planted through storytelling are turned over to ministers who are a product of Bible schools, it is likely that church growth will stagnate and rapid multiplication of new churches will be halted. In short, there needs to be a mix of leaders, some of whom have been trained in formal Bible schools and others in the oral Bible program—and many who have been trained in both. In either case, recognition and status should be awarded on the basis of merit, not according to educational achievement. The primary standard of measurement should be proven effectiveness toward reaching the agency's goals of evangelization and church-planting.

Finally, I recommend that this program be implemented on a broader scale. My hope is that readers will build on what I have done by adapting this work to new contexts and other geographical locations. It is likely that many of the world's oral learners are not, after all, resistant to the Christian message. Rather they resist the literate form in which it is presented to them. If gospel workers can be trained to simply tell them the stories of the Bible, undoubtedly many will come to Christ.

Appendix A
Where Stories Were Told

This survey was taken during the second training module when the new storytellers returned from completing their first field assignments. All the participants told Bible stories at Christian meetings such as church, Sunday school, cottage meetings, ladies prayer, fasting prayer, youth meetings, and so forth. The table below illustrates some of the other places they told the biblical stories. The figures for Batch 1 and Batch 2 indicate the number of storytellers who told in a particular context. (An "x" indicates the question was not asked to Batch #1).

Place, Person, or Occasion	Storytellers: Batch		Additional Information
	1	2	
To spouse and children at home	21	15	
To other relatives	X	13	
To non-family person at my home	19	6	Batch #2: two beggars (1 m, 1 f), a Hindu saddhu, a Hindu priest, a Buddhist guru, and a religious worker
At a neighbor's home	16	15	Both Christian and non-Christian neighbors
At a school	4	3	Batch #2 told in primary schools; the Creation twice, and Cain & Abel once
At a shop (store)	10	0	
A clinic/hospital	4	3	
Bus / bus stand	16	6	While on a bus (11); at bus stand (11)
RR / Train station	13	13	While on train (19); at RR station (7)
In a shared taxi	1	2	
Work place	2	8	Mostly to agriculture and day laborers
Tea stall	4	0	
At a telephone call shop	4	2	
At river while bathing	3	2	
Under a tree	X	7	
At market	4	0	

| Place, Person, or Occasion | Storytellers: Batch | | Additional Information |
	1	2	
While cycling	8	1	
At a special event	5	0	A funeral, a wedding, birthday, a retirement, and two Independence day programs
Evangelistic mini-crusade	11	5	
Government adult education centers	X	10	They are invited to tell at breaks
Well-washing	X	1	While storyteller is waiting at the well to wash clothes (told to both men & women)
To Muslims	X	4	
To Buddhists	X	4	
To nominal Christians	X	14	

Some other places where the stories were told are community sports fields, at a children's club, at tutoring centers, to sick people, at a school for the blind, at a computer cafe, to 15 leper families at a government leprosarium, at an office, on a ferry, to policemen, to Hindus who had gathered at a shrine for worship, and to shepherds watching their flocks.

APPENDIX B
TWO ACCOUNTS OF VIOLENCE AGAINST CHRISTIANS

Two reports from the agency with which I partnered illustrate the dangers that Christian workers face. These attacks focus particularly on traditional ways of evangelizing. This is a primary reason the agency asked us to begin a program of biblical storytelling training for its workers.

1. Four indigenous workers had gone to a village for a special meeting. The anti-Christian activists learned about this meeting and went to the village in search of the gathering place. They interrupted the meeting and forcibly entered into the audience and took out the workers. After pulling them out, they beat them up inhumanly. Two of the brothers became unconscious. Then the activists turned to the believers who attended the meeting and brutally beat and harassed them. The workers who were beaten were taken to the District Hospital around 9 pm. It is more than 35 miles away. Three of the workers are under treatment but one is very serious and is still not recovered from the trauma.

2. Two workers were conducting discipleship training for new believers. On the third day an activist came into the meeting place. He started to ask questions and looked at every piece of literature of the believers. Sitting there he made a few telephone calls on his mobile telephone. Sensing trouble, the leader, Bro. Daniel, closed the meeting but the fanatics arrived in front of the church. About 60 of them went to the authorities and demanded that everyone must be arrested.

    They took some people to their office and questioned them. They were all fearful of physical attack – that did not happen. Thereafter the activist leaders came to the church and with the help of the police broke open the church and took away whatever literature they could find. They took song books and notebooks of the 20 people who were doing the discipleship training and their New Testaments. They got their names from the notebooks and immediately they went to their homes and took all of them into police custody. At 5.30 pm police arrested 15 of them. But after the questioning they were released at 12.30 am.

    The police particularly wanted to get one man who is a high-caste convert to Christianity and is now a worker. We remember the trouble they gave him on his wedding day. They saw the marriage invitation and they chased his marriage party asking how come he is marrying a Christian girl. He was immediately counseled to leave the area and stay elsewhere with his wife. Their motorcycles are also kept elsewhere fearing attack on their vehicles.

The anti-Christian activist leader referred this matter to the state government home minister and there was heavy pressure from the minister's office on the police. Bro. Daniel was asked to report to the police every day. Later he was told to be available whenever they will call him. He is afraid to go out of his house as he could easily be attacked. Please continue to pray for the workers and for the 20 believers who went through the discipleship training and were ready to take baptism.

The situation became critical during 2007-2008. In a period of widespread and severe persecution 300 villages were "cleansed" of Christians. Hundreds of churches and thousands of homes were burned and tens of thousands of believers had to flee into the jungle. At the end of 2008 in this agency alone 2,316 believers from 472 families and 36 churches were living in refugee camps or hiding in the jungle for fear of losing their life. Many lost everything they owned when their homes were burned by fanatical anti-Christian mobs.

APPENDIX C
SAMPLE FIELD REPORT FORM WITH MNEMONIC SYMBOLS

Adam	Gen 1:1 .... 2:4	Genesis 2:5 .... 3:24	4:1-12, 16-17, 25-26	Noah	Genesis 6:5 .... 9:29	Genesis 11:1-9
Where?						
How many people?						
Where?						
How many people?						
Where?						
How many people?						

Abraham	Gen 12:1-8; Gen 13:2-18	Gen 15:1-9,18; Gen 16:1-16	Genesis 18:1 .... 19:29	Genesis 21:1-7; Gen 22:1-19
Where?				
How many people?				
Where?				
How many people?				
Where?				
How many people?				

The storytellers were required to fill out field reports and return them when they came for subsequent training modules. Each story was represented by a mnemonic symbol and included the Scripture reference (the fingers represent the primary story character). Storytellers were asked to list three occasions that they told each story and the number of listeners.

APPENDIX D
STORIES LEARNED

OLD TESTAMENT STORIES

	Scripted length
Adam (3 stories)	
Genesis 1:1 to 2:4	(775 words)
Genesis 2:5 to 3:24	(1175 words)
Gen 4:1-12, 16-17, 25-26	(380 words)
Noah (2 stories)	
Genesis 6:5 to 9:29	(1370 words)
Genesis 11:1-9	(225 words)
Abraham (4 stories)	
Genesis 12:1-8; Gen 13:2-18	(500 words)
Gen 15:1-14, 17-18; 16:1-16	(650 words)
Genesis 18:1 to 19:29	(1450 words)
Genesis 21:1-7; 22:1-19	(580 words)
Jacob (5 stories)	
Genesis 25:19-34	(340 words)
Genesis 27	(1000 words)
Genesis 28:10-22	(350 words)
Genesis 29	(620 words)
Gen 31:1-3; 32:3-32; 33:1-4, 17, 20	(850 words)
Joseph (4 stories)	
Genesis 37	(825 words)
Genesis 39 and 40	(935 words)
Genesis 41:1-49	(900 words)
Genesis 41:53 to 46:7	(2100 words)
Moses (5 stories)	
Exodus 1:1 to 2:22	(920 words)
Exodus 2:23 to 7:13	(1500 words)
Ex. 7:14 to 11:10; 12:1-15, 29-42	(2900 words)
Exodus 13:17 to 14:31	(650 words)
Exodus 19:1-20, 20:1-2	(800 words)
Joshua (3 stories)	
Joshua 1:1-11; 2:1 to 4:11	(1177 words)
Joshua 5:13 to 6:25	(529 words)
Joshua 7:1 to 8:30	(1122 words)

Samuel / Saul (2 stories)*
1 Samuel 1; 2:1-11, 18-21, 26   (739 words)
1 Samuel 3   (578 words)
[1 Samuel 4:1 to 6:15]
[1 Samuel 9 and 10]
[1 Samuel 15]
Saul / David (2 stories)
1 Samuel 16:1-13; chap 17   (1386 words)
[1 Samuel 18 and 19]
[1 Samuel 24 and 26]
[1 Samuel 28 and 31]
2 Samuel 11 and 12   (990 words)
Solomon (1 stories)
1 Kings 3   (630 words)
[1 Kings 11 and 12]
Elijah, Elisha (6 stories)
1 Kings 17   (620 words)
1 Kings 18   (870 words)
1 Kings 19   (510 words)
2 Kings 2   (450 words)
2 Kings 4   (1000 words)
2 Kings 5   (810 words)
Daniel (0 stories)
[2 Chron. 36:15-20, Daniel 1, Dan. 2, Dan. 3, Dan. 5, Daniel 6.]

NEW TESTAMENT STORIES

Birth Narrative
1. Isaiah 9:2, 6, Luke 1:5-25   6. Luke 2:8-20
2. Luke 1:26-38   7. Luke 2:22-38
3. Mat. 1:18-25   8. Mat. 2:1-12
4. Luke 1:57-67, 76-77, 79-80   9. Matt 2:13-23
5. Luke 2:1-7   10. Luke 2:40-52

Baptism of Jesus   (Mat. 3:1-17)
Testing of Jesus   (Luke 4:1-15)
Water Into Wine   (John 2:1-11)
Fishers of Men   (Luke 5:1-11)

* Stories in brackets [ ] represent Old Testament stories that were included in the pilot project, but because of a reduced number of training days were not taught in the oral Bible basic track.

Leper Healed	(Mark 1:40-45)
Paralytic Healed	(Mark 2:1-12)
Doing God's Will	(Mark 3:31-35; Luke 6:46-49; Mat. 21:28-31)
Man Who Lived Among the Dead	(Mark 5:1-20)
Nicodemus	(John 3:1-10, 14-21)
The Lord's Prayer	(Mat. 6:5-15)
Forgiving Others	(Mat. 18:21-35)
God's Provision	(Mat.6:25-33)
Herod Beheads John	(Mark 6:14-29)
Feeding 5,000	(Mat. 14:13-21)
Walking on the Water	(Mat. 14:22-33)
Jairus' Daughter and Woman with Bleeding	(Mark 5:22–43)
A Sinful Woman Anoints Jesus	(Luke 7:36-50)
Foreign Woman's Daughter	(Mat. 15:21-28)
Blind Bartimaeus	(Mark 10:46-52)
The Unjust Judge	(Luke 18:1-5)
Unfailing Prayer	(Luke 11:5-13)
Man Born Blind Healed	(John 9:1-41)
Money	(Mark 12:41-44; Mat. 25:14-30)
Story of the Good Neighbor	(Luke 10:25-37)
Zacchaeus	(Luke 19:1-10)
Faith of a Roman Army Captain	(Luke 7:1-10)
The 70 Sent	(Luke 10:1-24)
Woman at Well	(John 4:3-30, 31-38, 39-42; omit v.22)
Lost Sheep & Coins	(Luke 15:1-10)
Story of the Lost Son	(Luke 15:11-32)
Rich Man and a Beggar	(Luke 16:19-31)
Ten Lepers Healed	(Luke 17:12-19)
Forgiveness of Adulteress	(John 8:2-11)
The Transfiguration	(Luke 9:28-33, Mat. 17:5-9)
Epileptic Healed	(Mark 9:14-28; Mat. 17:20-21)
Resurrection of Lazarus	(John 11:1-8, 11-30, 32-46)
Story of the Sower	(Mark 4:1-10, 13-20)

Passion Narrative

1. Luke 19:28-40
2. Luke 22:54-62
3. Luke 23:32-43
4. Mat. 27:57-61
5. John 20:19-29
6. Luke 22:1-6; 39-53
7. Luke 23:1-5; 13-25
8. Luke 23:44-49
9. Mat. 28:1-10
10. Acts 1:4-5, 8-11

APPENDIX E
FACIAL EXPRESSIONS THAT PORTRAY HUMAN EMOTIONS

Abstraction, Meditation, Thought. Lower eyelids raised; eyes vacant. Perplexity sometimes raises hand to chin or rubs brow or taps forehead.

Admiration. Eyes open and bright; a smile.

Affirmation. Nodding several times. Negation expressed by moving head away or by shaking head.

Anger, Hate. Nostrils raised; mouth compressed; head erect; possibly clenched fists; protrusion of head and body (as in women quarreling).

Anxiety. Eyebrows oblique, mouth corners drawn down. Forehead muscle like a horseshoe.

Cheerfulness. Eyes open, head erect, no frown.

Contempt. Slight uncovering of canine tooth on one side, with consequent appearance of smile; or by smile alone; or by turning eyes away; or by half-closed eyes; or by nose turned up which follows from upturned lip. Finger-snapping, loud or gentle; or simple frown; or even by spitting or saying "ugh"; or by shudder; cf scorn, disdain, etc.

Decision. Closed mouth, tightened lips.

Devotion. Eyes raised; and sometimes hands raised and joined or open; body standing or kneeling.

Envy. *Cf.* Jealousy, Avarice, Revenge, Suspicion, Deceit, Slyness, Guilt, Vanity, Conceit, Ambition, Pride, Humility. Darwin doubts if we can fix these, though they are recognizable. Guilt and slyness show odd looks in the eyes. Perhaps pride shows puffing up, nostrils open, lower lip turned out.

Fear. Heart beating; eyes and mouth open; figure at first motionless; crouching down; pallor; perspiration; mouth is dry; trembling; fixation of eyes on object of fear; possible convulsions and arms raised; if fear becomes terror, a possible scream. . . . Sometimes the body shrinks, pushing fear away; shudder. (Actors raise shoulders and press arms to sides closely, bending the arms).

Helplessness. Hands open outward with elbows pressed to sides; shrugging; head on one side; mouth open; resignation is sometimes shown by hand folded on abdomen.

Ill-Temper. Frown; closed mouth. Sulkiness shows a pout.

Modesty. Flushing; turning the face; occasional tears; hiding all the face.

SOURCE: Charles Darwin, *Expression of the Emotions* in Burrell, 43–44.*

---

* Arthur Burrell, *A Guide to Story Telling* (London: Sir Isaac Pitman & Sons, 1926, 1975), 43-44.

APPENDIX F
STORY-SONG EXAMPLES

ORIYA STORY-SONGS

Jairus (first verse only)

Soma joro bodo loko jona jae roso boli namo thila.
Sota ki namo thla, Taro toki bemare hoye,
More baro bato dhire rala, Mone mone bhali ane tane buli.
Jesu kata aba suni dala so taki suni dela,
Tome asi moro tokhi chuye kore aba niko kora.

English translation:
In town, one big man his name is Jaeroso.
His daughter is sick and about to die.
He thought in his mind and went here and there,
And listened and went to Jesus.
"Please come and heal my daughter." (February 2007)

Syrophoenician Woman

Chali jiba agoru Jesu toma suni dekho
    Daya kori moro dekho tuma bhuji dekho
Daodo Santano mo binoti suno
    Bede nare maguchi koruchi pranamo
Jiyu moro bhuto grosto diyo tume takususto
    Israilo gono moro santano
Dibi tanko paye moro mono prono
Tanko paye moro chito
    Daya naye aou toma prati manarakho

English translation:
Before going Jesus please listen and see,
Please understand my pain.
Son of David, please listen to my request.
I am asking with pain and bowing down before you.
My daughter, she is demon possessed.
For Israeli people I will give my life
And time for them my heart is giving.

For you I have no kindness. Remember me. (February 2007)

Story of the Miraculous Catch of Fish (Luke 5:1–11)

Song Chorus (repeated twice after each verse):
   A buaa a maa bhai bhaini
   Ita kaekata hela, suna e katani

1) Jisu relathane relay
   Gadek loke
   Dehi delay Jisu jal dhaibalok [repeat twice]
   Arr kay hela janas
   Jisu Simon donga thane, bosi sighya delani
   Chorus: *Ita kaekata hela* — [Sing chorus two times]

2) Simon dure jal poka,Jisu kohile
   Helaa tamar kata boli pokai dele [repeat twice]
   Tar poehe bujhlas —-
   Gadek machh aslakaje,
   Jal phatlani -
   Chorus: *Ita kaekata hela* — [Sing chorus two times]

3) Odua hela boli pitar, dahi areko
   Jacob John aso dekhi, hele abako [repeat twice]
   Tar pochhe sunlas ——
   Chhania hai kohi baslay
   Jisu kay kolas ne -
   Chorus: *Ita kaekata hela* — [Sing chorus two times]

4) Jisu suni tanko bani, puni kohile
   Nachh thone thanie mane dhoru baele
   Tar pochhe sunlas ——
   Helas agee thanu tame
   Kata manaani —
   Chorus: *Ita kaekata hela* — [Sing chorus two times]

English translation:
Chorus: Oh, father, Oh mother, brother and sister,
   What has happened? Listen to this story.

1) Where Jesus was, there was a crowd, a number of people.

Jesus saw two people, those who were washing their nets.
What has happened? Do you know what happened then?
By sitting in the boat of Simon, Jesus is teaching.
[Sing chorus two times]
2) Jesus told Simon, "Throw your net far [away] from you."
　　"Let your will be done," [said Peter].
　　Then what happened? Do you know?
　　By many fishes coming, the net started to tear.
　　[Sing chorus two times]

3) What is happening? Peter called the others.
　　James and John became amazed by seeing this.
　　Then what happened? Then listen.
　　With wonder, they started to say,
　　"What did you do, Jesus, with us?"
　　[Sing chorus two times]

4) By listening to their words Jesus said, "I made you fishers of men,
　　from fishermen."
　　Then what happened? Do you know?
　　From today, this type of people you became.
　　Then listen carefully.
　　[Sing chorus two times]
—Written and translated by Pitambar Khamari (January 2007).

BHOJPURI LANGUAGE STORY-SONG

This is sung in the traditional Bhojpuri bardic style slowly and with much repetition by alternating the phrases or lines of the story (first singing it, then telling it clearly). Ismail Hembrom observed, "When Ganesh tells a story in the villages, he does it like this. His people listen carefully until they all understand the story. As it is sung, they also dance and play their instruments. They love to hear these stories; everyone listens very carefully, and they keep coming back to hear the stories again."

John the Baptist (by Ganesh Lal Yadav)
　　English translation:
　　A man came from God. His name was John. He came from God.
　　He came to give the testimony about the Light. But he was not the
　　　　Light.
　　John says, "Here, sister, I am just giving water baptism.

But the One Who is coming after me — He is a very powerful God
　　and He will give you baptism with the Holy Spirit and fire."
John says, "The One Who will come after me — He is very powerful.
He has kept the axe near to the tree. That tree which does not give
　　good fruit,
he will cut that tree down and put it in the fire."
John says, "See that winnowing basket. See that basket you are using to
　　winnow,
to sift and clean your rice. That basket is in His hand."
John says, "The one Who will come after me — He will sort out the
　　good grain from the chaff,
which looks like powder, which gets blown away by the wind.
He will sift out the good grain and carefully put it aside.
But He will throw that useless powdery chaff.
Yes, He will throw that useless chaff into the fire."
　　-Ganesh Lal Yadav (March 2005)

APPENDIX G
COMPARISONS OF STORYTELLING WITH BIBLE SCHOOL TRAINING

The agency has two levels of formal full-time residential Bible training. One is a kind of basic training that lasts ten months. It is conducted every year in many different divisions in local church facilities or rustic mission stations. In addition to academic studies relating to the Bible, this training serves to socialize the students into the agency's culture, its worship forms and the discipline that will be expected of the students later. The particular language used depends on the area of the country where the training is being conducted. For most of the students it is a second language and not their mother tongue.

A more sophisticated level of training takes place in a centrally located campus that is comparable to accredited Bible schools found in many places all over the world. Currently two-year and four-year programs are offered. All classes and study materials are in English, so in addition to their theological studies, students must also master an intensive program of language learning.

The students are not required to pay tuition or room and board to attend either of these training programs. They do have to be recommended by the agency, and meet other requirements, such as performing two years of service with the agency after completing their study program. Theological study can be a career track for these workers, most of whom have very limited options for educational advancement and jobs in their home context. Each academic degree they earn qualifies them for a higher level and more status within this organization (or, because many agencies are on the lookout for workers, with a different agency).

Even the founder of the agency admits that graduates of the central Bible school have been less effective in meeting the primary goals of the organization such as soul-winning, baptisms and church-planting, than are the village pastors who only completed a short training program. Studies have been done in various parts of the world that indicate the reasons for this. Here I will look only at the juxtaposition of the storytelling equipping model and the Bible School model.

Up to now, status, recognition and qualification for leadership have been awarded not by measuring a worker's performance in reaching the goals of the organization, but according to academic achievement. There are, of course, exceptions to this, but in general it is true. In order to be accepted as a worker of the agency, it is necessary to complete at least the minimum ten month training course. So new leaders who come forth from the storytelling process—who may excel as effective storytellers and proven leaders at the local level—nevertheless will also be required to demonstrate their ability at academic studies in order to qualify for support and an official position within the agency. This, of course, eliminates anyone who cannot learn to read and write at a significant level of skill.

Without discounting the need for academic study, it would be beneficial for the agency to seek some way to recognize the contributions of workers like the biblical storytellers who are most productive in reaching the goals of the organization. While it is true that the agency needs a certain number of academically trained workers, some mixture of the two types of training would seem to be needed; status should not be granted solely on the basis of academic achievement without corresponding successful and productive fieldwork. However, until changes are made, storytellers who wish to advance in the organization will have to put in their time in the recognized academic programs in order to be seen as worthy of promotion.

The following assessments were solicited as part of my research on the oral Bible pilot project in 2002. Five men volunteered to talk about their experiences in Bible school and compare them to the oral Bible project. All the responses were similar—four are reproduced here. The question asked them was: "How does this oral Bible program compare with Bible school?"

1. "We studied in a different way in the Bible Institute—it was just like school. But here we learn and we keep it in our heart. In the Bible school we would learn and they gave us notes to take with us when we would go back home. Then sometime, we would forget about that. But in biblical storytelling we don't have any written notes, we just note it down in our hearts. Due to this, it is very easy for us to work in the field. For this reason, it's very helpful for us." (T.)

2. "In the Bible Institute I learned the Bible like history—how we can know more about the Bible. But in this biblical storytelling training, we study and just keep it in our mind, so that we can use it in our field. And it's very easy for us to learn the Bible this way." (S.)

3. "In the Bible school we studied just like in public school. We take notes, and during exam time we study those notes and give answers. But in this biblical storytelling program, we just sit and read and then in a few minutes, we tell. Because of this, it has become very much easier for us to work in our field. Whoever we meet, we tell the stories that are stored in our heart *in the way that person is accustomed to knowing*; and this has become very helpful." (C.)

4. "I had never thought that I would take part in this biblical storytelling

training. I always had a thirst in my heart to know God's Word. Students would come back and tell me what they learned in the Bible school. Later, I even became a teacher in a Bible school myself. We would give the students notes and they would write the notes and show us. But in this oral Bible program, we just learn the Word of God and we go back to our fields—then we use it in a practical way. After telling the stories many miracles are happening just as we have heard in the testimonies. By telling the Word of God, it is very effective and has become very helpful for us." (L.)

APPENDIX H
COMPARING STORYTELLING WITH OTHER METHODS

27 STORYTELLERS SPEAK

In their own words these storytellers contrast storytelling and other methods such as preaching, teaching, tracts, films, witnessing or Bible reading. Their descriptions bring to life the huge difference storytelling has made for these gospel workers in their own contexts.

STORYTELLER #1:
Age 34; Christian 16 years; 12 years school; 1 year Bible school.

SYNOPSIS: People in this pastor's area are not interested in preached messages nor can they understand them. But they are very interested in stories. So now he shares the Gospel only by telling biblical stories. His new church has started growing. He has taught two other men to also tell the stories. One is a Hindu doctor; the other works for Reliance mobile telephone.

"After attending this storytelling program there have been many changes in my ministry. Now I have gotten a clear idea how to deliver the message. In my area the people are not interested to listen to preached messages. It is an area that is very bound by Satan. I started a church there seven months ago and at first nothing happened. They were not understanding me. But because of these stories, now these Sidi Sai Baba and Amba Bhai sect people are coming to the church. And they are regularly coming to prayer meetings. They are very interested to come and sit and listen to the stories. They cannot read or write because they are very poor. So now I share the gospel through stories only. . . . I have also made two storytelling disciples. One is a man who works for Reliance mobile telephone. And the other is a doctor named Dilip. He is telling the stories to the sick people who come to his clinic."

STORYTELLER #2:
Age 26; Christian 8 years; 15 years school; 2 years Bible school.

SYNOPSIS: Storytelling equips new leaders effectively even in low-literacy contexts. They can lead the church by telling biblical stories. Storytelling enables every church member to know the Bible.

"Dayalusun is the elder of my church. He was not knowing anything, but he was listening to everything for that [reason]. Little, little only he was able to read and write, but I did tell him the stories. After learning all the stories, now he is leading our church by only telling the stories. In this way, they are coming up in Christ. Every one of the church people knows the stories."

STORYTELLER #3:
Age 24; Christian from childhood; 10 years school; 2 years Bible school.

SYNOPSIS: Nonliterate people cannot understand sermons that use abstract or propositional terminology. But through biblical storytelling they can understand deep spiritual truths and grow spiritually.

"When I completed Bible School, after going back to my field, I was usually speaking in theological words. But in the interior area where I am working the people are uneducated, and they could not understand. After learning the Bible stories, I started telling stories instead of preaching. And they were so happy to hear the stories. Through the stories, now they have understood about the spiritual life. Through these stories, their spiritual life is developing. And this is how my church is developing."

STORYTELLER #4:
Age 34; Christian 19 years; 14 years school; 1/2 year Bible school.

SYNOPSIS: In many areas people strongly resist tracts and preaching. But with storytelling it is very easy to make friends. Everyone—young and old, even high caste people —like to listen to stories. So that makes it very easy to approach them and tell them stories from the Bible.

"Before learning these stories, we were finding it hard to distribute tracts and preach the word of God. But it is very easy to make friends and tell the stories. Wherever I go, if I get some people and ask them, 'I want to tell you a story,' then I start telling them the story. Before I had a fear to preach the word of God to higher caste people. But there is one custom in our state of Karnataka: everyone from children to old people, they all like to hear stories. So it is a very easy way to tell them the Bible stories. So now we can easily approach the higher caste people to tell them the Bible stories."

STORYTELLER #5:
Age 28; Christian 19 years; 5 years school; 1 year Bible school.

SYNOPSIS: In many areas carrying a Bible or using it to preach is a red flag for anti-Christian groups. But biblical storytellers—with no need to carry their Bibles because the stories are in their hearts—are welcomed in these places. Previously when they had gone to distribute tracts no one would even listen to them. *But the stories worked! There is no hindrance to sharing the stories.* "Through this storytelling program, I can understand deeply about the story and really tell the word of God.... It is the way to reach the Hindu people. It is the easy way. Through storytelling, we can reach the unreached people of any caste."

In my field it is very difficult to take the Bible and preach because there are many fanatical anti-Christian groups there. If they see someone preaching or carrying a Bible, they will take out his Bible, and tear it up, and beat that man and throw them out. It happened one day to one of our Junior Leaders. He had gone there for outreach. They took away his Bible, tore it up and threw him out. So in that place it is very difficult to share the good news and reach the people. But by the grace of God, as we learned these stories, without carrying our Bible, we are going and sharing those stories, whatever we are learning here. And we are reaching the Hindu people through these stories. There is no hindrance to sharing the story. So we are telling the stories to them.

Q. You say 7 people took baptism. Had you gone there before the storytelling?

A: We had gone before to distribute tracts, but they did not even listen to our words. But after the storytelling training, we went and shared the stories, and the stories worked. On August 10, they accepted Jesus Christ.... Really through this storytelling program, I can understand deeply about the story and really tell the word of God.... It is the way to reach the Hindu people. It is the easy way. Through the storytelling, we can reach the unreached people of any caste.

STORYTELLER #6:
Age 33; Christian 10 years; 12 years school; 1/2 year Bible school.

SYNOPSIS: People in this area are not receptive to tracts or preaching. But storytelling is effective for discipling people. In turn it is easy for the new disciple to tell the stories to parents and siblings and enfold them into the church also. A literate model of worship causes uneducated believers to feel shamed. But storytelling makes it possible for everyone—readers and nonreaders alike—to fully participate in the life of the church. This attracts more nonliterate people to the church.

After attending these two storytelling training sessions, we went back to our ministry place. When we had been distributing tracts and preaching there, the people were not ready to accept the tracts. There was one youth and I told him the stories, one by one. And he is so eager to learn the stories. Now he is coming with me to help me. And before that the boy was attending the church alone. But after that I told that boy, "Bring your family, your parents and your brother and sisters." Now they all are attending the church.... The situation in my church is like this: about 50% of the people are illiterate. When I used to preach to them, those who are educated people would open their Bible and read. But those who were uneducated got ashamed and they feel guilty within themselves. But when I learned the stories from here and I shared the stories, then they were also getting interested and they were not feeling guilty. And one of those families was a backward Hindu family. But now they are taking interest in coming in our church. And in this way our church is increasing. And we are so much blessed by the stories.

STORYTELLER #7:
Age 26; Christian 10 years; 12 years school; 1 year Bible school.

SYNOPSIS: The storyteller's description of his context reflects the use of inadequate / incorrect communication methods. He says that people are hard-hearted toward the word of God, but they are not hard-hearted toward stories. So apparently their resistance is only to preaching. He identifies storytelling as a very good way to form friendships with non-Christians. In a new church where he was transferred, he found that people had stopped attending because they were fed up with listening to preaching which they did not understand. By changing to a storytelling model, this pastor was able to slowly rebuild church attendance.

"Where I am working, the people are so hard-hearted. They oppose the word of God and refuse to hear the gospel. You can say that place is like Sodom and Gomorra. Even the parents encourage their sons and daughters to do bad things. And so it is very hard to preach the word of God among them. So this storytelling method is a very good method to make friendship, and tell them the stories and bring them to Christ.... There were at least ten pastors from our agency who had been transferred there before me. At one time there used to be least 8 or 9 families who attended the church there. But one by one, they all stopped coming. My coordinator transferred me there, so I went there to see why the people are not coming. It is because the people are fed up listening to preaching. The people are not interested to hear the preaching. For that reason, the people are not coming. So I gathered the small children together. I taught them the stories, the dramas, and the songs. Each Sunday I would switch and do something different. So the children started to come and they would share this with others. Slowly the adults also began to come back to see, 'What are the children doing?' So one by one the people are coming back. And whenever I preach [on the fourth Sunday], then the people are sitting and listening to my preaching there also. Now more than 15 adults are attending, both men and women."

STORYTELLER #8:
Age 31; Christian 18 years; 9 years school; 2 years Bible school.

SYNOPSIS: This storyteller's wife refers to the status accorded to literate communication forms, even when they are less effective than storytelling. Other Christians were equating storytelling with something less than literate presentation. The teller replies by defining biblical stories; they are real, not fiction, fable, myth, etc.

"After I learned these stories here, I went back home and shared them with my wife. Afterward she asked me this question: 'Nowadays all the other ministers are preaching about prayer and deeper things, but you are telling stories. Why are you doing this different storytelling method? What will the people think?' . . . Then some Christians told me, 'You should not tell stories.' I replied, 'This story is a true instrument; it really happened.' "

STORYTELLER #9:
Age 27; Christian 8 years; 12 years school; 4 years Bible school.

SYNOPSIS: This pastor became very discouraged because people were not listening to his preaching. But then he realized that whether people are Christian or non-Christians it is better to share a story—it makes it easier to approach them. Now people are listening attentively even in spite of language barriers. And for the first time people from outside the Christian community have started to listen, too. Before, whenever he had to be absent from his pulpit, there was no one to take over. But after he started telling stories from the Bible, it became easy for the believers to carry on the ministry when he is away.

"When I was going out preaching, people were not listening. I had become very discouraged about that. But after Uncle and Auntie taught us to tell the stories, now I realized that whether they are Christian or non-Christians it is better to share a story, which makes it easier to approach them. So I have started to tell the stories. And now these people are listening attentively. So now I know it is a helpful benefit for doing ministry in any language. Before this when I was just preaching, the people from outside were not listening. But when I started to tell the stories, Hindu people also came to listen. And it has benefited my program and many people who are not Christians have come to listen. Before I learned stories, when I was in my church and conducting meetings, I was preaching. And when I was absent from my church, my believers were not able to handle things. They were not able to preach, because the interpretation was very hard for them. But when I learned stories, and started sharing stories in my church, in my absence also, they are able to handle it easily."

STORYTELLER #10:
Age 25; Christian from childhood; 6 years school; 4 years Bible school.

SYNOPSIS: This pastor realized that his way of preaching had made it seem he was angry. So he began telling the stories in a loving way that was attractive. He found that not only can uneducated people not read; they cannot understand sermons either. In this area there are strong barriers of multiple languages and low literacy that make it very difficult to preach—nobody liked to listen and even the few who did could not understand. But through storytelling it became very easy to make them understand. People listened very attentively; through the stories they learned the Word of God and started attending the church. Now even without a Bible he can go and tell the stories effectively. He stated, "Whenever I get the chance, wherever I can go, I am telling the stories."

"After going home from the first story training, I told the stories to my wife. Then I told them to the small children in Sunday School. But this time, I did not tell like I was angry; instead, I told with love, as we had learned from Uncle and Auntie a good model for how to tell stories in an attractive way . . . In the field where I am working, there are many nonliterate tribal people. And there are many different tribal languages spoken there in those villages. So it is very difficult to preach the word of God. Nobody used to like to hear the preaching. Because they are uneducated people, even if you preach, they will not understand anything. But it is very easy to make them understand through the stories. Now they are listening very carefully, and learning the word of God, and those people are attending the church. And more than that, through this story program in my own life also I could experience the blessing of God. Now without a Bible I can go somewhere to preach and I can tell the stories from the Bible. Before I could not tell the stories or preach the word of God. Before I used to preach, and was teaching all the things. But after learning these storytellings, I can use only stories. Whenever I get the chance, wherever I can go, I am telling the stories."

STORYTELLER #11:
Age 28; Christian 8 years; 14 years school; 1 year Bible school.

SYNOPSIS: People tended to quickly forget sermons. Church members showed little interest in listening to the word of God. But now they like the Bible stories. They listen with interest and can remember all of the details. Before the believers were not willing to invite family or neighbors to listen to the sermons. But now they bring them to listen to the stories.

"Before when I would share a message with my people, they would forget it after two or three days. But they like the Bible stories. And they can remember them. I asked one of my believers about the Noah story. And he could remember all the exact measurements, how high, long and wide the ark was when Noah built it.... Before learning these Bible stories from here, my church members were not taking much interest in listening to the word of God. But now after learning the stories from here and teaching them from these stories, now they are taking interest and they are listening and they are also bringing their relatives or neighbors, likewise. But before they were not so much interested in that."

STORYTELLER #12:
Age 34; Christian from childhood; 21 years school; 1 year Bible school.

SYNOPSIS: Uneducated people find it difficult to understand preaching. But through the storytelling method, now they are able to understand everything. This has made them strong in their faith.

"The people in my place are uneducated. They are unable to read and write. And they cannot understand the message [preaching] very easily. But from the day I started to tell them the stories, they are telling me, 'The stories are so nice and we can understand them.' Before that, it was difficult for them to understand. But now they are understanding everything, through the storytelling way. And they are very strong in faith."

STORYTELLER #13:
Age 30; Christian 21 years; 12 years school; 1 year Bible school.

SYNOPSIS: Barriers of multiple languages and low literacy kept people from understanding this pastor's sermons or remembering what he had said. But after he began telling them Bible stories, they told him, "When you used to speak to us in sermons, we could not understand them very well and we could not remember anything from those messages. But now that you have started telling us the stories, we can keep those stories in our mind and we can remember them."

"I am working in a village where most of the people are uneducated tribal people. There are several different tribal languages which are spoken by the people living in this village. Before, whenever I would preach a message to them, they could not understand or remember much from my previous messages. After I attended the first storytelling training event, I started to tell them the stories we had learned here last month. And then the people began to tell me, 'Oh, pastor, previously when you used to speak to us in sermons, we could not understand them very well and we could not remember anything from those messages. But now that you have started telling us the stories, we can keep those stories in our mind and we can remember them.' Every

Sunday, I started asking the tribal people questions, and they could easily remember the answers from the stories I had told them.... Since attending this storytelling training, God changed my ministry. Previously I delivered the message [by preaching]. But nowadays I deliver the message by means of storytelling. We can really see the many impacts in our ministry." [He describes how he told the Nicodemus story and believers came to know they needed to be baptized and how he has made a disciple in that highly resistant village who is going around telling all the stories there].

STORYTELLER #14:
Age 26; Christian 13 years; 12 years school; 2 years Bible school.

SYNOPSIS: Storytelling the Bible is a way to spontaneously plant new home groups.

"I was trying to share the gospel in my village but the people there were not understanding. Then I entered one home and shared the story of Noah. After telling that story to them, then the lady and her husband called some of the children in the family. Now another family is coming, and other students are also coming, and they are having worship in their own home."

STORYTELLER #15:
Age 32; Christian from childhood; 9 years school; 1 year Bible school.

SYNOPSIS: In this pastor's context, storytelling has power to bring about personal transformation that sermons did not, even in the life of a hardened wife beater. People used to come for worship and then leave when the sermon started. But after this pastor started telling the Bible stories, everyone began to stay and listen. In fact, now they are so eager to learn the latest story (and story-song) that they are coming an hour early! Using storytelling, this pastor is able to take the Christian message to a fanatical anti-Christian village. He leaves his Bible at home and just starts at the beginning, telling them the creation story. The people are very hospitable to him, pressing him to come again and again to tell them more Bible stories. So he goes and tells them one story each day.

"There is one man whose name is Dev Kumar. And every day he was always beating his wife. He would never let one day pass without beating her. And many people had told the gospel to him, but nothing had happened. I began to think, 'What can I do for him?' Then I started to tell him the stories about Adam and Eve. I told the story seven times. After listening to this story, now he is not beating his wife anymore. Many pastors had come there, and had preached, but nothing had happened. Yet after hearing the story, he has changed his mind. Now he and his wife are living together very fine.... In that place most of the people are uneducated and cannot read and write. They are day laborers. After I would read from the Psalms, then the people would give their offering and then would begin to go out (one at a time they would slip away rather than sitting to listen to my preaching). But now after the Psalm and the offering, I am telling the stories instead of preaching. So now all those people are staying, sitting and listening in a nice way. The starting time for Sunday service is 8:30 a.m. But the people are now coming an hour early because they want to learn the new songs and the newest stories.

"Five miles from my place, there is a village where no one could go to preach the word of God. In days before, they had beaten up the Christians and torn their Bibles. It is a very difficult area, because there are many fanatical Hindu people who live there. But now after I have learned these stories, there is no need for me to take my Bible. I take some tracts and distribute them. Then I start telling the stories. I started at the beginning, by telling them the creation story. And I have been telling them all these stories. And they are offering me much hospitality in a nice way. And they are asking me to come again to tell them more stories. And they are very eager to hear these stories. So one by one, I am telling one story per day when I go there."

STORYTELLER #16:
Age 28; Christian from childhood; 10 years school; 1 year Bible school.

SYNOPSIS: This pastor's personal testimony is that even he himself could not remember sermons when he needed help. He says, "Those messages were not working in my heart." But a story is always there in his heart when he needs it, bringing him faith and courage. Before, people in his church had no interest in reading the Bible for themselves. And they could not understand or remember what he was teaching. But now when he tells them a story they can understand, and faith comes so they can believe.

"Before this, I was hearing sermons from others. But those messages were not working in my heart. I was simply forgetting them. Even though one brother may have given us a very good sermon, I may have forgotten it later when I was having a problem. But after learning these stories, whenever I am going through such a problem, then I am reminded of those stories and this brings me courage and brings faith in my heart. . . . Before, the people in my church would not read the Bible, even though they did own Bibles. And they were not able to understand or remember the things I was teaching them. . . . I have one new believer who was a Muslim. He is a new believer. Last month, he was very sick and he was in bed. And his son phoned me and told me, 'My father is so ill.' . . . So I went to them and I told them the story of the paralyzed man. And how he believed on Jesus and how he was healed. And so I told them the story. And they were having no other way, because they have no money. So they had to believe. And within two days that person was healed. And on the seventh day, he went back to work, building houses. Even though the doctor had said you have to be admitted at least eight days. If I had preached to them, I don't think they would have believed or gotten healed. But I told them this story and they believed. And God healed him."

STORYTELLER #17:
Age 34; Christian 16 years; 17 years school; 3 years Bible school.

SYNOPSIS: The believers were experiencing strong resistance in one village until they started telling the Bible stories. Then people began listening "nicely."
"There is a village where our people were going for worship [outreach]. The village people beat them and sent them away from that village. But we did one trick. We went to that village and started to teach the literacy program there. Then we started to tell them the Bible stories and they listened nicely among them."

STORYTELLER #18:
Age 31; Christian from childhood; 20 years school; 3 years Bible school.

SYNOPSIS: People who have never responded to witnessing respond to stories. People who cannot get anything from sermons are able to understand stories.
"One day I went to a man named Govind. Even though I had spoken the gospel message to him again and again, he had never responded before. So this time, I asked him, 'Do you want to hear a story?' And he responded, 'Yes.' After I told him the story of Sarah, I came to know that his wife had been barren for ten years. Then he asked me to pray for him. . . . Another day, I told stories to my adult education people. And then I asked them, 'Honestly, what did you get from these stories?' And they told me, 'We used to hear your sermons and messages. But we are not getting them; we are not understanding most of those messages. But when we heard these stories, now we are getting something. We understand these stories.' "

STORYTELLER #19:
Age 26; Christian 4 years; 13 years school; 1 year Bible school.

SYNOPSIS: Before learning to use storytelling, this pastor had found it very difficult to share the Gospel with non-Christians. But now they eagerly accept the stories he tells. A new believer showed no interest in reading the Bible but likes listening to the Bible stories. A man who was a member of a fanatical Hindu organization had opposed this pastor. But when he began listening to the stories, he repented, was baptized and soon began telling the stories himself.

"Before this, I could not share effectively with any Hindu families. But now we can share these stories, and they [the Hindus] are also accepting these stories as stories, in a very good way. So this program is very useful to us.... In my area there is a believer named Mallari. He and his wife have two daughters. He is a normal [average] believer; he has been a Christian for a year. He took baptism but he was not interested in reading the Bible. But he is interested in hearing the Bible stories. [He found faith for his wife to safely deliver twins when she had previously miscarried three times].... One man was against me when I used to be preaching the word of God and he was putting up many obstacles. He belonged to a fanatical anti-Christian movement. But when I told the stories, then slowly after hearing those stories, he repented and he took baptism. Now he is my good disciple."

STORYTELLER #20:
Age 24; Christian from childhood; 13 years school; 2 years Bible school.

SYNOPSIS: Preaching did not work in this pastor's context. But when he told the stories to a 10th grade student, this young man began telling them everywhere. He brought many of his friends to listen to the stories. And he went house to house telling the stories. People even called for him to come and tell them the stories.

"Before this I had tried to preach but it did not work in my place. Then I started to tell the stories there in my tutoring classes. And I told one of my students, whose name is Srabon, and he shared the stories with his parents. Then he went and told the stories to many of his friends. And he brought more of his friends to tutoring class for listening to the stories. All of them are Hindu. But after learning the stories, they are feeling good. They like the stories. He also went house to house and told the stories, and some people they also called him for telling the stories. After seeing it, I feel very happy because I was trying to preach to them, even though they were not listening. But through the stories, many people are eager to listen."

STORYTELLER #21: Age 35; Christian 9 years; 12 years school; 1 year Bible school.

SYNOPSIS: This minister is starting a new church in a highly resistant area. He began by trying unsuccessfully to teach the Bible to the children. When he started telling them Bible stories, Sunday School attendance jumped. Not only that, his wife and his own children have learned to tell the stories as well. When his wife tells the stories in Sunday School, "... then the children are very happy, as they are in the presence of God then." Even the Hindu parents have seen the changes in their children. So now some of them have started attending the church.

"It is very difficult to do ministry in my new place. At first I had gone with my family and visited that area and called the small children and started to teach them the Bible. I did not see much interest as I shared the word of God. But after attending this storytelling seminar, I came to know how to deliver the message, the word of God. So through this same way, I started to share the stories. Now 30 children are regularly attending Sunday School.... I have four children, three sons and one daughter. And already my three sons have learned those ten stories. And my wife learned more than ten stories. When she teaches Sunday School, she teaches the stories to the children. And then the children are very happy, as they are in the presence of God then. The Hindu parents have seen these changes in their children; now those Hindu people are very happy. And these Hindu parents are respecting these Christians brothers very much. So new families are coming now."

STORYTELLER #22: Age 33; Christian from childhood; 12 years school; 2 years Bible school.

SYNOPSIS: Storytelling is an excellent way to center conversations around the Bible and spiritual things. The uneducated people in this pastor's church were unable to understand his preaching. Some were obviously bored by it. But they happily listen to the stories. After he tells a story they say, "Today the story was very nice, very wonderful. We understand it." And then they go out and tell it to others.

"I used to take a teenager named Purushtum with me to go somewhere for maybe helping in my ministry. And while he was coming with me, we were talking about so many worldly things. But slowly, I started to tell him the Bible stories which we have learned here. So that boy used to ride the bicycle. And I would sit on the back and tell him the stories as we were going here and there, different places. After that, he received Jesus Christ as his personal savior and he took water baptism. And he is my first storytelling disciple. . . . In my church most of the people are uneducated. Whenever I used to preach, they could not understand. But this story program has helped me a lot. Now I tell the stories to them, and they are listening very interestedly. And they are very happy to hear the storytellings. One day I was conducting a cottage meeting at one house. And mostly it was older people who were sitting there. After worship I asked them, 'Now I will preach or shall I tell a story?' And they all shouted, 'No, No, No. Now, you can share the story.' Then I told the story and they are very interested to listen. Whenever I used to preach, one or two of them were getting bored. But whenever I am telling the stories they are very interested and they are listening nicely. And after finishing the program, when they are coming outside, they tell me, 'Today the story was very nice, very wonderful. We understand it.' And they are also telling it to others. So really, through this storytelling program, I am very blessed by God."

STORYTELLER #23: Age 29; Christian from childhood; 5 years school; 2 years Bible school.

SYNOPSIS: This pastor found storytelling to be so effective that he stopped preaching sermons without also telling Bible stories. Even though most of the people in his church can read, and can understand his sermons, they are benefiting even more from the storytelling. He uses an interactive format to get them talking about the story afterward. Because some members are literate and others are not, the story method makes it possible for everyone to participate equally.

"Nowadays I left preaching behind. I am not preaching now. In my church and cottage meetings I am only telling the stories.... Through this storytelling program I have learned so much. Most of the people in my church are educated. When I used to preach they can understand. But even so, when I started sharing the stories, they are very interested to learn the story and they are listening very carefully and really they are blessed by the stories. After I tell the story, then I ask them, 'How is this story today? Do you like it? Do you understand it? Did that story touch you or not?' And they are answering me, 'Today, what you were preaching, along with that you shared a story. And the stories are touching us and really we are blessed by God. We are understanding very clearly, and for remembering, the stories are very helpful for us.' So really through this story program we are blessed and in the coming days I can do better through this program."

[The interpreter adds: This pastor also asks them questions like, "In this story, there are so many characters or people. Which person in this story do you like?" So they might say, "We like Peter," and then they would tell why. Some of them are literate but others are not—so they are all able to participate, even those who are uneducated].

STORYTELLER #24: Age 36; 2 years Bible school.

SYNOPSIS: Even in pagan strongholds where there are famous temples such as this temple to the monkey god, storytelling is an effective way—perhaps the only way—to share the word of God.

"After I came to faith, I faced a lot of problems when trying to preach the Gospel. But by the grace of God, I came into this storytelling program. And after learning the stories here, then I went back to my place and I started to tell the stories. And there is one place where there is a Hannuman temple. Every day, about 300 kilos of coconuts are burned as an offering there. It is a very difficult place. One day my wife and I went there. We visited a house and asked for a drink of water, and came to know that a middle aged widow lady lives there. So we shared the story of Elijah and the widow of Zarephath. That Hindu widow's children and grandchildren also started to listen to the story. There are 14 people living in that house. So after sharing that story, we told them, 'There is one real God, and he will really help you.' And after listening to the story, those people were so happy. Because this is a Hindu dominated area, and there is a big temple there, it is not possible to openly share the Gospel. But through these stories, we are able to share the word of God with them."

STORYTELLER #25: Age 33; Christian 14 years; 13 years school; 2 years Bible school.

SYNOPSIS: Before showing the Jesus film, this pastor told Bible stories. Some people liked the stories even better than the film. As a result, four people came to the Lord.

"In one place, I told some Bible stories before I showed the Jesus movie. Some of the people were more interested to hear the stories than to watch the picture. I told them the stories of Creation, Adam and Eve, the Flood and Sodom and Gomorrah. I told them how the people were sinning. And as their sin continued to rise on the earth, then God became angry at their sin. So then God destroyed those who were sinning. I encouraged them to have faith. Four people believed from Kumar's family. They feared and then they trusted God."

STORYTELLER #26:
Age 36; Christian 10 years; 16 years school; 2 years Bible school. (female)

SYNOPSIS: The story way is a good way to reach resistant areas with the Gospel.

"After my teacher friend listened to the stories and saw my dramatic acting while I was telling the stories, then she realized this is a good method. She said, 'This is a very good idea. In this area, the Hindus will persecute you if you try to distribute tracts or carry a Bible. But this story way is a very good idea.' "

STORYTELLER #27:
Age 36; Christian from childhood; 12 years school; 1 year Bible school.

SYNOPSIS: No matter what this pastor preached, "people would immediately forget everything." But now that he is telling stories, for the first time they easily remember his messages, including all the details.

"Before I attended this storytelling program, whatever I preached, the believers would immediately forget everything. But after this first training event, I started telling the message through storytelling. Now they can easily remember the messages which I have taught in story form. Since I am now telling the stories, this is the first time they have been able to remember anything I have ever told them. I go to one village where there is a man, a believer, who is named Mansingh. Before, Mansingh would always forget all my messages. But now that I have started telling the stories, he remembers everything. And now Mansingh is so totally blessed that he has given his whole life to God. He especially liked this one story, the story of when Noah built the Ark. So even now, Mansingh remembers the entire story of Noah. He will tell all the details, and give all the exact measurements, when he tells about how high, how wide and how long the ark was, when Noah built it. So we are very happy."

APPENDIX I
THEMES IN THE VERBATIMS

Over the two-year program, hundreds of oral accounts of the storytellers' experiences were recorded and transcribed. From these, I identified and coded more than 50 significant themes. The list below includes the category name, my unique four-letter code and a short description.

Adult education program ADED
Any reference to the adult education program that was carried out in tandem with the oral Bible project.

Application of story APPL
What the storyteller says after telling the story, or what the listener understands it to mean. Often this takes the form of concrete comparisons: "In the same way ..." or "We should be like ..." or "We should not be like ..."

Bible interest (as a book) BIBL
When storytelling/listening leads to interest in reading the Bible; when storytellers read the Bible to prepare for a story performance; when storytellers thank God that now they do not have to first read from their Bibles to talk to others about Christ.

Bible school BSCH
Any reference to a formal Bible school (see Appendix G).

Character CHAR
When a listener or teller identifies with a Bible character.

Church Growth CHGR
When storytelling produces church growth through conversions and/or the planting of new congregations

Comparison with Storytelling PRCH
Comparisons between storytelling and any other more traditional Christian methodology for evangelization and/or discipling; i.e., preaching, teaching, tracts, films, witnessing or Bible reading.

Conversion   CNVR
When a told story or stories results in the conversion of an individual, a family or families. To be considered conversion, it is usually accompanied by water baptism.

Evolution/Creation   EVOL
Any mention of evolution. This was found only during the first period of fieldwork when the Creation story was being told.

Faith came to them   FAIT
There are many instances of faith coming to the hearers through the stories; also instances when the storytellers themselves express great faith in God through the stories.

Family of Storyteller   FMLY
Many reported that they first told the stories to their own wife and children, and many made storytelling disciples of their wife, and some of their children. In the reports of provision, among others, it is evident that story takes center place in the discipling of the minister's family.

Felt Needs
God often chooses to demonstrate His love and power to needy human beings by meeting their most basic physical needs supernaturally which can then become a door for spiritual needs to also be met.

Felt need: Childlessness	FCHD
Felt need: Death	FDTH
Felt need: Demonization	FDMN
Felt need: Exam	FXAM
Felt need: Fear	FLFR
Felt need: Relationships	FGHT
Felt need: Financial	FLT$
Felt need: Healing	FLHL
Felt need: Witchcraft curse	FWTC
Felt need: Other	FOTR

Intentionality   INTN
This includes both story selection and ways the teller recast the story in a particular situation.

Intentionality (not)   UINT

Instances when tellers told a particular story not knowing that it was going to be especially applicable to someone who was listening. It seems there were few instances of this after the first training event, perhaps because the storytellers quickly learned the knack of using stories intentionally.

Judgment Stories   JUDG

Stories told with the intention of showing God's judgment on sin. The accounts often include repentance/conversion by the story listeners.

Language barriers   LANG

After low literacy, language is the greatest barrier to the use of literate communication methods to share the gospel in India.

Literacy, illiteracy   READ

Where a storyteller specifically mentions literacy or illiteracy; i.e., educated, not educated, etc.

Lord's Supper   EUCH

The Eucharist was celebrated during each training module accompanied by the telling of the Passover story from Exodus and/or the first Lord's Supper from the Gospels.

Making new storytellers   CHEL

Cases where a storyteller specifically says he or she is teaching another person(s) to learn and tell the stories.

Money $$$$

When a storyteller points to increased giving as a result of storytelling, either as an individual gift in response to hearing a story, or congregational giving.

Multiplying storytellers   MULT

Where new GEN3 storytellers are being created not one by one but in some program of multiplication. This was usually connected with training adult literacy workers as storytellers.

Negative comment   NEGT

Anywhere a storyteller or listener makes a negative comment about the method of storytelling (only three references were found, all by Christians).

New Leader   NLDR
Where a new leader of a church or home group comes out of the storytelling process itself.

Personal application   PRSNL
When the storyteller gives an interpretation that applies the biblical story in some way to him or herself.

Question by listener   Q???
When a story listener responds with a question.

Real story?   RLST
One of the marks of oral learners is that they don't trust abstract or propositional statements. It is the first-hand experience—either personal or vicarious—that makes something concrete, hence trustworthy. Once they are satisfied that it is a "real story" they are comfortable identifying with the character(s) and believing that this God could do something similar for them.

Religious worker listener   RELI
Cases where stories were told to a high religious person of another faith.

Repetition   RPET
When the storyteller specifically says the same story was repeated for any reason. Oral learners do not value novelty like print communicators do. Instead, that which is familiar is most welcomed. A story is like a well-loved song.

Response of listener   RESP
When a storyteller describes the response of a listener (or a personal response) to the story; i.e., a deep description by the storyteller of a story listener's response to the story. It may also be something the listener did or said in response to a story.

Resistance   RSIS
When a storyteller indicates an area is difficult, hard, or resistant due to the people's adherence to another religious system. In the village literacy/storytelling program this is addressed by not carrying artifacts associated with Christianity, such as a Bible or hymn book, and through the use of stories to share the gospel instead of traditional Christian preaching or teaching.

Story-Song use S-NG
When the storyteller mentions the use of a song in conjunction with the telling of a story.

Story requested again 2XST
When a story listener asks that a previously told story be repeated. This is different from REPT in that it is a specific request by the listener.

Example of a told story T-LD
When a storyteller describes or illustrates telling the story, repeating parts of it within the verbatim.

Story (+2 digits) OT_ _
A particular Old Testament story that was told.

Story (+2 digits) NT_ _
A particular New Testament story that was told.

Techniques TECH
Communication techniques used by a storyteller beyond the mere words of the story. Also programmatic training or telling techniques; i.e., "We taught them in the same way we learned here." or "And they called the people. And however they heard it from us, then in the same way they are also telling."

Telling to children CHLD
Instances where a storyteller says that a biblical story was told to a child or to children. Often after children heard the stories, they told them at home to their parents, and then the parents became interested and started attending the church.

Theological truth THEO
The use of story to teach a theological doctrine; for example, judgment, one God creator of all, creation *ex nihilo*, faith, God's omnipotence, God's love, salvation or the temporal nature of this world; i.e., when a storyteller or listener indicates an understanding of a theological truth by restating a story's meaning.

Third generation telling GEN3
A storytelling by a person who heard the story from someone whom I had trained. Storytelling equips new believers to become effective witnesses and

evangelists immediately while relationships with non-Christian friends, relatives and business associates are still strong and vital.

Fourth generation telling GEN4
Instances where a biblical story is told by someone who learned it from a GEN3 teller.

Transformed TRSF
Instances where a storyteller or story listener indicates a personal transformation in response to a story.

Witnessing WITN
Instances where a story or stories are used to point people to Christ.

Women WOMN
Instances where a woman or women are mentioned significantly in connection with storytelling.

APPENDIX J
CASE INSTANCE EXAMPLES

Selected case instances representing eleven of the categories identified by the process of coding the verbatims database.

1. APPLICATION OF STORY

a) By Simon Pargi; told September 2007

A believer had been praying for five years for water for a well. Their neighbor was a Hindu and he was against them. These Hindu neighbors were not permitting them to take water from their well. So I told them the story about Isaac when he was in Canaan, where he dug wells in the desert. And wherever Isaac dug, he found good water there (Genesis 26). I told them, "In this same way, God will do it here also." Then I prayed for them for that well. After that God spoke in my heart to tell them, "You should dig a well in this particular place." As they started digging the well there, I went around this well and prayed again. When they had finished digging the well, they found very good water coming from it. It was a spring! So after that, what happened is this: those people who were against them by not allowing them to take water from the well—their own well totally dried up.

A man from my church had a water buffalo who was giving milk every day. But suddenly, one day that buffalo was not giving milk. Instead, lots of blood was coming out from the udder and they were so worried about that. But I went there and prayed for that buffalo, and then the blood stopped coming out. After that, the milk started to come again. The buffalo became healed. I had told them about the flock of Jacob, how God blessed his livestock (Genesis 30). More than 45 people are attending in my church now. But before that, only three people were coming. It was after I took this storytelling training that the 45 people began to attend. This growth all happened in the past six months.

b) By Sunil Kumar; told February 2007

Again and again, I have been learning these Bible stories during these training events. And then I go back home and the first thing I do is tell all these same stories to my own wife and my two children. So one day, this is what happened. My wife told me, "Today, we want to have chicken." I told her, "Yes, it is true; but first I have to tell you once again the story of Elijah" (1 Kings 17:6). She said, "I have listened to this story so many times. And again you want to tell me this story?" I said, "Yes. Let me tell it to you again.

Because this God of Elijah will also provide for you." So I told her the story and then I went out from my house. When I came home again at noon, there was still no chicken in my home. When I came home again that evening, my wife asked me, "Where is the chicken? I want to prepare it."

I told her, "The God of Elijah will give it for you." Then I left to go to the home meeting. My wife prepared some rice and she kept quiet. While I was at the home meeting, my brother came to my house. He brought one kilo of chicken that he had bought and he gave it to my wife. So she began to cook the chicken. When I came home after the meeting, I asked her, "Did the God of Elijah provide you with any chicken?" She said, "Yes, the God of Elijah has provided me with the chicken." I said, "Let me see. Maybe you are joking with me." This brother had never given me anything before that time. He was just like a crow, always snatching things from my hand. But that day he gave me one kilo of chicken. It was a miracle!

Now we used to give our children a cookie every day. But one day the cookies were all finished and we had no money in the house. So my wife said to me, "Please buy some cookies for the children." I told her, "We have no money, not even one coin. We have zero money. How can I provide anything?" And the children, my one-year old child and my other child, they began to cry. My wife said, "You should get cookies for the children. Go to the believer's shop and borrow it." But I said, "No, I will never borrow." So two or three days later, I was outside walking along the road when a believer rode by on his motorcycle. He stopped and greeted me. Then he drove on to a store where he bought the biggest package of cookies they had and brought it back and gave it to me. I cried when he gave it to me. When I went home and showed it to my wife, she also cried. Our two children have been daily eating those cookies, and that big package of cookies has lasted more than a month. You see, our God of Elijah, he has provided us with everything we have needed both bread and meat.

2. BARREN WOMEN WHO CONCEIVED

In this culture, the shame associated with a woman's failure to bear children can lead to divorce, suicide, or even murder. So it is not surprising that some of the most heart-wrenching prayer requests are from barren women.

a) By Simon Pargi; told September 2006
There were three barren women. Two of them were barren for ten years and one was barren for five years. I told them the stories about Abraham, Rebekah and Hannah and other such stories. And they believed. Now two of the women have given birth to sons; the other woman is going to deliver next month.

b) By Bhim Singh Bamania; told September 2006
One day, I told a story from the word of God to the owner of the house where I am renting, He and his wife were not able to have a child for the past four years. So I told them the story about Abraham and Sarah. After telling them the story, they believed and we have prayed for them. Now that house owner's wife is four months pregnant.

c) By Bibhuti Bhusan Pani; told September 2006
There was a woman who was barren for four years. That woman's mother said to me, "You should pray for my daughter who is barren." So I told them the story about the barren lady in the Bible, Isaac's wife. I told them how Isaac prayed for Rebekah and then God granted the child. The next Sunday I prayed for that woman that God may give her a child. Then this last Sunday, that woman's sister was telling me, "Brother Bibhuti, you prayed for my elder sister. Now she is pregnant!"

d) By James Korkora; told January 2007
We told the story of Creation in a village called Hattivena where Gond people live. There are two brothers there whose wives had not been able to have children for four or five years. They had worshipped many idols and gone to the different shrines, and made sacrifices before idols also. But nothing happened. After hearing this, we gladly told them the story of Abraham and Sarah, how God miraculously gave Sarah a baby when she was old. We began going to that place every week telling them the stories of Joseph's life and many other stories. As we learned these stories so we told them. Then both women became pregnant! After seeing this, seven people came to the Lord. Now there is a regular worship service going on there. One of the women gave birth to a boy, and the other is ready to deliver—this is her last month.

3. CONVERSION

a) By Prakash; told January 2007
I made a disciple named Sribash Harijan. In his village, there was a man who was doing witchcraft. He was doing many powerful and miraculous things, even healing sick people and curing mad people through the power of this evil spirit. Then I went there and told him the story of the flood (Noah). I told him, "God destroyed this earth by a flood because of sin. But Noah and his family were saved because he was a righteous man in the sight of God. Noah and his family worshiped God and obeyed all things that God had commanded him. So God saved that particular family." The man who was doing the witchcraft told me, "I always do this for others, but still we

do not have any peace in my own family. We do not have any financial breakthrough in our household. We also do not know where our money is going. So now through this story, I came to know that whatever we are doing is not good. It is a sin against God. Now we know that Jesus is the real and living God and He will take care of his children." He said, "I will leave all these idols and evil things." He cut them down, threw them out and accepted Jesus Christ. From that day onwards, he gave up all his witchcraft and came to faith. He and his family [ten people] have taken water baptism. When this witchcraft man received Jesus Christ, his four brothers also came to Christ along with him. Altogether from these four families, ten people have taken water baptism.

b) By James Korkora; told January 2007

There is a village in my mission field where nobody knows about Jesus Christ. One day I went there and told the stories to the small children. A young man named Sukhda also came and sat there with the children to listen to the stories. I told all of the stories starting from creation. I also told them the story of Naaman, the Syrian army officer who was healed of leprosy. Sukhda was listening very carefully. After hearing the stories, he asked me, "Sir, will you please come to our home?" (He is from another village). So I went with him. For the past two years, Sukhda's father had been itching all over his whole body. They had taken him to different doctors and hospitals and he had taken medicine, but he was no better. Sukhda told me, "Sir, if you pray for my father and he gets healed, then we will believe in Jesus Christ." So I told that same story of Naaman there at Sukhda's home. He said again, "If your God heals my father, then we will follow Him, and we will attend your church services and join the church." Afterward I went back there regularly to tell them more stories from the Bible. Before long they believed, and God healed that man's father. Sukhda's entire family is now attending Sunday worship. Through them another new family in that same village is also attending. This week after returning home from storytelling training, I will baptize them all.

4. FINANCIAL NEED

a) By Luke Kumar; told January 2007

In our home there was a financial problem—we had no money. We were suffering because there were only two rupees in our house. So we had no money to give an offering on the first Sunday of 2007. We were thinking about this with disappointment. But I told the story of Elijah to my wife and my dear children, how God had miraculously provided both meat and bread to Elijah at the brook, before he met with the widow of Zarephath (1 Kings 17). I told my family that story and talked to them at that time. They were in faith [believing]. Also, we would have liked to eat meat, but we had no money to purchase any, nor to prepare and eat it. On Saturday, while we were sitting together talking with all the believers, one believer brought us half a kilo of mutton. He also brought a new Turkish towel and then gave us 200 rupees! It was such a great miracle for our family. I praise the Lord for this miraculous provision.

b) By Rajat Kumar; told January 2007
Sometimes my wife and I quarrel. During November, we had a quarrel. She is a little bit rich, from a wealthier family. One day, we were out of everything; we had nothing and no money in our house. So she got angry at me. I looked at her and laughed at her. I told her, "Please, come sit over here and I will tell you a story." So I told her the story of Elisha and the miraculous provision for the prophet's widow (2 Kings 4). Then I told her, "Please bring your purse and your money bag over here, and let us pray over it, and God will provide what we need." One day soon after that, my brother (who is an engineer) came to our home and he gave me 300 rupees. And then a few days later, my monthly pay was increased! So now my wife has seen that, "Really our God is a mighty God and he is providing for all our needs."

c) By Sabat Kumar; told January 2007
One day this past December, we did not have any money in our family. And especially in December, everyone wants to wear a new outfit for Christmas. My wife was telling me, "Look, everybody has new clothes except for us. We do not have a new dress for Christmas day. How can we tell our believers they must have faith, yet we are not having anything new to wear on Christmas Day?" So I told my family, "Believe in God and he will provide for you." I am always telling them these stories, such as the stories about the faith of Abraham. On the night of December 24, one believer gave 800 rupees, by which I purchased a new outfit for each of our four children. My wife said, "Our children got a new dress, but what about me and you?" I told her, "Do not worry about your *saree*. God will provide for you and me." And we prayed that God would provide for us. That night we went to a cottage meeting, and there was a widow woman there who had purchased a piece of cloth for a shirt and pants and she gave it for my new clothes. But still my wife said, "You got new clothes, but what about me?" I told her, "Do not worry, God will provide for you." And we prayed again. Then one sister brought the best quality *saree* from a city, the kind that my wife likes. So she also bought the cloth for the blouse and gave it

to the tailor to prepare it for my wife. So she gave that best quality *saree* and blouse to my wife. So she got her new dress, too! So after that I told my wife, "Our God provided it."

d) By Prashant; told January 2007

My family and I live in a rented house. Last month we had no money. The house owner is a widow lady and she is a miser also. When she came to collect the rent, I went into the bedroom to escape her. I wanted to avoid having to talk to her, so I was arranging my story program papers on the bed. But then she came into our bedroom and saw me arranging my papers on the bed. She asked my wife, "What are these pictures on these papers?" She did not know we are Christians and we are doing this kind of ministry. So my wife told her, "We are sharing the word of God in stories." Now she was suffering chronic [migraine] pain in her head. As she was sitting on the bed looking at the pictures, my wife told her the story of the woman in 2 Kings 4 whose son had head pain and when the prophet Elisha prayed he was healed. So then the landlady asked my wife, "If I will believe, then your God will heal me?" She answered, "Yes, if you will believe, then God will heal you." (By that time, I had left to go somewhere else). So my wife prayed two times for her. The next day the landlady came again and told my wife, "Your God has healed me!" The first time she came it was to collect the house rent, but at that time we were having no money. Now she said, "Your God has healed me, so I will not collect the house rent for this month."

5. The Dead Raised

a) By Dasrath; told January 2007

There is a Hindu man named Umesh who is about 25 years old. He is married and has one child. In December Umesh decided to commit suicide. So he ate poison and he was going to die. His parents came to me and asked, "If you know a doctor, could you please help us?" I went with them and they admitted Umesh to the hospital. (Recently, another man there had committed suicide by taking poison. His body was being prepared for the funeral pyre at that same time. So the parents were afraid because they had seen how that other man had died and they were terrified this same tragedy would happen to their own son). They pleaded with me again and again, asking me if there was any way I could help them. So after that, I told them, "Yes I'll do my part. I will do whatever I can do." But after that the doctor said, "I have done all I can. I cannot do any more." When the doctor said this, the mother and father and everyone started crying. By hearing these words of the doctor, they were so discouraged, thinking, "Our only son will be lost!" So in this situation, I prayed to God. And I told them a story from the life of Elijah in the Bible in 1 Kings 17, how he had healed the son of the widow, raising him up from the dead. I shared that story with them and prayed for them. And I gave them hope.

Umesh was already lying there like he was dead. So we prayed that God would raise him up, too. They had told everyone about Umesh having taken poison; they were all Hindu people. The parents were grieving. But finally, more than 60 hours after he had taken the poison, Umesh came back to life. He came back to life and became totally well. All the people saw this, and that it had happened after we'd prayed for him. He was totally healed by God. He got his life back from God. He was raised from the dead. So we thanked God for that. It was a blessing from God. Father God gave him back. When we prayed, that dead son was raised up again from the dead just like the story of Elijah who prayed for the dead son of the widow. We told all the people about this story how Elijah had prayed for that dead son. Many people have now come to the Lord and are coming to my church because they heard about this. I thank God that this miracle happened because of this story. By telling the stories, great, great miracles are taking place. It is my privilege to learn these stories and then go to the villages to teach them how to tell the stories.

b) By Simon Pargi; told September 2006
Since we were last here for storytelling training, there were three dead people who were raised up from the dead. One teenager had totally died and they took him to the hospital and the doctor gave him the injection and the saline but even though the saline bottle had not finished, the doctor declared that the man had died. Then they brought the dead youth back to his family. The boy's father at one time had been a believer in Jesus Christ, but his family was not following Christ at that time. They informed me by telephone and when they prayed for the boy he became raised up to life. Now I have been teaching the stories to that boy, and he has been learning the stories very quickly. He is so enthusiastic to learn the stories because God has healed him. And he is studying in his school. In days to come he wants to be a good storyteller.

There was also a woman who died. She did not have any fever or any kind of sickness. But one day suddenly while she was walking near her house, she fell down suddenly and she died. She had three children, and one of her children ran to her and was crying because his mother had died. The woman's father saw it from a distance and he was asking his grandchild, "What happened to your mother?" So then everybody saw that she as dead. They took her to the hospital and when they admitted her, the doctor said "I cannot do anything because she already died." So they were angry, demanding that the doctor should give her medicine so she can get well. The doctor said, "Am I God that I can heal her? I cannot heal her. You have to take her back to your home."

Her husband was away, so they took her back to her parents' home. The dead woman's father is a member of my church. He had been hearing the stories of the Bible in the church and also I had told them stories in their home, especially the story of Elisha and the boy who died of head pain and the story of Lazarus in John 11. So when he prayed for his dead daughter, she came back to life again. When the doctor learned that the woman had come back to life, he was astounded. Later when I went there, he asked, "What kind of God are you worshipping? He is such a powerful God. You people are just praying and even the dead people are rising up. It is a miracle." So then I told him stories from the New Testament about Jesus Christ.

Another woman is from a village called Keda. She was not a believer, although sometimes she attended our church. One day her son was playing near a small river and he fell into the water. It was so deep that the boy's arms were moving like he was swimming even though he did not know how to swim. His friend's father and mother were watching him from above and they were thinking that maybe he was just playing with another child down there under the water. But he had already died. When he floated up to the surface they brought the dead boy to his parents. They took him to the headman of the village, saying, "Someone killed our son and then put him in the river."

Even though they were Hindu, they thought, "No, we will not take him to anyone else. We will take him to a man who is a servant of God, who prays for the people. Maybe if he prays for our son, he may come to life. So they brought their son to my house. At that time, I was out. But two of my believers were there, a man named Natu and a lady named Santi. They had faith that, "If we pray, then Jesus Christ will heal him." So they began praying for the boy. While they were praying, he came back to life. They were praising God and the boy's parents believed in Jesus Christ. They said, "My son came to life, so now we want to be Christians. We will receive Jesus Christ." And they did.

The boy who was raised up from the dead has an uncle named Dipesh. I told Dipesh the stories about Elijah and he believed these stories. So he got a chance to learn the stories. Now he is my storytelling disciple. I was explaining how Elijah laid upon that dead boy and prayed for him and then he came to life. Seven times he laid on the boy. Now because of these miracles, people are coming to my church.

6. Is This a Real Story?

a) By Sanjeeb; told April 2006

After this training in February, I went back to my home village and started sharing these stories to different people. One day I went to a man named Govind. Even though I had spoken the gospel message to him again and again, he had never responded before. So this time, I asked him, "Do you want to hear a story?" And he responded, "Yes." So I started telling him several stories. Then I shared the story about how Sarah had been barren for so many years before God finally gave her a son (Genesis 18, 21). He surprised me when he asked me, "Is it a real story?" I said, "Yes, it is a real story. Why?" He said, "Since ten years ago, my wife has been unable to have any child." So he asked me to pray for him, and I prayed for him then.

b) By Higuram; told April 2006

When I went back to my mission station, I started telling these stories to many people. They are laborers and are mostly illiterate. These Hindus believe people are made in the image of a monkey. But when I told the story about Creation and how God made Adam and Eve, the people listened very well. They were very interested and very pleased to hear these stories. Then one man named Ram Lal, asked me, "It is true? This really happened?" So I told them, "Yes, it is a true story—it really happened." Then they believed. So, now many people are coming to the church there.

c) By Sudhir; told September 2006

One day we were traveling on the train for a monthly meeting. There was a lady who was traveling alone, so we gave her a seat. After she sat down we told her Bible stories.... That lady was so happy to hear about the Creation story. She was surprised and said, "Is it really like this that God created this world and every man and every thing like that only? It is the real story. I believe this story. Surely I will tell this story to my husband also."

7. Peace in Human Relationships

a) By Prakash; told April 2006

I started conducting a small tutoring class in a village for the children where I told the story of Cain and Abel. That story really touched their hearts. So then the children went home and told that story in their own families. Now there was a man living there who had two wives. His grown children were always fighting and arguing over how his land was going to be distributed among them and they had no peace and joy in that family. The next day, those two women came and asked me to tell them that story. So I went with them and told the story of Cain and Abel in their home. And God did a work in their lives, because that story really touched their hearts. They started to think and discuss among themselves, "Every day, we are quarreling and arguing over this land, and there is no peace and joy in our lives." So the next day they came to me and said, "We don't want this land; let them take it. But we want peace and joy in our family." There are many brothers in that family. One of those brothers, who is named Govind Bagh, has now started attending my church with his family. There are five people in his family, and now all five are ready to take baptism.

b) By Sabat; told September 2006

There is a man in the church named Dev Kumar. Everyday he would always beat his wife. He would never let one day pass without beating her. Many people had spoken to him from the Bible, but nothing changed. I began to think, "What can I do for him?" So I started telling him the stories about Adam and Eve. I told the story seven times. After listening to this story over and over, now he is not beating his wife anymore. Many pastors had come there and had preached to him, but nothing had changed. Yet after hearing this story, now he has repented and they are living together very fine. His wife's name is Sukanti. Even though he was a church believer, he was beating his wife. But after learning the stories, now they are doing well and living in peace for many months. In that village, all the people know what this person was like. But thank God he has changed.

c) By Sangram; told January 2007

Since starting in this storytelling program, I have shared all these Bible stories with the people in my church. I told them the stories of creation, Adam, Cain and Abel, Noah and Abraham. One family was greatly blessed and changed by hearing the story about Cain and Abel. Before that, the members of this family were always very angry. But after they heard about Cain and Abel, they said, "No, we should not be angry like Cain. That is not good." So now they have become very humble.

8. FELT NEED FOR HELP WITH SCHOOL EXAMS

The academic environment in India creates intense pressure on students each year when they sit for their final exams. The results of an exam determine not only if a student advances, but also which school they will be permitted to attend. It is no exaggeration to say that less than satisfactory marks on a crucial exam can affect the remainder of a student's life. During exam season, nothing has higher priority in a student's family. Fathers stay close to home while mothers prepare special meals for the students. Everything possible is done to give them a crucial edge. Lamentably, another predictable result each year is a spate of suicides by children who were unable to bear up under the pressure. Hence help with school exams is a need that is felt strongly by both parents and students. In the oral Bible pilot project, this came up repeatedly since women participants often asked prayer for their children's exams and several of the participants were also school students. The following account was given by Pitambar:

> I want to tell you about my storytelling disciple, Ranjeet. God did a wonderful thing—through him ten young men received Christ, and through Jesus Christ they were able to pass their tenth standard exam. When Ranjeet was telling the creation story to them, he said, 'From nothing, something has happened.' This made the ten young men who were listening understand that there is a God who can do something out of nothing. So they prayed to God for help and as a result they all passed their exams. Now 20 or 25 people are coming to hear Ranjeet when he is telling the stories. He is also leading a congregation by telling Bible stories. Through him more people have decided to take baptism. Recently he called me to come for the baptism ceremony. It will be soon. (Pitambar; February 2007).

9. NONLITERATES AND STORY LEARNING

Because the GEN2 participants were all able to read, it is important to ask whether the stories will transfer to nonliterates using this oral Bible model. Following are some accounts that address this:

a) By Dasrath; told April 2006
My disciple, Goondapa, is illiterate. He used to tell stories of evil spirits and idols, satanic stories, which bring fear into the people's lives. But since I have been teaching him the Bible stories, now he is telling them in [chronological] order like a series to other people. So far I have told him 25 stories. Out of these, he tells ten stories to others. Goondapa is 75 years old.

b) By John S.; told February 2007
About 50% of the people in my church are illiterate. When I used to preach to them, those who are educated would open their Bible and read. But those who were uneducated were ashamed and felt guilty within themselves. When

I learned the stories from here and started telling the stories then the illiterate members also were interested and were not made to feel ashamed (one of those families is a low-caste Hindu family). Now they are eager to come to church, and the church is growing.

c) By Rajeth Korkora; told February 2007
The people there are uneducated and people. They are unable to read and write; it is not easy for them to understand the preaching. But from the day I started to tell them the stories, they tell me, "The stories are so nice and we can understand them." Before that, it was difficult for them to understand. But now they are understanding everything, through the storytelling way. And they are very strong in faith."

d) By Amruth; told February 2007
I started planting a church seven months ago in a village where there are many cults, such as those who worship *Sidi Sai Baba* and *Amba Bhai*. The people cannot read or write because they are very poor. At first nothing happened. When I preached they were not able to understand me. But then I went and shared a story with them. Since I started to tell them stories, now they can understand. So now these *Sidi Sai Baba* and *Amba Bhai* people are regularly attending the meetings. They work in the day time and can attend the meetings only in the evenings. But they are very interested to come and sit and listen to the stories.

10. APPLICATION BY STORYTELLERS OF MAT. 6:5–15 AND 18:21–35

a) By A___; told January 2007
This week we learned the story about forgiving others. I have always been a hot-tempered man; I was always arguing and shouting at others. Even this morning, I fear I may have accidentally offended my brother Rajeet. I was just joking around, but maybe he was offended. I told him, "Brother, this is my habit. I always used to be fighting with others, so please forgive me." Learning this story really touched my heart. It taught me that I must forgive others. From now on, no matter what problem may come into my life with others, I have made a decision to always be ready to forgive others.

b) By B_____; told January 2007
When I was attending school, I joined a Kung Fu training program, for the purpose of taking revenge against those who bullied me. While I was practicing those methods, I accidentally kicked a friend so he fell down. I did not say anything to him after that. But this story taught me how many

times I must forgive my brother. It taught me that I must go and ask them to forgive me, because Jesus said, "If you don't forgive others, then your heavenly Father won't forgive you either." So now I have made a decision to go find this man and ask his forgiveness for what I did.

c) By Ranjeet; told January 2007
I was touched by the Forgiveness story. Just like Peter, I used to have anger against my neighbors. One day my brothers and I went to preach the gospel. But the people beat us very badly and they imprisoned us. My younger brother helped me because he is able to defend himself very well like a Kung Fu master. Then again on the 23rd of November, 2005, some people filed false charges against me. But this story has taught me that I need to forgive. So now I have decided to forgive them.

d) By Ramesh Barela; told January 2007
In the past three days we have learned so many stories. Last night I was lying on my mat and could not sleep. As I was thinking about these stories, the Holy Spirit spoke to me through them. I fell asleep and had a dream. I was in my church, and there were some church elders there and I was washing their feet. Then today while we were learning this Forgiveness story, our trainer, Nileswar, asked us, "How often have you washed your wife's feet?" So I thought, "Last night, God showed me this dream, so this must be connected." Now I have made a decision when I go back to my home that I will do according to the vision of God. I will wash the feet of others."

e) By U____; told January 2007
I was touched by this story about forgiveness. The story reminded me that I need to forgive my brother (this brother is just like the Gadarene demoniac). I had been bothered all week by a strong feeling of tension within myself. In fact, I was so tense that I could not even eat lunch today. The tension was because for a long time I have not had forgiveness in my heart. But now after learning this Forgiveness story, I am feeling free and blessed.

11. RESISTANCE TO THE GOSPEL OVERCOME

a) By Amruth; told September 2006
This storytelling process is very helpful for me in my ministry because I can teach the people the word of God through these stories very easily. Because people are bound and blinded by Satan in my area, if I share directly about Jesus Christ, they will get angry at me and may do me some harm. So after attending this program, I am teaching the word of God

through stories only.

b) By Byju P. John; told September 2006

One of my apprentices named Rajesh is working in an area where there is much Hindu opposition against the Gospel. But those same Hindu people are not opposed to him whenever he is telling the stories. One man from that place got saved and is ready for baptism now.

c) By Dasrath; told April 2006

One day I was walking through a field when I saw a Hindu family of four people who are living there. They are very Hindu—fanatical Hindu. I asked them for a drink of water, and they gave me some good water to drink. Then I asked them, "Do you want me to tell you a story?" They replied, "Yes, we are interested to hear that story." So I told them the story about Creation. They liked my Creation story very much. "This creation story of yours—it is different from our own Hindu creation story. Why is it different from our story?" So I told them, "My Creation story that I am telling—it is written in the Bible. It is a true story." They were very interested to hear it. So that man (Sharanappa is his name) said, "When are you going to come back to our home again? Whenever you come by here again, we are ready to hear more such stories from you." So they have invited me to please come and share more stories with them in the coming days.

d) By Dasrath; told September 2006

Before learning these stories, we were finding it hard to hand out tracts and preach the word of God. But it is very easy to make friends and tell the stories. Wherever I go, if I get some people and ask them, "I want to tell you a story," then I start to tell them the story. Once we were traveling from Hyderabad to Bidar, and there was a man from a Muslim background who was sitting in the train with me. His name is Sayed. He was trying to get water, but could not. So I gave him a water bottle and he was so grateful. We visited with each other and started discussing about religion, from the Quran and also from the Bible. I gave him a chance to first tell me about his Quran. Then I said, "Let me tell now about our Bible and about the word of God. So I told him the stories. I told him about the creation and Adam and Eve, and he listened very carefully. Three or four other passengers were also sitting there, and they were also eagerly listening to the stories. Then I told him at last about Jesus Christ, how Jesus Christ came to this world as a sacrifice for us, to take away the sin from us, and to make us children of God. After telling these stories, we even sang a song about Adam—it has many verses. Those people were listening to that song and they were so interested to hear it. This is the chorus:

Where did you come from?
One day you will go there only.
You came from dust.
Again you will go to dust.

In this way our ministry is growing through this storytelling program. Before, I had a fear of preaching the word of God to higher caste people. But there is a custom in our state: everyone, from children to old people, they all like to hear stories. So it is a very easy way to tell them the Bible stories and now we can easily approach the higher caste people.

e) By Ishwar; told April 2006

One day, when I was walking along the road, one family shouted, "Oh, a Christian is going there. One Christian is there." Immediately I stopped, because I was so surprised to hear them shouting like that. So I went over to the family and asked, "What is the problem?" A sick girl was there so I prayed for her and I also started telling the Creation story. But the man of that house, the girl's father, was not at all interested to hear the Good News. He shouted at his wife, "Why did you invite these kind of people into our house?" So he was shouting about it. And he was totally against hearing the Gospel. He opposed us completely. Somehow I was able to finish telling the creation story. I told it like this: "God formed man out of the dust. And God took so much care when He did this. He came down and took some of the dust of the earth, some of the mud—in His holy hand. And out of that dirt, He formed man in His own image, with great love. So you and I, we are the creation of God." I finished the story and went back to my home.

After some days, the man who had opposed me came to see me. He called me, saying, "Oh, Christian, come out." I was afraid because I thought, "This is the man who opposed me. When I went to his house, he was very much against me. So now he is calling me again. So maybe he is going to beat me." So I was very much afraid. But when that man came into my house, he said, "Christian, tell me this story once again." So I started to tell him the same story. It began to touch his heart, and slowly, slowly, his entire life changed. He began telling that story to others and it started to spread among the people. Now he has committed his life to God. And not only that; more of his family members have started to come. So now they are also hearing the stories. About 20 new people have started to attend my church. That man's name is Rathnakar.

APPENDIX K
COMPREHENSIVE EXAM SCORES

BATCH A (ORIYA LANGUAGE)

STORY TELL-ER	Apprentice Score	Chronology	Multiple Choice	ORAL1 (OT)	ORAL2 (NT)	ORAL3 (OT & NT)	FINAL SCORE
S.K.B	77.8	100	97	86.1	87.8	91.7	90.1
S.K.S.	89.9	100	99	93.3	76.1	77.2	89.3
K.D.N.	81.6	100	99	80.4	83.3	82.5	87.8
P.K.	76.6	100	99	83.3	86.7	72.9	86.4
P.C.K.	82.4	100	100	71.7	80.8	80.6	85.9
P.K.K.	67.3	100	92	70.4	84.2	87.5	83.6
S.K.D.	72.1	90	91	77.5	76.7	84.2	81.9
S.K.T.	66.6	80	90	82.5	71.3	81.7	78.7
S.K.S.	0	100	99	88.3	89.6	90	77.8
P.K.M.	78.4	100	94	48.8	77.9	61.7	76.8
S.R.G.	80.8	100	90	63.8	59.6	66.7	76.8
J.K.	83.8	90	86	65.7	53.8	74.2	75.6
R.S.K.	0	100	99	71.7	74.6	88.1	72.2
R.S.	0	100	100	65.8	84.6	81.9	72
A.K.	0	100	99	69.2	75.4	85	71.4
B.P.	0	100	100	73.8	72.1	76.3	70.4
R.P.	0	75	89	68.3	75.8	85.8	65.7

BATCH B (MULTIPLE LANGUAGES)

STORY TELLER	Apprentice Score	Chronology	Multiple Choice	ORAL1 (OT)	ORAL2 (NT)	ORAL3 (OT & NT)	FINAL SCORE
B.B.P.	93.2	100.0	98.0	99.0	77.0	77.0	90.7
S.S.	81.6	100.0	95.0	97.5	83.9	83.9	90.3
D. M.	75.6	100.0	95.0	97.5	85.6	85.6	89.9
D.N.W.	53.6	100.0	100.0	100.0	83.9	83.9	86.9
P.K.	82.0	100.0	98.0	99.0	67.9	67.9	85.8
J.S.	70.3	100.0	82.0	91.0	85.3	85.3	85.6
K.D.A	80.7	82.0	96.0	89.0	73.9	73.9	82.6
S.V.S.	79.3	100.0	96.0	98.0	59.4	59.4	82.0
A.N.	67.3	70.0	93.0	81.5	85.8	85.8	80.6
P.S.A.	0.0	100.0	99.0	99.5	85.7	85.7	78.3
P.M.J.	0.0	100.0	99.0	99.5	80.4	80.4	76.5
A.M.	0.0	100.0	96.0	98.0	80.0	80.0	75.7
V.H.G.	52.3	86.0	97.0	91.5	56.7	56.7	73.4
I.G.Y.	0.0	82.0	91.0	86.5	65.0	65.0	64.9
M. T.	0.0	64.0	81.0	72.5	78.1	78.1	62.3
D.N.	49.7	10.0	37.0	23.5	45.2	45.2	35.1

APPENDIX L
MULTIPLE CHOICE QUESTIONS

The multiple choice segment of the storytellers' final exam was comprised of 108 statements covering every story learned in the course. Each statement was followed by a choice of four story symbols, only one of which represented the correct story (see #1 below).

1. In this story a man dreamed a dream about angels.

2. In this story God spoke to Moses on a mountain.
3. In this story a prophet was taken to heaven.
4. In this story a boy was separated from his parents on a journey.
5. "Lord, if my brother keeps sinning against me, how many times do I have to forgive him?"
6. In this story a man asked Jesus, "Who is my neighbor?"
7. In this story Jesus said, "I am the resurrection and the life."
8. In this story a small stone killed God's enemy.
9. In this story Jesus said, "Where your treasure is, there your heart will be also."
10. In this story a man prepared food for his father.
11. God said, "Stretch out your hand over the sea and divide it."
12. In this story God spoke to a prophet in a still, small voice.
13. In this story a king commanded to kill all the little children two years old or younger.
14. In this story the disciples asked Jesus to teach them to pray.
15. In this story a man said, "I was afraid, and went and hid your money in the ground."

END NOTES

1 [online] The Indian Evangelical Team, <http://www.ietmissions.org/>.
2 Now Fuller Theological Seminary School of Intercultural Studies.
3 Grant Lovejoy, "Chronological Bible Storying: Description, Rationale and Implications" (Nairobi, Kenya: Non-Print Media Consultation, June 2000), 5.
4 Walter J. Ong, *Orality and Literacy: The Technologizing of the Word* (London and New York: Routledge, 1982), 42.
5 Suggested by J. O. Terry; private email message, June 1, 2007.
6 Lucien Levy-Bruhl, *Primitive Mentality* (Boston: Beacon, 1966), 433.
7 Tom Steffen, *Passing the Baton: Church Planting That Empowers* (La Habra, CA: Center for Organizational & Ministry Development, 1997), 122.
8 Mary Drewery, *William Carey: A Biography* (Grand Rapids, MI: Zondervan, 1978), 30.
9 Louis J. Luzbetak, The Church and Cultures: New Perspectives in Missiological Anthropology (Maryknoll, NY: Orbis Books, 1988), 374.
10 William Carey biography. *A Candle in the Dark*, Gateway Films, 1998.
11 Lois-ellin Datta, "Case Study Evaluations," [online] GAO Program Evaluation and Methodology Division, 1990, accessed October 2003, <http://www.ojp.usdoj.gov/BJA/evaluation/guide/documents/documentee.html>.
12 Davydd J. Greenwood and Morten Levin, *Introduction to Action Research* (Thousand Oaks, CA: Sage, 1998), 6.
13 Ibid., 73-81.
14 Ibid., 19.
15 Ibid., 106.
16 Ibid., 6.
17 Charles H. Kraft, Christianity in Culture: A Study in Dynamic Biblical Theologizing in Cross-Cultural Perspective (Maryknoll, NY: Orbis Books, 1979), 147.
18 Charles H. Kraft, *Communication Theory for Christian Witness* (Maryknoll, NY: Orbis Books, 1991), 16-17.
19 Ong, Orality and Literacy, 78.
20 Richard A. Jensen, *Thinking in Story* (Lima, OH: CSS, 1993), 31.
21 Richard A. Jensen, *Preaching Matthew's Gospel: A Narrative Approach* (Lima, OH: CSS, 1998), 18.
22 Michael Cole et al., The Cultural Context of Learning and Thinking: An Exploration In Experimental Anthropology (New York: Basic Books, 1971).
23 Michael Cole and Sylvia Scribner, *Culture and Thought: A Psychological Introduction* (New York: John Wiley & Sons, 1974), 160-164.
24 James B. Slack and J. O. Terry, *Chronological Bible Storying: A Methodology for Presenting the Gospel to Oral Communicators* (Ft. Worth, TX: Southwestern Baptist Theological Seminary, 1997), 42.
25 Harry Box, "Communicating Christianity to Oral, Event-Oriented People" (Ph.D. diss., Fuller Theological Seminary, Pasadena, CA, 1992), 25, 59.
26 Ibid., 314.
27 Ibid., 150.
28 Harry Box, "Central Issues in Communicating the Gospel in Melanesia" (M.A. thesis, Fuller Theological Seminary, Pasadena, CA, 1982), 192.
29 Slack and Terry, 9.
30 National Adult Literacy Survey (NALS) 1992. This has been succeeded by the 2003 National Assessment of Adult Literacy (NAALS).

31 Lovejoy, 7.

32 C. J. Daswani, *Linguistic Diversity and Literacy in India* (New Delhi: International Literacy Institute, Second Asia Regional Literacy Forum-Innovation and Professionalization in Adult Literacy: A Focus on Diversity, February 9-13, 1998).

33 William A. Graham, *Beyond the Written Word* (Cambridge: Cambridge University Press, 1987), x, 80, 88-92.

34 J. P. Losty, *The Art of the Book in India*, 14; quoted in Anne Pellowski, *The World of Storytelling* (New York: R. R. Bowker, 1977), 12.

35 BBC News, April 4, 2002

36 Kirin Narayan, *Storytellers, Saints, and Scoundrels: Folk Narrative in Hindu Religious Teaching* (Philadelphia: University of Pennsylvania, 1989), 46.

37 http://www.nbtindia.org.in/world_bookfair.shtml; http://www.delhiprinter.org/bookpub.htm; accessed October 2007.

38 Ong, Orality and Literacy, 41.

39 David Filbeck, *Social Context and Proclamation: A Socio-cognitive Study in Proclaiming the Gospel Cross-culturally* (Pasadena, CA: William Carey Library, 1985), 107.

40 Ibid., 107-109.

41 Ibid., 108.

42 S. Estborn, *Our Village Christians: A study of the life and faith of village Christians in Tamilnad* (Mysore, India: Wesley Press, 1959), 2.

43 Robert Alter, *The Art of Biblical Narrative* (n.p.: BasicBooks, 1981), 107.

44 Jacob Loewen, *Culture and Human Values* (Pasadena, CA: William Carey Library, 1975), 134.

45 Susan Niditch, *Underdogs and Tricksters: A Prelude to Biblical Folklore* (San Francisco: Harper & Row, 1987), xi.

46 Ibid., xi, 48.

47 Ibid.,149.

48 B. F. Skinner, *The Technology of Teaching* (New York: Appleton-Century-Crofts, 1968), 110.

49 James L. Crenshaw, *Education in Ancient Israel* (NY: Doubleday, 1998), 3.

50 Susan Niditch, *Oral World and Written Word: Ancient Israelite Literature* (Louisville, KY: Westminster John Knox Press, 1996), 5.

51 Eric A. Havelock, "The Alphabetic Mind: A Gift of Greece to the Modern World;" *Oral Tradition Journal*, 1/1 (1986): 134-150.

52 John D. Harvey, *Listening to the Text: Oral Patterning in Paul's Letters* (Grand Rapids, MI: Baker Book House, 1998), 50-51.

53 Louis L'Amour, *Sackett's Land* (NY, Bantam, 1974), 189-190 (in a preview of *Smoke from the Altar*).

54 N. T. Wright, *The New Testament and the People of God* (Minneapolis: Fortress Press, 1992), 40.

55 Catherine Hezser, Jewish Literacy in Roman Palestine: Texts and Studies in Ancient Judaism (Tubingen: Mohr Siebeck, 2001).

56 Crenshaw, *Ancient Literacy*; (Cambridge and London: Harvard University Press, 1989) 44.

57 Meir Bar-Ilan, *Illiteracy in the Land of Israel in the First Centuries* c.e. Essays in the Social Scientific Study of Judaism and Jewish Society (S. S. a. A. G. S. Fishbane. New York, Ktav, 1992), II: 46-61.

58 William Barclay, *Educational Ideals in the Ancient World* (Grand Rapids, MI: Baker Book House, 1974, 1959), 23.

59 Hezser, 473.

60 Crenshaw, *Education in Ancient Israel*, 38.

61 Whitney Shiner, *Proclaiming the Gospel: First-Century Performance of Mark* (Harrisburg, PA: Trinity Press International, 2003), 13, 14.

62 *Exegesis of the Sayings of the Lord* (recorded in Eusebius, Hist. Eccl. 3.39).

63 John Dominic Crossan, *Jesus: A Revolutionary Biography* (New York: HarperCollins, 1994), 24-26.

64 Harvey, 283f.

65 Acts 7

66 Acts 9, 22, 26, Galatians 1, 1 Tim. 1:12-16; etc.

67 Acts 13:16f

68 E. E. Ellis, *Paul's Use of the Old Testament* (Grand Rapids, MI: Eerdmans, 1957), 10. In Harvey, 83.

69 Rom. 4, Gal. 2, 1 Cor. 10:1-11, 15:22, 45-49; etc.

70 N. T. Wright, 79.

71 Hans Ruedi Weber, *The Communication of the Gospel to Illiterates* (London: SCM Press, 1957), 64.

72 Mark Ellingsen, *The Integrity of Biblical Narrative: Story in Theology and Proclamation* (Minneapolis: Fortress Press, 1990), 18.

73 Charles H. Kraft, lecture delivered to Fuller School of World Mission Ethnotheology class, 15 Oct 1997, Fuller Theological Seminary, Pasadena, CA.

74 Acts 8:4

75 Acts 6:7, 12:24, 19:20

76 Gary B. McGee, "Pentecostal Phenomena and Revivals in India: Implications for Indigenous Church Leadership," *International Bulletin of Missionary Research* 20:3 (July 1996): 112.

77 J. O. Terry and Tom Steffen, "The Sweeping Story of Scripture Taught Through Time," *Missiology: An International Review*, no. 35 (3) (July 2007).

78 Ruth A. Tucker, *From Jerusalem to Irian Jaya* (Grand Rapids, MI: Zondervan, 1983), 66.

79 John L. Nevius, *Methods of Mission Work* (New York: Foreign Mission Library, 1895), 33, 39. (Etext edition, 1995 by Clyde C. Price, Jr.).

80 Stephen Neill. "The Christian Catalyst Collection from the 20th Century." Video recorded at the Overseas Ministries Study Center, 1984. Distributed by Vision Video, Box 540, Worcester, PA 19490, Tape 1, Lecture 2.

81 Weber, 18.

82 Ibid., 39.

83 Trevor McIlwain, *Building on Firm Foundations*, vol. 1, (Sanford, FL: New Tribes Mission, 1987).

84 Tom Steffen, *Reconnecting God's Story to Ministry: Cross-cultural Storytelling at Home and Abroad* (La Habra, CA: Center for Organizational & Ministry Development, 1996).

85 J. O. Terry, "The Roots of CBS," *Journal of Bible Storytelling* (email publication), no. 1 (July 2004): 7.

86 Loewen, 370-376.

87 International Orality Network, accessed June 2006, <http://www.oralbible.com/>.

88 Lynne A. Abney, *Chronological Bible Storying for Muslim Arabic Speakers* (International Mission Board, Northern Africa and the Middle East, 2000), 1-5 (paper).

89 Peter Chang, "Steak, Potatoes, Peas and Chopsuey," in *Missions and Theological Education in World Perspective*, ed. Conn, Harvie M., and Samuel Rowen (Farmington, MI: Associates of Urbanus, 1984), 113.

90   Boomershine, 52.

91   Jerome Bruner, *Actual Minds, Possible Worlds* (Cambridge, MA: Harvard University Press, 1986), 11.

92   Ibid., 25.

93   Ibid., 26.

94   Wolfgang Iser, *The Act of Reading* (Baltimore, MD: John Hopkins University Press, 1978), 21, 61; quoted in Bruner, 25.

95   Bruner, 35.

96   Ibid., 36.

97   Ibid., 13.

98   "From Control to Power: A Fresh Look at Leadership," Dr. Nick Begich [online], cited May 2007, available from <http://www.earthpulse.com/src/subcategory.asp?catid=8&subcatid=5>.

99   Shiner, 63.

100 Ibid., 64.

101 Ibid., 65, 66.

102 Ibid., 67.

103 J. Stephen Lang and Mark A. Noll, "Colonial New England: An Old Order, New Awakening," *Christian History* 8 (1985).

104 Patrick N. Allitt, "(Lecture 8: The Second Great Awakening)," *American Religious History*, (Chantilly, VA: The Teaching Company, 2001), videocassette.

105 James Stephens, *The Crock of Gold* (New York: Macmillan); quoted in Ruth Sawyer, *The Way of the Storyteller* (New York: Viking Press, 1942), 16.

106 Maarten Wisse, "Narrative Theology and the Dogmatic Use of the Bible" (Helsinki: ESPR Conference, 2000).

107 Ibid.

108 Jonathan Wilson, email newsletter, December 26, 2002.

109 *Encyclopedia Britannica*, Britannica CD. Version 97th ed., s.v. "Human Learning and Cognition: The Physiology of Transfer of Training."

110 Andrew Fletcher of Saltoun (1653–1716), *Works—Letters to the Marquis of Montrose*, 266.

111 Ben Okri, *Birds of Heaven* (London: Weidenfeld & Nicolson, 1995).

112 Santosh Soren, March 2005.

113 Michael Goldberg, *Theology & Narrative: A Critical Introduction* (Nashville, TN: Abingdon, 1981), 234.

114 N. T. Wright, 77.

115 Kevin M. Bradt, *Story as a Way of Knowing* (Kansas City, MO: Sheed & Ward, 1997), viii.

116 S. Y. Shah and C. J. Daswani, *Adult Education in India: Selected Papers* (New Delhi: UNESCO, 2000), 19. [online] accessed July 2007, available from <http://unesdoc.unesco.org/images/0012/001213/121314eo.pdf>.

117 Anonymous, private email message to author, May 2000.

118 J. O. Terry, private email message to author, March 20, 2004.

119 Abney, in Lovejoy, 7.

120 Jakob Nielsen, "Lower-Literacy Users," [online] Jakob Nielsen's Alertbox, 2005, accessed July 2007, available from <http://www.useit.com/alertbox/20050314.html>.

121 Edward R. Dayton and David A. Fraser, *Planning Strategies for World Evangelization* (Grand Rapids, MI: Eerdmans, 1990), 163.

122 Ibid.

123 Paul G. Hiebert, *Anthropological Insights for Missionaries* (Grand Rapids, MI: Baker

Book House, 1985), 129.

124 Clark Bouton and Russell Y. Garth, ed., *Learning In Groups* (San Francisco, CA: Jossey-Bass, 1983), 75.

125 Ibid., 32

126 Max McLean, "Why I Love the Bible: An Interview with Max McLean," [online] The Listener's Bible, 2000, accessed April 15, 2003, available from <http://www.listenersbible.com/cgi-bin/merchant2/live_events.asp>.

127 Beatrice Silverinan Weinreich, ed., *Yiddish Folktales* (New York: Pantheon Books, 1988). (Originally a famous story told by Jacob Kranz, the Maggid of Dubno, an 18th century rabbi in Eastern Europe).

128 LaNette Thompson, "The Nonliterate and the Transfer of Knowledge in West Africa" (M.A. thesis, University of Texas, Arlington, TX, 1998), 11.

129 David Straker, "Belief Bias," [online] Changing Minds.org, 2004, accessed January 1, 2005, available from <http://changingminds.org/explanations/theories/belief_bias.htm>.

130 Tom Steffen, private email message to author, Sept. 23, 2007.

131 N. T. Wright, 40.

132 Henry Ward Beecher, *Yale Lectures on Preaching* (1872-1874); quoted in Thomas H. Troeger, *Imagining a Sermon* (Nashville, TN: Abingdon, 1990), 114.

133 Nancy Durrant, "It's the way they tell them," *London Times*, May 27 2006, [online] TIMESONLINE, accessed July 2007, available from <http://www.timesonline.co.uk/article/0,,22874-2193450.html>.

134 Pablo Friere, *Pedagogy of the Oppressed* (M.B. Ramos, transl. New York: Seabury, 1970), 58.

135 Gordon Wells, "Dialogic Inquiry in Education: Building on the Legacy of Vygotsky," in *Vygotskian Perspectives on Literacy Research: Constructing Meaning Through Collaborative Inquiry*, Lee, Carol D., and Peter Smagorinsky, eds., (Cambridge: Cambridge University Press, 2000), 67.

136 *Missions and Theological Education*, ed. Harvie M. Conn and Samuel F. Rowen (Farmington, MI: Associates of Urbanus, 1984), 38.

137 Boomershine, 21.

138 Ibid., 106.

139 Kraft, *Christianity in Culture*, 163-164.

140 LaNette Thompson, private email message to author, 28 February 2002.

141 Lee and Smagorinsky, *Vygotskian Perspectives*, 6.

142 Vera P. John-Steiner and T. M. Meehan, "Creativity and Collaboration in Knowledge Construction," *Vygotskian Perspectives*, 35.

143 Bryan R. Wamick, *Imitation and Education: A Philosophical Inquiry into Learning by Example* (Albany, NY: State University of New York Press, 2008), 55.

144 Ibid., 59.

145 Ibid., 32.

146 Ibid., 17.

147 Ibid., 26.

148 Ibid., 27, 18.

149 Ibid., 38-43.

150 Arden Glenn Sanders, "Learning styles in Melanesia: Toward the Use and Implications of Kolb's Model for National Translator Training" (Ph.D. diss., Fuller Theological Seminary, Pasadena, CA 1988). 193.

151 George W. Patterson, *Church Multiplication Guide* (Pasadena, CA: William Carey Library, 1993), 26.

152   Earl D. Radmacher, Ronald Barclay Allen and H. Wayne House, *The Nelson Study Bible: New King James Version* (Nashville, TN: Thomas Nelson Publishers, 1997), 1 Sam. 27:11.

153   Slack and Terry, 9.

154   Wonsuk Ma, "Toward an Asian Pentecostal Theology," *Asian Journal of Pentecostal Studies* (January 01, 1998): 1.2.1.

155   Ronald F. Youngblood, F. F. Bruce and R. K. Harrison, "Biblical Theology," in *Nelson's Illustrated Bible Dictionary* (Nashville, TN: Thomas Nelson Publishers, 1995).

156   Veli-Matti Karkkainen, "Evangelization, Proselytism, & Common Witness: Roman Catholic-Pentecostal Dialogue on Mission, 1990-1997," *International Bulletin of Missionary Research* 25:01 (2001): 16.

157   Walter J. Hollenweger, "Charismatic Renewal in the Third World: Implications for Mission," *Occasional Bulletin of Missionary Research* [now IBMR], 4:2 (April 1980): 69.

158   L. Grant McClung, Jr., "Theology and Strategy of Pentecostal Missions," *International Bulletin of Missionary Research* 12:01 (1988): 2.

159   Veli-Matti Karkkainen, "Mission, Spirit and Eschatology: An Outline of a Pentecostal-Charismatic Theology of Mission," *Mission Studies* 16:01 (1999): 78.

160   Ma, 1.0.

161   Charles R. Taber, "The Limits of Indigenization in Theology," *Missiology: An International Review* 6:1 (January 1978): 65.

162   Sverre Holth, (1968) "Towards an Indigenous Theology" Ching Feng 11(4):5-26; cited in "The Limits of Indigenization in Theology" by Charles R. Taber, *Missiology: An International Review* 6:1 (Jan 1978): 65.

163   John Hercus, *Pages from God's Casebook* (Chicago: Intervarsity Press, 1962), 16-17.

164   Loewen, 3-4.

165   Ibid.

166   de Mesa, 1.

167   Ma, 3.1.1.

168   Paul G. Hiebert and Frances F. Hiebert, *Case Studies in Missions* (Grand Rapids, MI: Baker Book House, 1987), 17.

169   de Mesa, 10.

170   Van E. Sanders, "A Theological Study of Point of Contact Theory," *Global Missiology, sec. Contemporary Practice* (July 2004), [online] available from <www.globalmissiology.net>.

171   David J. Hesselgrave, *Communicating Christ Cross-Culturally: An Introduction to Missionary Communication* (Grand Rapids, MI: Zondervan, 1991), 598.

172   Steffen, *Passing the Baton*, 157-158.

173   Jack W. Hayford, "Healing Divine, The Ministry of," in *Hayford's Bible Handbook*, (Nashville, TN: Thomas Nelson Publishers, 1995), 630.

174   William Barclay, *The Daily Study Bible Series* (Neptune, NJ: Loizeaux Brothers, Inc.; Bible Companion Software), Romans 1:16-17.

175   William E. Vine, Merrill F. Unger and William White, *Vine's Complete Expository Dictionary of Old and New Testament Words* (Nashville, TN: Thomas Nelson Publishers, 1996), 2:547.

176   Jack W. Hayford and Rebecca Bauer, *Praying in the Spirit: Heavenly Resources for Praise and Intercession*, Spirit-Filled Life Kingdom Dynamics Study Guides, ed. Hayford, Jack W. (Nashville, TN: Thomas Nelson Publishers, 1997), 1527–1528.

177   R. Edward Miller, *Thy God Reigneth: The Story of the Revival in Argentina* (Burbank,

CA: World M.A.P, 1964), 41.

178 Charles H. Kraft, "Contextualization in Three Dimensions," lecture delivered at installation as Sun Hee Kwak Chair of Global Mission, October 20, 1999, Fuller Theological Seminary, Pasadena, CA.

179 J. Herbert Kane, *Wanted: World Christians* (Grand Rapids, MI: Baker Book House, 1986), 215.

180 Paul G. Hiebert, "The Flaw of the Excluded Middle," *Missiology* 10:1 (January 1982): 35-47.

181 C. Zechariah, "Missiological Strategy for the Assemblies of God in Tamil Nadu" (D.Miss. diss. Fuller Theological Seminary, Pasadena, CA, 1981), 208.

182 Mark Naylor, "How Do We Train the Trainers?," [online] Northwest Baptist Seminary, 2003, cited September 2003, available from <http://impact.nbseminary. com/archives/12>.

183 J. Oswald Sanders, *Spiritual Leadership* (Chicago: Moody Press, 1974, 1994), 150.

184 Malcolm S. Knowles, *The Adult Learner: A Neglected Species* (Houston TX: Gulf Publishing, 1973).

185 Mel Silberman, Active Training: A Handbook of Techniques, Designs, Case Examples, and Tips (San Francisco, CA: Jossey-Bass Pfeiffer, 1998), xi, 1.

186 Ong, *The Presence of the Word* (New Haven, CT: Yale University Press, 1967), 30.

187 J. O. Terry, *Good News for Those with Stories of Grief* (International Mission Board, SBC, 1999).

188 Wilbur Smith, *Blue Horizon* (London: Pan Macmillan, 2003), 671.

189 Plato, *Phaedrus*, trans. Benjamin Jowett (World Library, Inc, 1991) [CD-ROM].

190 Frances A. Yates, *The Art of Memory* (London: Pimlico, 1966).

191 Grant Lovejoy, private email message to author, June 21, 2007.

192 Pellowski, 171.

193 "Bengali Story Scrolls at Santa Fe Museum of International Folk Art," [online] , 2006, cited 7 October, 2007, available from <http://www.imeem.com/ballanpr/ blogs/2006/07/23 /Bh1mRgpq/bengali_story_scrolls_at_santa_fe_museum_of _international_folk_art>.

194 Jack Goody, *The Interface Between the Written and the Oral* (Cambridge: Cambridge University Press, 1987), 178.

195 Marcel Jousse, *Oral Style* (Paris: Beauchesne, 1925), 95. In Harvey, John D.; *Listening to the Text: Oral Patterning in Paul's Letters* (Grand Rapids, MI: Baker Book House, 1998), 3.

196 Susan Wittig, "Formulaic Style and the Problem of Redundancy," *Centrum* 1 (1973), 128, 131. In Harvey; *Listening to the Text*, 42.

197 Tom Steffen, "Foundational Roles of Symbol and Narrative in the (Re)construction of Reality and Relationships," *Missiology: An International Review*, no. XXVI: 479.

198 Scot McKnight, "Five Streams of the Emerging Church," *Christianity Today*, February 2007. [Online] accessed July 2007, available from <http://www. christianitytoday.com/ct/2007/february/11.35.html>.

199 Steffen, "Foundational Roles of Symbol and Narrative," 484.

200 N. T. Wright, 40.

201 Viggo Søgaard, *Audio Scriptures Handbook* (Reading, England: United Bible Societies, 1991), 13.

202 Steffen, "Foundational Roles of Symbol and Narrative," 478.

203 Charles H. Kraft, "What Kind of Encounters Do We Need in Our Christian Witness?," *Evangelical Missions Quarterly, Vol.* 27 (July 1991): 258-265.

204 Charles H. Kraft, "Dynamic Equivalence Churches: An Ethnotheological Approach

to Indigeneity," *Missiology* (January 1973): 43.

205 Ibid.

206 Alter, 182.

207 Ibid., 116-117.

208 Chuck Larkin, "What is Storytelling?" [online], cited 6 October 2004, available from <http://www.eldrbarry.net/roos/st_is.htm>.

209 Pellowski, 193.

210 Ibid., 206.

211 Jousse, *Oral Style* (Paris: Beauchesne, 1925), 95. In Harvey; *Listening to the Text*, 3.

212 Frederick Buechner, *Now & Then: A Memoir of Vocation* (San Francisco: Harper & Row, 1983), 15-16.

213 Ruth Finnegan, *Oral Literature in Africa* (London: Oxford, 19070), 5; quoted in Klem, 128.

214 Klem, 127.

215 Arthur Burrell, *A Guide to Story Telling* (London: Sir Isaac Pitman & Sons, 1926), 41.

216 Chuck Larkin, "What is Storytelling?"

217 J.E. Lesslie Newbigin, A South India Diary; quoted in S. Estborn, Our Village Christians: A study of the life and faith of village Christians in Tamilnad (Madras: Christian Literature Society, 1959), 42.

218 Ralph D. Winter and Steven C. Hawthorne, *Perspectives on the World Christian Movement* (Pasadena, CA: William Carey Library, 1992), B-157 to B-175.

219 Daniel Shaw, *Transculturation: The Cultural Factor in Translation and Other Communication Tasks* (Pasadena, CA: William Carey Library, 1988), 28.

220 Hesselgrave, 46.

221 Kraft, *Communication Theory*, 92.

222 Shaw, 31.

223 Thompson, 38.

224 Paul G. Hiebert, *Anthropological Reflections on Missiological Issues* (Grand Rapids, MI: Baker Book House, 1994), 147.

225 Ibid., 149.

226 Ibid.

227 F. Hrangkhuma, *Christianity in India: Search for Liberation and Identity* (New Delhi: CMS/ISPCK, 1998), 78.

228 Donald A. McGavran, *Understanding Church Growth* (Grand Rapids, MI: Eerdmans, 1990), 155, 239.

229 Donald A. McGavran, *The Bridges of God* (New York: Friendship Press, 1968).

230 Ong, *Orality and Literacy*, 42-43.

231 N. T. Wright, 7, 51.

232 Ellingsen, 28-29, 64.

233 Ong, Presence of the Word, 22.

234 Niditch, *Oral World*, 4, 1.

235 *Midrashim* are stories of the ancient Jewish rabbis. See Louis Ginzberg, *The Legends of the Jews*, trans. Henrietta Szold (Philadelphia: The Jewish Publication Society, 1909 and 1937), IV: 3

236 William G. Archer, *The Hill of Flutes: Life, Love, and Poetry in Tribal India: a Portrait of the Santals* (London: Allen & Unwin, 1974), 48. [Field Date: 1942-1946].

237 Marcus Murmu, Fr., "The Santals: Their Traditions and Institutions in Bangladesh," (2004), 3. Available from Bishop's House, Post Box No. 5, Dinajpur –5200, Bangladesh.

238 Marla Magaha, private email message to author, July 3, 2007.

239 Crenshaw, *Education in Ancient Israel*, 1.
240 *I Am Sam*. Avery Pix, released January 2002, film.
241 Dennis Dewey, "Rediscovering Biblical Narrative as Storytelling in the Digital Age," Lamblight Lecture, October 7, 2004, Trinity Western University.
242 Ong, *Orality and Literacy*, 32-33.
243 Ibid., 74.
244 Box, "Communicating Christianity," 346.
245 David Kornfield, "Seminary Education Toward Adult Education Alternatives," in *Missions and Theological Education In World Perspective*, ed. Conn, 187.

Index of Authors

INDEX OF VERBATIMS BY THEME

Index of Topics

REFERENCES

Alter, Robert. *The Art of Biblical Narrative. n.p.*: BasicBooks, 1981.

Archer, William G. *The Hill of Flutes: Life, Love, and Poetry in Tribal India: a Portrait of the Santals.* London: Allen & Unwin, 1974.

Barclay, William. *Educational Ideals in the Ancient World.* Grand Rapids, MI: Baker Book House, 1974, 1959.

Boomershine, Thomas E. *Story Journey: An Invitation to the Gospel As Storytelling.* Nashville, TN: Abingdon, 1988.

Bouton, Clark, and Russell Y. Garth, ed. *Learning In Groups.* San Francisco, CA: Jossey-Bass, 1983.

Box, Harry. "Central Issues in Communicating the Gospel in Melanesia." M.A. thesis, Fuller Theological Seminary, Pasadena, CA, 1982.

_____. "Communicating Christianity To Oral, Event-Oriented People." Ph.D. diss., Fuller Theological Seminary, Pasadena, CA, 1992.

Bradt, Kevin M. *Story as a Way of Knowing.* Kansas City, MO: Sheed & Ward, 1997.

Brown, Richard D. "Designing Programs for Oral Cultures." *Notes on Literature in Use and Language Programs* 46 (December 1995).

Bruner, Jerome. *Actual Minds, Possible Worlds.* Cambridge, MA: Harvard University Press, 1986.

Buechner, Frederick. *Now & Then: A Memoir of Vocation.* San Francisco: Harper & Row, 1983.

Burrell, Arthur. *A Guide to Story Telling.* London: Sir Isaac Pitman & Sons, 1926, 1975.

Cole, Michael, and Sylvia Scribner. *Culture and Thought: A Psychological Introduction.* New York: John Wiley & Sons, 1974.

Cole, Michael, John Gay, Joseph A. Glick and Donald W. Sharp. *The Cultural Context of Learning and Thinking: An Exploration In Experimental Anthropology.* New York: Basic Books, 1971.

Conn, Harvie M., and Samuel Rowen, eds. *Missions and Theological Education In World Perspective*, ed. Farmington, MI: Associates of Urbanus, 1984.

Costas, Orlando. *Christ Outside the Gate: Mission Beyond Christendom.* Maryknoll, NY: Orbis Books, 1982.

Dayton, Edward R. and David A. Fraser. *Planning Strategies for World Evangelization.* Grand Rapids, MI: Eerdmans, 1990.

de Mesa, Jose M. "Making Salvation Concrete and Jesus Real: Trends in Asian Christology." *SEDOS* (January 1999).

Ellingsen, Mark. *The Integrity of Biblical Narrative: Story in Theology and Proclamation.* Minneapolis: Fortress Press, 1990.

Filbeck, David. *Social Context and Proclamation: A Socio-cognitive Study in Proclaiming the Gospel Cross-culturally.* Pasadena, CA: William Carey Library, 1985.

Finnegan, Ruth. *Oral Literature in Africa.* London: Oxford, 1970.

Friere, Pablo. *Pedagogy of the Oppressed.* New York: Seabury, 1970.

Goldberg, Michael. *Theology & Narrative: A Critical Introduction.* Nashville, TN: Abingdon, 1981.

Goody, Jack. *The Interface Between the Written and the Oral.* Cambridge: Cambridge University Press, 1987.

Graham, William A. *Beyond the Written Word.* Cambridge: Cambridge University Press, 1987.

Greenwood, David J., and Morten Levin. *Introduction to Action Research*. Thousand Oaks, CA: Sage, 1998.

Harvey, John D. *Listening to the Text: Oral Patterning in Paul's Letters*. Grand Rapids, MI: Baker Book House, 1998.

Havelock, Eric A. "The Alphabetic Mind: A Gift of Greece to the Modern World," *Oral Tradition Journal*, 1/1 (1986).

_____. *The Muse Learns to Write*. New Haven, CT, Yale University, 1986.

Hayford, Jack W. "Healing Divine, The Ministry of." In *Hayford's Bible Handbook*. Nashville, TN: Thomas Nelson Publishers, 1995.

_____., and Rebecca Bauer. *Praying in the Spirit: Heavenly Resources for Praise and Intercession*. Nashville, TN: Thomas Nelson, 1997.

Hercus, John. *Pages from God's Casebook*. Chicago: Intervarsity Press, 1962.

Hesselgrave, David J. *Communicating Christ Cross-Culturally: An Introduction to Missionary Communication*. Grand Rapids, MI: Zondervan, 1991.

Hezser, Catherine. *Jewish Literacy in Roman Palestine: Texts and Studies in Ancient Judaism*. Tubingen: Mohr Siebeck, 2001.

Hiebert, Paul G. *Anthropological Insights for Missionaries*. Grand Rapids, MI: Baker Book House, 1985.

_____. *Anthropological Reflections on Missiological Issues*. Grand Rapids, MI: Baker Book House, 1994.

_____. "The Flaw of the Excluded Middle." *Missiology* 10:1 (January 1982).

_____., and Frances F. Hiebert. *Case Studies In Missions*. Grand Rapids, MI: Baker Book House, 1987.

Hollenweger, Walter J. "Charismatic Renewal in the Third World: Implications for Mission." *Occasional Bulletin of Missionary Research*, no. 4 (April 1980).

Jensen, Richard A. *Preaching Matthew's Gospel: A Narrative Approach*. Lima, OH: C.S.S. Publishing, 1998.

_____. *Thinking in Story*. Lima, OH: C.S.S. Publishing, 1993.

Jones, E. Stanley. *Christ at the Round Table*. New York: Abingdon, 1928.

Kane, J. Herbert. *Wanted: World Christians*. Grand Rapids, MI: Baker Book House, 1986.

Karkkainen, Veli-Matti. "Mission, Spirit and Eschatology: An Outline of a Pentecostal-Charismatic Theology of Mission." *Mission Studies* 16:01 (1999).

Klem, Herbert Viele. "Toward The More Effective Use of Oral Communication of the Scriptures in West Africa." Ph.D. diss., Fuller Theological Seminary, Pasadena, CA, 1977.

Knowles, Malcolm S. *The Adult Learner: A Neglected Species*. Houston TX: Gulf Publishing, 1973.

Koehler, Paul. "Telling God's Stories with Power: Biblical Storytelling in Oral Cultures." D.Min. thesis, United Theological Seminary, Dayton, OH, 2007.

Kraft, Charles H. *Christianity in Culture: A Study in Dynamic Biblical Theologizing in Cross-Cultural Perspective*. Maryknoll, NY: Orbis Books, 1979.

_____. *Communication Theory for Christian Witness*. Maryknoll, NY: Orbis Books, 1991.

_____. "Dynamic Equivalence Churches: An Ethnotheological Approach to Indigeneity." *Missiology* (January 1973).

_____. "What Kind of Encounters Do We Need in Our Christian Witness?." *Evangelical Missions Quarterly* 27 (July 1991): 258–265.

_____. Lecture delivered to Fuller School of World Mission class, 15 October 1997. Fuller Theological Seminary, Pasadena, CA.

————. "Contextualization in Three Dimensions." Speech delivered at the Install as Sun Hee Kwak Chair of Global Mission, October 20, 1999. Fuller Theological Seminary, Pasadena, CA.

Lee, Carol D., and Peter Smagorinsky, ed. *Vygotskian Perspectives on Literacy Research: Constructing Meaning Through Collaborative Inquiry,* Cambridge: Cambridge University Press, 2000.

Levy-Bruhl, Lucien. *Primitive Mentality.* Boston: Beacon, 1966.

Loewen, Jacob A. *Culture and Human Values: Christian Intervention in Anthropological Perspective.* Pasadena, CA: William Carey Library, 1975.

Lovejoy, Grant. "Chronological Bible Storying: Description, Rationale and Implications." Nairobi, Kenya: Non-Print Media Consultation, June 2000.

Luzbetak, Louis J. *The Church and Cultures: New Perspectives in Missiological Anthropology.* Maryknoll, New York: Orbis Books, 1988.

Ma, Wonsuk. "Toward an Asian Pentecostal Theology." *Asian Journal of Pentecostal Studies* (January 01, 1998).

McClung, L. Grant, Jr. "Theology and Strategy of Pentecostal Missions." *International Bulletin of Missionary Research* 12:01 (1988).

McGavran, Donald A. *The Bridges of God.* New York: Friendship Press, 1968.

————. *Understanding Church Growth.* Grand Rapids, MI: Eerdmans, 1990.

McGee, Gary B. "Pentecostal Phenomena and Revivals in India: Implications for Indigenous Church Leadership." *International Bulletin of Missionary Research* 20:3 (July 1996).

McIlwain, Trevor. *Building on Firm Foundations.* Vol. 1, Sanford, FL: New Tribes Mission, 1987.

Narayan, Kirin. *Storytellers, Saints, and Scoundrels: Folk Narrative in Hindu Religious Teaching.* Philadelphia: University of Pennsylvania, 1989.

Nevius, John L. *Methods of Mission Work.* New York: Foreign Mission Library, 1895.

Niditch, Susan, *Oral World and Written Word: Ancient Israelite Literature.* Louisville, KY: Westminster John Knox Press, 1996.

————. *Underdogs and Tricksters: A Prelude to Biblical Folklore.* San Francisco: Harper & Row, 1987.

Ong, Walter J. *Orality and Literacy: The Technologizing of the Word.* London and New York: Routledge, 1982.

————. *The Presence of the Word.* New Haven: Yale University Press, 1967.

Patterson, George W. *Church Multiplication Guide.* Pasadena, CA: William Carey Library, 1993.

Pellowski, Anne. *The World of Storytelling.* New York: R. R. Bowker, 1977.

Sawyer, Ruth. *The Way of the Storyteller.* New York: Viking Press, 1942.

Shaw, Daniel. *Transculturation: The Cultural Factor In Translation and Other Communication Tasks.* Pasadena, CA: William Carey Library, 1998.

Shiner, Whitney. *Proclaiming the Gospel: First-Century Performance of Mark.* Harrisburg, PA: Trinity Press International, 2003.

Silberman, Mel. *Active Training: A Handbook of Techniques, Designs, Case Examples, and Tips.* San Francisco, CA: Jossey-Bass Pfeiffer, 1998.

Skinner, B. F. *The Technology of Teaching.* New York: Appleton-Century-Crofts, 1968.

Slack, James B., and J. O. Terry. *Chronological Bible Storying: A Methodology for Presenting the Gospel to Oral Communicators.* Ft. Worth, TX: Southwestern Baptist Theological Seminary, 1997.

Søgaard, Viggo. *Audio Scriptures Handbook.* Reading, England: United Bible Societies, 1991.

Steffen, Tom. "Foundational Roles of Symbol and Narrative in the (Re)construction of Reality and Relationships." *Missiology: An International Review*, no. XXVI.

_____. *Passing the Baton: Church Planting That Empowers*. La Habra, CA: Center for Organizational & Ministry Development, 1997.

_____. *Reconnecting God's Story to Ministry: Cross-cultural Storytelling at Home and Abroad*. La Habra, CA: Center for Organizational & Ministry Development, 1996.

Taber, Charles R. "The Limits of Indigenization in Theology." *Missiology: An International Review* 6:1 (January 1978): 53–79.

Terry, J. O. *Good News for Those with Stories of Grief*. International Mission Board, SBC, 1999.

_____. "The Roots of CBS." *Journal of Bible Storytelling (email publication)*, no. 1 (July 2004).

_____, and Tom Steffen. "The Sweeping Story of Scripture Taught Through Time." *Missiology: An International Review*, no. 35 (3) (July 2007): 315–335.

Thomas H. Troeger, *Imagining a Sermon*. Nashville, TN: Abingdon, 1990.

Thompson, LaNette. "The Nonliterate and the Transfer of Knowledge in West Africa." M.A. diss., University of Texas, Arlington, TX, 1998.

Troisi, Joseph, *Tribal Religion: Religious beliefs and practices among the Santals*. New Delhi: Manohar Publishers, 1979, 2000.

Weber, Hans Ruedi. *The Communication of the Gospel to Illiterates*. London: SCM Press, 1957.

Winter, Ralph D., and Steven C. Hawthorne. *Perspectives on the World Christian Movement*. Pasadena, CA: William Carey Library, 1992.

Wright, N. T. *The New Testament and the People of God*. Minneapolis: Fortress Press, 1992.

Yates, Frances A. *The Art of Memory*. London: Pimlico, 1966.